Pak's Britannica

Pak's Britannica

Articles by and Interviews with David Dabydeen

EDITED BY
LYNNE MACEDO

University of the West Indies Press
Jamaica • Barbados • Trinidad and Tobago

University of the West Indies Press
7A Gibraltar Hall Road   Mona
Kingston 7   Jamaica
www.uwipress.com

© 2011 by Lynne Macedo

All rights reserved. Published 2011

A catalogue record of this book is available
from the National Library of Jamaica.

ISBN: 978-976-640-256-3

Cover photograph of David Dabydeen
courtesy of the University of Warwick.

Book and cover design by Robert Harris.
Set in Adobe Garamond 11/14.5 x 27
Printed in the United States of America.

FOR MOSES AND SURYA,
THE NEXT GENERATION

Contents

Acknowledgements ix

Introduction xiii

Part 1 Articles by David Dabydeen

1 Eighteenth-Century English Literature on Commerce and Slavery 3

2 On Not Being Milton: Nigger Talk in England Today 21

3 On Cultural Diversity 34

4 Teaching West Indian Literature in Britain 43

5 From Care to Cambridge 59

6 On Samaroo's *Tempus Est*: The Earliest Colonial Rewriting of Shakespeare's *The Tempest* 67

7 Hogarth and the Canecutters 80

8 West Indian Writers in Britain 86

9 Introduction to Edward Jenkins's *Lutchmee and Dilloo: A Study of West Indian Life* 106

Part 2 Interviews with David Dabydeen

10   A Talk with David Dabydeen   123
     Felicity Hand

11   Interviewing David Dabydeen   133
     Chelva Kanaganayakam

12   "A Certain Obligation": An Interview with
     David Dabydeen   141
     Clarisse Zimra

13   David Dabydeen Talks to Mark Stein   156
     Mark Stein

14   Getting Back to the Idea of Art as Art: An Interview
     with David Dabydeen   163
     Lars Eckstein

15   A Forced Indianness: An Interview with David Dabydeen   173
     Letizia Gramaglia

16   An Interview with David Dabydeen   184
     Karen Raney

     Notes   199

Acknowledgements

Note: Several of the articles by Professor Dabydeen were originally written as lectures and not intended for publication. As a result, they do not necessarily contain full citation details.

Articles by David Dabydeen

"Eighteenth-Century English Literature on Commerce and Slavery". In *The Black Presence in English Literature*, edited by David Dabydeen, 26–49. Manchester: Manchester University Press, 1985.

"On Not Being Milton: Nigger Talk in England Today". In *The State of the Language*, edited by C. Ricks and L. Michaels, 3–14. Berkeley, CA: California University Press, 1989.

"On Cultural Diversity". In *Whose Cities*, edited by Mark Fisher and Ursula Owen, 97–106. Harmondsworth: Penguin, 1991. Copyright © David Dabydeen 1991.

"Teaching West Indian Literature in Britain". In *Studying British Culture*, edited by Susan Bassnett, 135–51. London: Routledge, 1997. Copyright © David Dabydeen 1997.

"From Care to Cambridge". In *Displaced Persons*, edited by Kirsten Holst Petersen and Anna Rutherford, 137–44. Aarhus, Denmark: Aarhus University Press, 1998.

Acknowledgements

"On Samaroo's *Tempus Est:* The Earliest Colonial Rewriting of Shakespeare's *The Tempest*". Talk given at the Royal Festival Hall, 8 November 2000; broadcast 11 November 2000 on BBC Radio 3. First published in this format in *Entertext* 1.1 (Winter 2000): 10–26. Copyright © David Dabydeen 2000.

"Hogarth and the Canecutters". In *"The Tempest" and Its Travels*, edited by Peter Hulme and William Sherman, 257–62. London: Reaktion, 2000.

"West Indian Writers in Britain". In *Voices of the Crossing*, edited by Ferdinand Dennis and Naseem Khan, 59–75. London: Serpent's Tail, 2000. Copyright © David Dabydeen 2000 and 2010.

"Introduction" to *Lutchmee and Dilloo*, by Edward Jenkins, 1–21. London: Macmillan, 2003. (Reprinted by permission of the publisher.) Copyright © David Dabydeen 2003.

Interviews with David Dabydeen

Felicity Hand, Universitat Autònoma de Barcelona, Departament de Filologia Anglesa i Germanística. "A Talk with David Dabydeen". *Links & Letters* 2 (1995): 79–86.

Chelva Kanaganayakam, University of Toronto. "Interviewing David Dabydeen". In *Configurations of Exile: South Asian Writers and Their World*, 27–33. Toronto: Tsar, 1995.

Clarisse Zimra, Southern Illinois University, Carbondale, IL. "A Certain Obligation". *Crab Orchard Review* 4, no. 2 (1999): 8–23. Interview conducted in summer 1997 at the University of Warwick.

Mark Stein, Open University. "David Dabydeen Talks to Mark Stein". *Wasafiri* 29 (Spring 1999): 27–29. Interview conducted on 29 June 1998.

Lars Eckstein, Universität Potsdam. "Getting Back to the Idea of Art as Art: An Interview with David Dabydeen". *World Literature Written in English* 39, no. 1 (2001): 27–36.

Acknowledgements

Previously Unpublished Interviews

Letizia Gramaglia, University of Warwick. "A Forced Indianness: An Interview with David Dabydeen". Interview conducted at the University of Warwick, 19 October 2009.

Karen Raney, University of East London, editor of *Engage* journal. "An Interview with David Dabydeen". University of Warwick, 29 July 1996; modified for publication 2010. (This interview was one of over thirty interviews conducted by Karen Raney between 1996 and 2001, as part of a research fellowship at Middlesex University to investigate visual literacy. The project was a collaboration between the Arts Council of England and Middlesex University. Raney's publications from this research include *Visual Literacy: Issues and Debates* [London: Middlesex University Press, 1997] and *Art in Question* [London: Continuum, 2003].)

Introduction

LYNNE MACEDO

TO ANYONE WITH AN INTEREST in Caribbean literature, the name of David Dabydeen will undoubtedly be familiar. As the author of three collections of poetry and six novels, to date, Dabydeen has won numerous prestigious awards, including three Guyana Prizes for Literature, the 2004 Rajo Rao Award for Literature, and the 2008 Anthony N. Sabga Award for Literature. Yet, in addition to being a leading Caribbean author, Dabydeen is also Professor of Literary Studies at the University of Warwick, and has published an extensive range of scholarly articles throughout his academic career. Until now, however, his academic writing has only been available in specialist journals or interspersed in collections of scholarly articles. *Pak's Britannica* is therefore the first book to be devoted solely to Dabydeen's academic works, and combines the best of his output together with a series of scholarly interviews from the past twenty-five years. Collectively they provide a unique insight into the mind of this acclaimed scholar.

Each of the articles in this collection bears testament to Dabydeen's desire to inform yet question received knowledge, while also illustrating the broad range of his views on culture, literature, history and art. They range in subject matter from a portrait of his own experiences while studying and subsequently working within Western academia; his complex and often challenging views on Shakespeare and eighteenth-century artists such as Hogarth; and his in-depth knowledge of the Indo-Caribbean experience. But whatever the subject matter, Dabydeen's abiding concern with highlighting the historical erasure of black history and culture in the West has continued to inform his writing from the earliest to the most recent article in this collection.

As both a writer and an academic, Dabydeen has always been aware of the debt that members of his generation owe to earlier Caribbean authors such as Brathwaite,[2] Harris, Naipaul and Walcott, all of whom are as renowned for their critical as for their fictional publications. He frequently cites their work as inspiration for both his subject matter and many of the stylistic techniques by which he reflects on issues, challenges and preconceived notions about the Caribbean people. It would be incorrect to imagine, however, that Dabydeen's academic work merely emulates or expands on that of his predecessors. Instead, both the academic articles and the interviews which are contained within *Pak's Britannica* reveal that his concerns are to transcend the specifics of an African- or Indo-Caribbean experience, and to highlight the ways in which Caribbean culture has helped to shape contemporary European society. From the very earliest stages of his career and irrespective of the subject matter, Dabydeen's voice is shown throughout this collection to be rich, provocative and constantly evolving. He emerges not only as a critical commentator whose work has been shaped by the migratory experience but also one that has contributed significantly to our understanding of the Caribbean and its diaspora.

The first section of *Pak's Britannica* begins with a detailed article on the role played by eighteenth-century English literature in supporting commerce and slavery. First published in 1985, Dabydeen provides an incisive survey of the literary response to this "age of commercial achievements",[3] focusing in particular on the ways in which the trade in Africans was justified and condoned on both moral and economic terms. The main points of his argument are illustrated with numerous examples from key literary figures of the age, whose poetic attacks on Africa and her peoples he reads as a strategy: "to reconcile their belief in the civilizing effects of commerce to the barbaric realities of the slave trade".[4] This is a closely and concisely argued article, one in which we can already begin to perceive the challenging nature of Dabydeen's scholarship in his suggestion that financial motivations often "compromised the literary expressions of both pro-commerce and anti-slavery writers".[5] It is easy to forget that, during the mid 1980s, his assertion that it was unrest amongst the slaves themselves which led to emancipation, not the hollow words of English poets and pamphleteers, was anything *but* the accepted view that resonates throughout critical writing on slavery today.

"On Not Being Milton: Nigger Talk in England Today" is perhaps one of the best known articles in this collection; extracts from it have appeared in several anthologies, including the *Routledge Reader in Caribbean Literature* (1996). The complete article from 1989 is reproduced here in order that Dabydeen's detailed views on creole and the development of black British poetry can be fully appreciated. The very title itself is, of course, deliberately provocative, and Dabydeen immediately highlights the kinds of "summary dismissal or parody"[6] to which "Nigger talk" is often subjected as a perpetuation of the stereotyping of black people that has operated from the seventeenth century onwards. Because language has historically been one of the features by which peoples have been judged civilized or barbarian, he asserts that the conscious use of an explicitly black idiom by poets such as Linton Kwesi Johnson, Mikey Smith or John Agard is a powerful and potent weapon against "the contempt and dehumanising dismissal by white people".[7] His closing remarks about the concept of "otherness" and its role in fuelling white racism throws down the gauntlet to British politicians like Powell and Thatcher, who warned against the alien nature of immigrants. Dabydeen's assertion that "I cannot feel or write poetry like a white man, however, much less serve him . . . I'd prefer to be simply peculiar, and to get on with it"[8] deliberately draws attention to himself as a member of that "alien" immigrant group, but one whose voice and views will not be easily silenced.

Unlike the first two articles in this collection, both Dabydeen's "On Cultural Diversity" and "Teaching West Indian Literature in Britain" have something of a different tone, as Dabydeen employs both satire and personal anecdotes to talk about racism and the role of Caribbean studies in Western academia. He considers not only how West Indians actively contributed to British society with their "willingness to take, transform and give back",[9] but just also how ironic it is that the popularity of West Indian Literature classes in British universities is often owed to white students' finding "their own culture jaded, lacking frisson and danger".[10] Not only does he suggest that it is British blacks who should be concerned about the impact that European integration might have on them in the future, but also that the Caribbean should concentrate on "the cultural values and practices that *survived* British colonization".[11] Only then, he contends, will the impact of colonialism be seen as something much greater than a simple, one-way "traffic" of British culture and values.

"From Care to Cambridge" has been included in the collection because it gives quite a different perspective to Dabydeen the scholar, largely because of its intimate, autobiographical style that stands in stark contrast to much of his other academic output. The article is primarily concerned with recounting Dabydeen's teenage years in London and his mostly unhappy time as an undergraduate at Cambridge in the early 1970s. Although it is inward-looking in subject matter, it nevertheless carries Dabydeen's trademark wit and mastery of language as he recalls, for example, his occasional pilfering of food from Sainsbury's and a local Asian shop. Revealing that he rarely attended lectures at Cambridge, Dabydeen describes how he spent much of his time alone in the university library, where he first began to make connections between the "sheer energy and nakedness of the dialect"[12] in Medieval poetry with his own Guyanese creole.[13] On (re)reading his three poems at the end of the article, it is easy to see just how important that revelation was to his own development, both as a poet and as an exponent of black British writing such as that previously considered in "On Not Being Milton".

As Dabydeen's academic career has progressed, so has his prominence as a public figure and social commentator with numerous appearances on radio and television, including several BBC 4 documentaries, such as *Painting the People*, and a six-part series entitled *Guyana: Trouble in Paradise*. "On Samaroo's *Tempus Est*" began as a talk given by Dabydeen at London's Royal Festival Hall. It was subsequently broadcast by BBC Radio 3 in November 2000, indicators of both the originality of the article's contents and its intellectual rigour. In this article, Dabydeen examines Shakespeare's *The Tempest* and shows how uncertainty about its origins and authenticity has led to inspiration for numerous rewritings and re-interpretations. He then turns his attention to an eco-critical interpretation of *The Tempest* through a detailed analysis of a rewriting from 1929 by an Indo-Guyanese called Samaroo. *Tempus Est* has been relocated to a devastated area of rainforest in Demerara, with its main characters transformed into bizarre creatures that completely lack sexual feelings. Dabydeen's analysis of Samaroo's work shows how commercial voracity and "the impulse to destroy"[14] have always been facets of the colonial experience, and that Samaroo's Prospero feels compelled to kill everything he encounters as a means of denying "kinship between the human and the non-human".[15] In his incarnation as Shiva, using a series of distorted lines from William Blake, Samaroo's Prospero embodies the catastrophic effects of materialism or "single vision", which eventually leads to "deforestation and ecocide".[16] Dabydeen contends that Samaroo was clearly a man ahead of his time, whose prescient concerns about the environment have even greater resonance today.[17]

There is a very direct connection between the previous article and "Hogarth and the Canecutters" – both of which were published in 2000 – as the latter is also concerned with *The Tempest*. Its main focus, however, is upon the visual representation of key figures from Shakespeare's play in Hogarth's 1735 painting of *A Scene from the Tempest*, a work that Dabydeen suggests has rarely enjoyed much in the way of critical attention. Dabydeen has a strong interest in visual representations and, in fact, worked extensively on Hogarth for his own doctoral thesis. His views on this painting – in particular the apparently grotesque rendering of Caliban – are therefore significant on a number of different levels. Dabydeen claims that, rather than being contemptuous of his creation, Hogarth was actually sympathetic towards and "relishing [of] his self-made creature".[18] Describing how Hogarth's subtle use of light and gesture can be seen as linking the figures of Miranda and Caliban, Dabydeen argues that Miranda's representation is actually deeply ambivalent, as she appears "caught between a honey-tongued Prospero fingering his wand and Caliban wielding curse and cudgel".[19] This notion of moral ambivalence is something that Dabydeen has explored in several of his own poems and, despite criticism, continues to believe is a valid response. While these poems may appear to show the female figure as "being simultaneously virginal and voracious",[20] he also implies that they carry a deeper, underlying message of "the possibility of tenderness between Miranda and Caliban, the oppressor's daughter and the broken slave".[21]

"West Indian Writers in Britain" begins on something of a personal note as Dabydeen considers the lasting impact that V.S. Naipaul's writing had on him after he first read *Miguel Street* (1959) as a schoolboy.[22] Describing how he has "wrestled" with Naipaul – whose influence can clearly be traced in several of Dabydeen's novels – Dabydeen claims that writers of his generation still owe a profound debt to those "ancestral voices" for providing "a living literary tradition that is distinctly West Indian".[23] Early arrivals like Mittelholzer, Lamming, Salkey and Selvon were able to find publishers in Britain, but Dabydeen shows, however, that critical reviews of their work were often patronizing or, at worst, downright racist in tone. He also points out just how ironic the situation was in which novels by West Indian writers were eagerly awaited in the 1950s and 1960s while, at the same time, racial tensions and violence were a regular occurrence in post-war Britain. In a postscript added in 2010, Dabydeen brings this article up to date by examining how a shift took place in the 1970s with black British writers like Linton Kwesi Johnson deliberately breaking their ties with a colonial past by "assert[ing] a particularized Black British identity".[24] In characteristic fashion, Dabydeen writes of how "Blackness was in danger of becoming a fetish",[25] but one which, he believes, was "emancipated" from this new form of enslavement by the publication of Steve Martin's *Incomparable World* in 1995. By writing a humorous novel about eighteenth-century Britain which shows that blacks were already an integral part of London society, Martin's writing is a dramatic shift away from the "Mope syndrome", and points the way for future writers to be liberated "from ethnic categorization . . . [and] from the logic of suffering".[26]

The final article in this collection is an abridged version of the introduction to a new edition of Edward Jenkins's *Lutchmee and Dilloo*, the first novel about Indo-Caribbean life, originally published in 1877. Throughout his career, Dabydeen has worked extensively on the Indo-Caribbean experience, and this article summarizes many of the difficulties that Indian migrants to the Caribbean faced. As Dabydeen explains, Jenkins wrote sympathetically about the plight of colonial subjects, and was also the author of a novel, *Ginx's Baby*, which was to become a Victorian best-seller. On returning from the Caribbean, Jenkins published *The Coolie: His Rights and Wrongs* (1871), which Dabydeen asserts was "the most comprehensive account of the indentureship system in the nineteenth century".[27] Although much of the material in this publication was widely criticized and many of Jenkins's claims dismissed as spurious, it appears that it was the malicious remarks about his literary abilities which subsequently stirred the author into creating *Lutchmee and Dilloo*. Dabydeen argues that the novel is groundbreaking for both its subject matter and the ways in which the Indian characters are psychologically developed, even though, ultimately, Jenkins's writing betrays him as a steadfast supporter of colonialism, despite his desire to eliminate injustices in the system.

In contrast to the measured and authoritative tone of Dabydeen's academic articles, the second part of *Pak's Britannica* contains the transcripts from a series of interviews with Dabydeen conducted by seven Caribbean scholars from universities across Europe, the United States and Canada. Drawn together for the very first time, these interviews cover a diverse range of topics and give a more intimate perspective into Dabydeen's extensive body of work – be it his poetry, his novels or his scholarly activities of the past twenty-five years. Collectively, these interviews highlight the ease with which Dabydeen freely transcends any sense of cultural, ethnic, linguistic or racial boundaries, while also allowing his playful sense of humour to undercut many of his more controversial pronouncements. Yet, above all this, the common thread which runs through each and every one of these interviews is an overwhelming sense of Dabydeen's abiding and undiminished passion for the very act of writing. As he commented in a 2005 magazine article, "I write because it is all I have ever wanted to do, since childhood . . . Without language, I'd be a beggar or a banker, so writing is a kind of benediction for me."[28]

The earliest of the interviews in this collection (chapter 10) – carried out in 1995 by Felicity Hand – is primarily concerned with the challenges facing "black" writers in Britain, and how Dabydeen dealt with issues such as identity and alienation in his first two novels: *The Intended* (1991) and *Disappearance* (1993). Even at this early stage in his career as a novelist, Dabydeen argues forcefully for a measure of imaginative freedom, to escape the burden of addressing issues of race merely because of his own ethnic background. Similar comments can be traced in several of the other interviews in *Pak's Britannica*, drawing the reader's attention towards the hybrid, multifaceted nature of Dabydeen's writing and away from what Dabydeen himself perceives to be the limitations of "hurts and history".[29]

The interviews by Chelva Kanaganayakam (chapter 11) and Karen Raney (chapter 16) were both conducted after the publication of Dabydeen's long narrative poem "Turner". Critical interest in Dabydeen's writing was undoubtedly heighted by the appearance of this work, described in its first edition in somewhat understated terms as "a dynamic, redemptive riposte"[30] to J.M.W. Turner's painting *The Slave Ship*. Not surprisingly, both the interviewers dwell at length upon the inspiration behind the poem and some of its more controversial facets, several of which were deliberately emphasized in the poet's own preface. Kanaganayakam's questioning also draws attention to the explicitly Indian references in the poem, notably the character of Manu and the centrality of the cow in the village. Dabydeen's reply is noteworthy, as he states that " 'Turner' is for me a very Indian *and* African poem",[31] a belief which clearly lies at the heart of his vision of Caribbean history as a pluralist, interconnected experience, unlike the essentialist views of some of his contemporaries. In Raney's interview, the line of questioning is much more focused on the visual impact that art has had upon Dabydeen's writing, and how his responses to Turner's *Slave Ship* served as a "trigger" for this particular poem. Dabydeen asserts that Turner's work undoubtedly has a strong narrative aspect to it, but one that was much more complex and inclusive in its engagement with the past than earlier critics had identified. As such, the painting not only calls out for "verbal interpretation" but the *particular* kind of hybrid interpretation that Dabydeen was able to create in his fusion of English, Indian and African imagery. His subsequent remarks about painting suggest that he views visual images as just another influence on his writing, and that, rather than aiming to subvert the work of particular artists like Turner or Hogarth, he aspires to acknowledge their inspiration, while also asserting his own artistic freedom to imaginatively "re-shape" their ideas in whatever manner he chooses.

The 1999 interview with Clarisse Zimra took place when Dabydeen was completing work on the novel *A Harlot's Progress*, which was published later that same year. Given the novel's explicit links to Hogarth's series of paintings of the same name, parallels can undoubtedly be drawn between some of Dabydeen's responses to Zimra's questions about the novel, and the answers he gave in the previous interview with Raney (cited above). The discussion about the ambiguous nature of the character of Mungo, however, moves into quite different territory by illustrating just how skilful Dabydeen's writing is in deliberately drawing the reader's attention to the fictional construction of the novel. By highlighting Mungo's inability to present the "truth" about his past, Dabydeen suggests that conflicting versions of the same story demonstrate how his character's life – and, by extension, that of millions of other slaves – must remain an enigma that can never be resolved. Issues of self-representation are also something of a mystery in this interview: when questioned by Zimra, Dabydeen stubbornly refuses to be tied to any specific notion of "blackness" or ethnicity, but refers back to the hybrid and flexible nature of Caribbean society in contrast to the more fixed notions of race that still appear to operate in the United States.

In the United Kingdom, the year 1999 marked the fiftieth anniversary of the arrival of the SS *Empire Windrush*. Mark Stein's interview therefore focuses on Dabydeen's academic role in these events, before considering his latest creative output. Dabydeen is quick to dismiss some of the complaints which dogged specific aspects of the celebrations as merely being part of the West Indian character, and counters that the celebrations had apparently been so successful in raising awareness amongst the population as a whole that he had received hate mail as a direct result! Moving on to discuss how West Indian immigrants have become an integral part of British society, Dabydeen also pinpoints the dichotomy he personally faces as an immigrant who spent his formative years in the Caribbean: "The non-writing part of me, the restrained part of me, is Britain. The imaginative part of me is Guyana."[32] Nevertheless, despite having what he identifies as a "kind of double consciousness"[33] which allies his creative imagination to many of the *Windrush* generation, he also calls for a more detached eye to be cast over contemporary black British and Caribbean writing, in place of the patronising, adulatory tones of much of the criticism it currently receives.

Lars Eckstein's 2001 interview explores in depth Dabydeen's continued interest in painting, and Dabydeen's replies link back with some of his earlier comments to Stein about the importance of his Caribbean childhood, which, he asserts, fostered a passion for the visual. Stating that he has little interest in music and that the Caribbean of his youth was a region devoid of fine art and galleries, Dabydeen enthusiastically recalls a visit to the Paul Klee Museum in Bern, Switzerland, and how it inspired him to try to write as well as Klee painted. Expanding upon earlier comments, Dabydeen goes on to assert that his writing – including both "Turner" and *A Harlot's Progress* – should not be viewed as a straightforward transfer from the visual to the page, but more as an "artistic correspondence"[34] which aims to go behind the image to an exploration of the ideas that originally inspired the artist. Reaffirming the need for Caribbean writers to move beyond "a kind of parade of grievances",[35] Dabydeen claims that motivations are not what should be judged in assessing such writing, but more the aesthetic quality of the output: "To write beautifully [is] the only responsibility a writer has."[36] However, he also inserts a few ironic words of caution in the closing stages of this interview about placing too much value on his comments about the writing process: "The sheer delight and anarchy on the page gets lost in an interview because you have to rationalize what you have done."[37]

The penultimate interview in this collection pinpoints the latest developments in Dabydeen's ongoing career as an academic, poet and novelist, and provides yet another perspective on his varied and cosmopolitan interests. Gramaglia's line of questioning is predominantly concerned with issues relating to Dabydeen's ethnic background, and how this has led him to actively promoting Indo-Caribbean studies as part of his academic role. Dabydeen explains that any "sense of Indianness"[38] he may have came about largely through the influence of cricket (Rohan Kanhai), V.S. Naipaul's novel *Miguel Street* and the political career of Cheddi Jagan. He is, however, quick to point out that his childhood was spent in an ethnically diverse environment – typical of much of the Caribbean – and that he has never felt constrained in his choice of writing material simply because of his origins: "To be a writer you must be eccentric not ethnocentric."[39] He mischievously suggests that he was really "pushed" into Indo-Caribbean studies after being chastised in the 1980s for giving a talk on the iconography of blacks in British art, an event which led him to compose poetry that dealt specifically with the East Indian experience. He closes this 2009 interview, however, by provocatively stating that, as of now, he is not particularly interested in Indo-Caribbean scholarship *per se*, only on eco-critical issues: "I would like to be a green writer because the future is not black nor brown, the future is green."[40]

Contemporary society presents us all with enormous challenges, whether it is the destruction of the planet's most precious resources, the increasing fragmentation of populations split by enormous wealth disparities, or growing religious tensions. Dabydeen's thoughts and writings touch on all these situations, a feature which places his work in a context not just of the Caribbean and its diaspora, but one of global stress and fracture. From the work included in this collection, it seems apparent that Dabydeen the scholar, the poet or the novelist will continue to surprise, confront and confound his colleagues and critics alike for as long as he continues to write. Never one to shy away from the more controversial aspects of race, ethnicity, identity and "belonging", his work will always challenge readers into re-examining their own views through a consciously provocative style that actively resists categorization. The "loose-tongued ambassador"[41] may have a few surprises in store for us yet.

Part 1

ARTICLES BY
DAVID DABYDEEN

CHAPTER 1

Eighteenth-Century English Literature on Commerce and Slavery (1985)

EIGHTEENTH-CENTURY BRITAIN EXPERIENCED a rapid expansion of commerce, with the growth of colonies, the spread of empire, and British domination of the trade in African slaves. "There was never from the earliest ages", Samuel Johnson wrote, "a time in which trade so much engaged the attention of mankind, or commercial gain was sought with such general emulation." One writer in the *Craftsman* of 1735 described the "Torrent of Riches, which has been breaking in upon us, for an Age or two past". John Brown wrote of "the Spirit of Commerce, now predominant", and Reverend Catcott preached breathlessly on the commercial supremacy of Britain:

> In a word, the whole earth is the market of Britain; and while we remain at home safe and undisturbed, have all the products and commodities of *the eastern and western Indies* brought to us in our ships and delivered into our hands... Our island has put on quite a different face, since the increase of commerce among us... In a word, commerce is the first mover, the main spring in the political machine, and that which gives life and motion to the whole, and sets all the inferior wheels to work.[1]

Addison, some three decades earlier, described London as "a kind of *Emporium* for the whole earth",[2] a view echoed, on a national level, in Defoe's *A Tour Thro' the Whole Island of Great Britain* (1724–26), with its sense of unbounded progress, agricultural, commercial and industrial.

The age, therefore, whilst being one of "high culture" (the rise of British art, the establishment of tastes for Italianate music and architecture, and a general cultivation of "civilized" values) was, to a greater extent, an age of commercial achievements. As J.A. Doyle puts it, "If the eighteenth century was the age of Addison and Horace Walpole, it was in a far more abiding sense the age of Chatham and Wolfe and Clive."[3] The great trading companies established in the previous century flourished and there was a general sense of the manifold possibilities of money-making, of financial development through international trade and commerce with the colonies. Schemes for making money by taking out patents on new inventions abounded, as did speculation in the stock of all kinds of companies, the mood of financial adventurism reaching a giddy height in the South Sea period of 1720, the South Sea disaster being the first great crisis in British capitalism.

"It is money that sells all, money buys all, money pays all, money makes all, money mends all, and money marls all"; "'tis Money makes the Man"; "All Things are to be had for Money"; "Money, th' only Pow'r . . . the last Reason of all Things"; "Money answers all Things" – these are the often repeated maxims of the age.[4] The greater proportion of this money was derived from the traffic in human beings, the buying and selling of African peoples and the enforced labour of these peoples. The slave trade was of vast economic importance to the financial existence of Britain. It was the revenue derived from slavery and the slave trade which greatly helped to finance the industrial revolution.[5] In seventeenth- and eighteenth-century opinion, blacks were "the strength and sinews of this western world", and the slave trade "the spring and parent whence the others flow", "the first principle and foundation of all the rest, the mainspring of the machine which sets every wheel in motion", "the Hinge on which all the Trade of this Globe moves on" and "the best traffick the kingdom hath".[6] The profits from the slave trade were seen as benefiting the whole British nation without exception: as one writer in 1730 stated, "*There is not a Man in this Kingdom, from the highest to the lowest, who does not more or less partake of the Benefits and Advantages of the* Royal African Company's FORTS AND CASTLES in Africa." Other writers told of the "immensely great" profits made by sugar planters who have "remitted over their Effects, and purchas'd large Estates in England", of the "many private Persons in England [who] daily gain great Estates in every Branch of the Trade" and of investors in the African Company who have "for Sixty Years past, got great

Estates out of the Subscriptions".⁷ West Indian merchants and planters educated their children in Britain and supported them in a state of opulence; thousands of black slaves were also brought to Britain by returning merchants and planters.⁸

The trade in black people was at the time justified on economic and moral grounds. Slavery was right and allowable, the argument ran, because it was profitable and therefore "necessary". According to Defoe, it was "an Advantage to our Manufacturers, an encreasing of the Employment of the Poor, a Support to our General Commerce, and an Addition to the general Stock of the Nation". Grosvenor in Parliament admitted euphemistically that the slave trade "was an unamiable one", but added with no recognition of the callousness of his comparison, "So also were many others: the trade of a butcher was an unamiable trade, but it was a very necessary one, not withstanding."⁹ The term "necessity" appears again and again in works excusing the slave trade. William Bosman for instance, writing in 1705, admits, "I doubt not but this Trade seems very barbarous to you, but since it is followed by meer [*sic*] necesity it must go on." William Snelgrave some thirty years afterwards echoed Bosman's sentiments: "Tho' to traffic in human Creatures, may at first sight appear barbarous, inhuman and unnatural; yet the Traders herein have as much to plead in their own Excuse, as can be said for some other Branches of Trade, namely, the *Advantage* of it."¹⁰ Such a brutal economic rationale was indicative of the materialist mood of the age, one which saw profit as the main criterion of behaviour, and morality only as a secondary consideration.

The moral justification of the slave trade ranged from the argument that the trade was "benevolent", in that it provided poor white people with employment, to the argument that the slave trade saved Africans from the bloody tyranny of their own countrymen and from being eaten by their fellow cannibals. As John Dunton put it, "They must either be *killed* or *eaten*, or both, by their barbarous conquering enemy"; likewise, James Grainger, James Boswell, Edward Long and others were all agreed on the compassionate nature of slavery, and used exactly the same arguments as Dunton.¹¹ One writer in 1740 spoke not of "enslaving" blacks but of "rather ransoming the Negroes from their national Tyrants" by transplanting them to the colonies, where, "under the benign Influences of the Law, and Gospel, they are advanced to much greater Degrees of Felicity, tho' not to absolute Liberty".¹²

Viewing the African as a primitive, sub-human creature was necessary to the whole business of slavery since it avoided or made easy any problems of morality: Christians were not enslaving human beings, for blacks were not fully human. Africans embodied all the qualities that Lord Chesterfield, a self-conscious gentleman of taste and culture, abhorred. According to Chesterfield, Africans were "the most ignorant and unpolished people in the world, little better than lions, tigers, leopards, and other wild beasts, which that country produces in great numbers".[13] It was thus morally acceptable "to buy a great many of them to sell again to advantage in the West Indies". An indication of the primitivism of the African was the supposed absence of manufactures, sciences, arts and systems of commerce within African society. It was repeatedly asserted that blacks were ignorant, unskilled and undeveloped creatures, their lack of scientific, industrial and commercial knowledge accounting for their savage morality.[14]

The Literary Response: Commerce and Civilization

Many eighteenth-century men of letters were directly involved in the business world, holding prominent government posts, holding investments in financial schemes and companies, or writing on money matters. Addison, Defoe, Cleland, Steele, Swift, Pope, Prior and Smollett, among others, were in one way or another connected with the world of commerce. Addison, for instance, was a commissioner of trade and plantations; Cleland, a commissioner of land tax and house duties; Smollett, once a surgeon on a slave ship, married a colonial, slave-owning heiress. Inevitably, perhaps, a great deal of eighteenth-century literature concerned itself with financial matters. As T.K. Meier has written,

> literary men of the seventeenth and eighteenth centuries, including Dryden, Pope, Steele, Thomson, most of the georgic poets, and a number of lesser dramatists, essayists, and poets did heap high praise upon both the concept of capitalistic business enterprise and upon businessmen who practiced it ... Commerce and industry had caught the literary imagination of the period and represented for a time at least, the progressive hope of the future.[15]

Bonamy Dobrée, in discussing eighteenth-century poetry, has described commerce as "the great theme that calls forth the deepest notes from poets of the period".[16] No other theme, Dobrée writes, "can compare in volume, in depth, in vigour of expression, in width of imagination, with the full diaspon of commerce".

Poets like James Thomson, Richard Glover, Edward Young, James Gaugh, George Cockings and John Dyer celebrated commerce as the catalyst of social, cultural and economic progress. Thomson's *The Castle of Indolence* (1748) views urban development, the establishment of empire and the expansion of markets in laudable ideals; his "Knight of Industry" is an imperialist and property developer who creates a city out of undeveloped land, just as Defoe's Crusoe transforms his desert island into a flourishing town:

> Then towns he quickened by mechanic arts,
> And bade the fervent city flow with toil;
> Bade social commerce raise renowned marts,
> Join land to land, and marry soil to soil,
> Unite the poles, and without bloody spoil
> Bring home of either Ind the gorgeous Stores.
>
> (Thompson, *Castle of Indolence*, canto II, stanza 20)

In *The Seasons – Autumn* (1730; II.22–150) Thomson traces approvingly the long historical process whereby the city rises out of the wilderness, with the evolution of man from the horrors of a primitive existence into a blissful state of commercial and scientific activity. Glover's *London: Or, the Progress of Commerce* (4th edition, 1739) celebrates, in a similar vein, the development of nature and the growth of the city through commerce:

> She in lonely sands
> Shall bid the tow'r-encircled city rise,
> The barren sea shall people, and the wilds
> Of dreary nature shall with plenty cloath.
>
> (Glover, *London* II.127–30)

It is commerce that has awakened the whole world from its primitive slumber, bringing development, progress and civilization:

> thou beganst
> Thy all-enlivening progress o'er the globe
> Then rude and joyless . . .
>
> (Glover, *London* I.173–75)

Urban development is the theme, too, in poems like Cockings's *Arts, Manufacture, and Commerce* (ca. 1869), Gaugh's *Britannia* (1767) and Young's *The Merchant* (1741). The sense of the limitless possibilities of expansion and gain is given perfect expression by Young as he urges Englishmen to seize the present opportunities of commerce:

> Rich *Commerce* ply with Warmth divine
> By *Day*, by *Night*; the *Stars* are Thine
> Wear out the Stars in *Trade*! Eternal run
> From Age to Age, the noble Glow,
> A Rage to Gain, and to *bestow*,
> Whilst Ages last! In *Trade* burn out the Sun!
>
> (Young, *The Merchant*, strain IV, stanza 19)

In this poem, Young's model of the world is a purely economic one – the relationship among earth, sea and air seen as a series of commercial transactions:

> *Earth's* Odours *pay* soft *Airs* above,
> That o'er the teeming Field *prolific* range;
> *Planets* are Merchants, take, return
> Lustre and Heat; by Traffic burn;
> The whole *Creation* is one vast *Exchange*.
>
> (Young, *Merchant*, strain III, stanza 26)

The kindling of commercial activity is compared to natural awakenings, to the rain from heaven which cheers the glebe, activates the bees and rouses the flowers. Blake may have seen "a Heaven in a Wild Flower" (*Auguries of Innocence*, I.2), but Young is more down-to-earth. Such a commercial response to nature is a distinguishing feature of much of eighteenth-century literature. Trees existed to be cut down and fashioned into merchant ships. When one writer described "beautiful forests", he meant not their aesthetic qualities but their commercial potential: "The farther one advances into the country, the more beautiful Forests are found, full of Gummy Trees, fit to make Pith for Ships; as also infinite Store of Tress fit for Masts."[17]

The consensus of opinion in many pieces of eighteenth-century literature is that commerce is a wonderful activity, creative of progress, culture and civilization. Glover writes of the mathematics, philosophy, poetry and laws that result from commerce:

> Barbarity is polish'd, infant arts
> Bloom in the desert, and benignant peace
> With hospitality, begin to sooth
> Unsocial rapine, and the thirst of blood.
>
> (Glover, *London*, II.209–12)

Young makes similar claims for the civilizing power of commerce:

> Commerce gives Arts, as well as *Gain*;
> By Commerce wafted o'er the Main,
> *They* barbarous Climes enlighten as they run;
> *Arts* the rich Traffic of the Soul!
> May travel *thus*, from Pole to Pole,
> And gild the World with Learning's *brighter* Sun.
>
> (Young, *Merchant*, strain II, stanza 1)

The contact between men as a result of mutual trade is seen as conducive to tolerance, morality and culture. The merchant, the agent of commerce, was also celebrated as the agent of progress and civilization, the embodiment of civilized standards derived from his commercial experience. No praise was great enough to lavish upon him, and all poetic eulogies fell short of their mark:

> Is *Merchant* an inglorious Name?
> No; fit for *Pindar* such a Theme,
> Too great for Me; I pant beneath the Weight!
> If loud, as *Ocean's* were my Voice,
> If Words and Thoughts to court my Choice
> Out-number'd *Sands*, I could not reach its Height.
>
> (Young, *Merchant*, strain III, stanza 24)

The merchant was also seen as a force for liberty, "liberty" being a key word in literature celebrating commerce. Commerce meant the rise of the middle class, which, as it gained political influence, sought protection from the tyranny and arbitrary laws of the aristocratic class, its main ambition being the legal protection of property. Hence Young's verse:

> *Trade*, gives fair *Virtue* fairer still to shine;
> Enacts those Guards of gain, the *Laws*;
> *Exalts* even *Freedom's* glorious Cause.
>
> (Young, *Merchant*, strain IV, stanza 14)

There was, as C.A. Moore has said, "one dark blot" in this bright picture of progress, civilization and liberty through commerce: "The one detail out of moral keeping was the slave traffic."[18] Slavery was such an undeniably crucial aspect of colonial and international commerce that the men of letters could not avoid touching on the subject. Their problem was how to reconcile their belief in the civilizing effects of commerce to the barbaric realities of the slave trade. Cornelius Arnold and John Dyer provided one way out of the dilemma. Arnold interrupts briefly his eulogy on commerce to express perfunctory regret at the fact of African slavery, but he blames the Africans for the existence of the slave trade, his argument being that Africans, in their civil wars, capture their fellow countrymen and sell them into slavery:

> Onward they [i.e., British merchants] steer their Course,
> To *Afric's* parched Clime, whose sooty Sons,
> Thro' Rage of civil Broils . . . hard Destiny!
> Forc'd from their native Home to *Western Ind*,
> In Slavery drag the galling Chain of Life.[19]
>
> (Arnold, *Commerce*, stanza 6)

Dyer's *Fleece* (1757) contains a similar, perfunctory pity for the condition of blacks, Dyer not wishing to appear inhumane and uncivilized. Nevertheless the black is shouldered with the blame for slavery:

> On Guinea's sultry strand, the drap'ry light
> Of Manchester or Norwich is bestow'd
> For clear transparent guns, and ductile war,
> And snow-white iv'ry; yet the valued trade,

Along this barb'rous coast, in telling, wounds
The gen'rous heart, the sale of wretched slaves;
Slaves, by their tribes condemn'd, exchanging death
For life-long servitude; severe exchange!

(Dyer, *Fleece*, book IV, I.189–96)

Young and Glover deal with the problem of slavery in different ways. There is, in Young's poem, a brief, scornful reference to blacks, describing, of all things, their laziness: "*Afric's* black, lascivious, slothful Breed, / To clasp their *Ruin*, fly from *Toil* . . ." (Young, *Merchant*, strain V, stanza 20). Africa is attacked because it does not practise the principles of capitalist development which Young celebrates, and the African is seen as being ignorant of the principles of science and commerce:

Of *Nature's* Wealth from *Commerce* rent,
Afric's glaring Monument:
Mid *Citron* Forests and *Pomegranate* Groves
(Curs'd in a Paradise!) she pines;
O'er *generous* Glebe, o'er *golden* Mines
Her *Begger'd, famish'd*, Tradeless Natives roves.

(Young, *Merchant*, strain V, stanza 21)

Young, in an indirect way, is saying that slavery is a benevolent institution, since it teaches the African the virtues of labour. Glover, though equally deceitful, is not so breathtakingly perverse. His poem, *London*, attacks the Spanish for enslaving and destroying the Indian natives, but he makes no reference to the British participation in slavery and British treatment of the Africans. (He wrote the poem in 1739, when anti-Spanish sentiment was running high in Britain, and British traders were not only angry at the liberties taken by Spanish merchants but also jealous of Spanish commercial rivalry, an opposition that erupted into the "War of Jenkins's Ear" in 1739.) Glover's reference to slavery, and Indian slavery at that, is therefore merely political.

Another way of reckoning with slavery whilst being faithful to the ethic of commerce was to minimize the brutality of the trade through careful choice of diction. James Grainger, for example, in his poem *The Sugar-Cane* (1764) strives to reduce the horror of slavery by wrapping it up in a napkin of poetic diction. *The Sugar-Cane* is as good an example as any of the way in which "the raw materials of human experience were habitually transmuted in eighteenth-century poetry".[20] Instead of "slave-owner", Grainger prefers to use the term "Master-Swain"; he prefers "Assistant Planter" to the term "slave". The use of poetical phrases such as "Afric's sable progeny" to describe the black slaves further softens the stark realities of their actual condition. It was callous abstractions of this sort that provoked Samuel Johnson's attack on Grainger's acceptance of slavery.

Picturesque descriptions of slave labour and the slave environment were another feature of pro-commerce literature. Grainger's *Sugar-Cane* contains idyllic descriptions of the golden cane fields with their contentedly laborious black swains, "Well-fed, well-cloath'd, all emulous to gain / Their master's smile, who treated them like men" (Grainger, *Sugar-Cane*, book I, II.611–12). The author of *The Pleasures of Jamaica*, written some three decades before, presented a view of slave plantations that was similarly picturesque:

> Hither retiring, to avoid the heat,
> We find refreshment in a cool retreat;
> Each rural object gratifies the sight,
> And yields the mind an innocent delight;
> Greens of all shades the diff'rent plants adorn,
> Here the young cane, and there the growing corn;
> In verdant pastures interspers'd between,
> The lowing herds, and bleating flocks are seen:
> With joy his lord the faithful Negro sees,
> And in his way endeavours how to please;
> Greets his return with his best country song,
> The lively dance, and tuneful merry-wang.
> When nature by the cane has done her part,
> Which ripen'd now demands the help of art,
> How pleasant are the labours of the mill,
> While the rich streams the boiling coppers fill.
>
> (Anon., *Pleasures of Jamaica*)

As one of the characters in La Vallée's anti-slavery novel explains to an African, avarice "borrows the voice and colours of fiction. Fiction gilds your chains".[21] The same "fiction" was being employed to describe the condition of England's peasants and workers – hence the masses of eighteenth-century pastoral verse which romanticized agricultural labour, erasing from it any notion of toil and exploitation. And if, as in *The Pleasures of Jamaica*, the African slaves trip over each other in their joyful haste to greet their returning master, so in Addison's version of country life are the English peasants gladdened by the approach of their squire, Sir Roger: "I could not but observe with a great deal of Pleasure the Joy that appeared in the Countenances of these ancient Domesticks upon my Friend's Arrival at his Country-Seat. Some of them could not refrain from tears at the Sight of their old Master; every one of them press'd forward to do something for him, and seemed *discouraged if they were not employed.*"[22] It is no wonder that abolition pamphleteers made frequent appeals to English workers, urging them to recognize in the servitude and distress of blacks the conditions of their own existence.

The fact is that many of the pro-commerce writers who either justified slavery or minimized its inhumanity were, in one way or another, involved in the profits to be made from slavery. Glover, for instance, was the son of a merchant, and also a member of Parliament, noted for his defence of West India merchants before Parliament. In 1742 a petition drawn up by Glover and signed by three hundred merchants, complaining of the inadequate protection of English trade, was presented to Parliament. Glover afterwards attended to sum up their evidence before the House of Commons. In 1775 he received a plate worth £300 from West India merchants in acknowledgement of his services to them. His will mentions property in the city of London and in South Carolina. Cornelius Arnold was, in later life, beadle to the Distillers Company, which had interests in West India sugar. Grainger, who died in St Christopher in 1766, was married to the daughter of a Nevis planter, and took charge of his wife's uncle's plantations; he invested his savings in the purchase of slaves.[23]

The involvement in the economic benefits of slavery meant a warped ethical response to it. We catch the sense of wealth beyond the dreams of avarice in William Goldwin's poem *Great Britain: Or, The Happy Isle* (1705), specifically in the compounded descriptive phrases like "Massy heaps of shining Treasure":

> See! How the Busie Merchant Ploughs the Main
> In Vessels big with weighty Heaps of Gain; ...
> Huge Loads of Wealth, the distant World's Encrease.

(p. 5)

The feeling of great wealth is carried over in Goldwin's *Poetical Description of Bristol* (1712), in which the sole reference to slavery is an indirect one – "Jamaica's Growth, or Guinea's Golden-dust", also in R.J. Thorn's *Bristolia* (1794): "Around the quays, in countless heaps appear, / Bales pil'd on bales, and loads of foreign ware."

The Alternative Response to Commerce

The alternative response to the wealth pouring into society took many forms. To begin with, there was a sense of the physical ugliness and the despoliation of the landscape resulting from commercial and industrial activity. Goldwin's response to the growing signs of industrialization, for example, is more ambivalent than Dyer's or Thorn's. In Dyer's *Fleece*, the smoke rising over Leeds is described as "incense" and praised as a sign of industrial activity. Thorn's poem on Bristol is also optimistic about industrial fumes. Standing upon Brandon Hill like a latter-day Moses upon Pisgah, he surveyed the promised land of money and machinery: "Here, whilst I stand, what clouds of smoke appear / From different work-shops, and dissolve in air!" (Thorn, *Bristolia*). Goldwin, however, in his *Poetical Description of Bristol*, while celebrating the city's commercial and manufacturing wealth, rejects the accompanying destruction of nature, the uprooting of Kingswood Forest and the rape of the earth as miners tear "Magazines of Coals from Nature's Bowel". The mine and miners present a "horrid" sight to the eye, and he launches into an attack on the ugliness and pollution of a glass manufacturing works: "Thick dark'ning Clouds in curling smoky Wreaths / Whose sooty Stench the Earth and Sky annoys, / And Nature's blooming Verdure half destroys" (Goldwin, *Poetical Description of Bristol*). The sulphur emitted from the factory's chimney "blasts the Fruit of fair Sicilia's Fields". Goldwin's poem ends with a paean on natural beauty, the "Grotesque" rocks and cliffs along the river which "afright the climbing Eye" in a different way from the "horrid" sight of the coalmine. Goldwin's anxieties about progress accumulate throughout the eighteenth century, and culminated in the next in Mrs Gaskell's polluted Milton in *North and South* and Dickens's Coketown in *Hard Times*, works that betray the same pessimism about progress so perfectly expressed in Hopkins's *God's Grandeur*.

Bound up with the feeling of disgust at the physical pollution created by "progress" was a sense of the city as a hideous, dirty, chaotic phenomenon. The pro-commerce writers may have celebrated the evolution of the city from the barren wilderness as a sign of civilization, but others – Pope, Swift, Gay, Smollett – depicted the city as corrupt, putrid and anarchic to the point of insanity. London, for example, is often portrayed as a gigantic Bedlam riddled with crime and disease, as Max Byrd in his recent study of the image of the city in eighteenth-century literature has shown.[24]

If the spirit of commerce was seen as having stimulated crime, it was also seen as having created inhumane attitudes in people, including selfishness and hardness of heart. R. Lovell, in *Bristol: A Satire* (1794), described the soullessness of Bristolians motivated only by "sordid wealth": "Foul as their streets, triumphant meanness sways, / And grovelling as their mud-compelling drays" (Lovell, *Bristol*). Bristolians have become mere emblems of money, devoid of "the nobler cares of mind", "soft humanities", "mild urbanity" and "sympathetic feeling": "In all his sons the mystic signs we trace; / Pounds, shillings, pence, appear in every face" (Lovell, *Bristol*). Another eighteenth-century observer of Bristolians described how "their Souls are engrossed by lucre", with the more gentle qualities of mind "banished from their republic as a contagious disease". Samuel Johnson noted the same quality in Bristolians: according to Johnson, Richard Savage's rejection at Bristol was because his wit, culture and conversation were not valued in this "place of commerce", with traders more conscious of "solid gain".[25]

Both Dyer and Thomson in their eulogies on commerce had asserted its benevolent effect upon the labouring classes in raising their standard of living to glorious levels. According to Thomson, commerce fuelled by the spirit of liberty has enriched the whole nation – "The poor man's lot with milk and honey flows" (*Liberty*, V.1.6). Although the principle of subordination still holds sway in society, the wealth derived from commerce is equally enjoyed, Thomson claimed. Dyer similarly described the national benefits of industry, which "lifts the swain, / And the straw cottage to a palace turns" (*Fleece*, book III, I.332). Other writers were more realistic than Thomson and Dyer, and recognized an unequal distribution of wealth and a stark division in society between the haves and have-nots. "Under the present Stage of Trade", John Brown wrote, "the Increase of Wealth is by no means equally or proportionally diffused: The Trader reaps the main Profit: after him, the Landlord, in a lower Degree: But the common Artificer, and still more the common Labourer, gain little by the exorbitant Advance of Trade."[26] Thomas Bedford, in a sermon bitterly attacking commerce, colonization and slavery, observed that, because trade and commerce had introduced inflation in Britain and a more expensive manner of living, "the bulk of its people may still continue poor, in the midst of a thousand like advantages".[27]

Those who attacked commerce as a force for squalor and degradation focused increasingly on slavery for the substance of their views. The bulk of British anti-slavery literature was written in the latter part of the century, spurred on by the propaganda of the abolition movement, but by 1750 there was already considerable public awareness of the brutality of the slave trade. Hence Postlethwayt, in 1746, produced a tract in defence of slavery, to counter the "Many [who] are prepossessed against this trade, thinking it *a barbarous, inhuman, and unlawful Traffic for a Christian Country to Trade in Blacks*". The "many" in the first half of the century included the Quakers, John Dunton, Ralph Sandiford, Jonathan Swift, Samuel Johnson, Charles Gildon, Joseph Warton, Richard Savage and others. Even Defoe had at one time written anti-slavery verse, denouncing the slave traders and their brand of Christianity.[28] Major poets like Wordsworth, Blake, Southey and Cowper would later make similar protests against slavery. William Blake, in addition to poems like *The Little Black Boy*, created some powerful engravings of slave abuse as illustrations for John Stedman's 1796 *Narrative of a Five Year Expedition against the Revolted Negroes of Surinam*. The production of poetry was spurred on by the formation of the Abolition Society in 1787, and the relationships that leading social crusaders sought to forge with eminent writers. The Reverend John Newton, for instance, an ex-Guinea merchant turned penitent, urged Cowper to put his pen to the service of black humanity. Cowper responded with some anti-slavery ballads which were instantly popular and distributed in thousands throughout the country. Wordsworth's contact with William Wilberforce and Thomas Clarkson (the former a close acquaintance of his uncle, the latter a fellow resident in the Lake District) led to verse supportive of their campaigns, such as the 1807 sonnet on Clarkson's Abolition Bill. Such poets, however, were merely being perfunctory in their anti-slavery productions – the triteness and laboured sentiments of their expressions betray an absence of deep, personal involvement or vision.²⁹ Indeed, Cowper in a letter of 1788 admitted that "the subject, as a subject for song, did not strike me much", and Wordsworth in a passage in the *Prelude* dealing with abolition agitation confessed,

> For me that strife had ne'er
> Fasten'd on my affections, nor did now
> Its unsuccessful issue much excite
> My sorrow . . .
>
> (Wordsworth, *Prelude*, A-version, book X.II.202–5)

The French revolution, being a white affair and closer to home, excited more profound and lasting interest than the Haitian revolution of the identical period. There were indeed a scattering of verses and pamphlets singing the courage and genius of Toussaint L'Ouverture, but it took nearly one hundred fifty years, with the appearance of C.L.R. James's *The Black Jacobins*, before a full assessment of the profundity of the Haitian revolution was made. (James is, significantly, a black West Indian: given the established and enduring European belief that black people have no history to speak of,³⁰ the burden of revelation has fallen on black scholars and slave-descendants like James.)

The lack of integrity on the part of English eighteenth-century writers can be startlingly glimpsed in Coleridge's attitude towards blacks. His first major poem was a Greek ode against the slave trade, which earned him the Browne Gold Medal at Cambridge University.³¹ He was to write that "my Greek ode is, I think, my *chef d'oeuvre* in poetical composition". Coleridge's interest, however, lay more in the exercise of scholarship than in the plight of blacks: slaves were mere fodder for conceptualization and poetical practice conducted in Greek with the aim of winning a coveted prize. His real attitude towards blacks is revealed in his nausea at Othello's embrace of Desdemona. It was one thing to sympathize spaciously and within the elegant, classical boundaries of a Greek ode with blacks, but quite another thing to have them marrying into the family. Similar hypocrisy can be imputed to other English writers. From the 1770s onwards England was deluged with anti-slavery verse, the sheer bulk of it, the bewildering variety of poetical expression (odes, pastorals, eclogues, sonnets, doggerel, even creole jingles) being an overwhelming aspect of the literary history of the period. There is little evidence, though, to suggest that any of these poets devoted any personal time or effort, or dug deep into their pockets, to support the abolitionist cause. Indeed, it is more probable that the theme of slavery fed them, providing an opportunity for grubs and hacks to indulge in sentiment, to try out verse techniques, and to make some money by either capitalizing on popular feeling or else by cashing in on the newspapers' latest sensational revelation of West Indian brutalities.

Unlike the black writers of the eighteenth century (Equiano, for instance, who trudged all over England organizing anti-slavery rallies and publicizing his slave autobiography), whose finances and very lives were bound up with their literary productions, English writers merely exploited the slave theme for their own gain and recognition. For Swift, the theme provided an opportunity for the exercise of wit and display of satirical prowess. He thunders against the brutishness and hypocrisy of the business of colonization: "Ships are sent out with the first opportunity, the natives driven out or destroyed, their princes tortured to discover their gold, a free licence given to all acts of inhumanity and lust, the earth reeking with the blood of its inhabitants: and this execrable crew of butchers employed in so pious an expedition, is a *modern colony* sent to convert and civilise an idolatrous and barbarous people" (*Gulliver's Travels*, book 4, chapter 12). Yet Swift was quite happy to invest hundreds of pounds, in 1720, in the South Sea Company, whose sole business at the time was to ferry African slaves to the Spanish colonies. In 1713, by the Treaty of Utrecht, Britain had gained the "Asiento" privilege of supplying the Spanish colonies with slaves, and this monopoly was granted to the South Sea Company. The "Asiento" privilege was considered at the time to be the "jewel" clause of the Treaty. To celebrate the Treaty, Alexander Pope in 1713 published his *Windsor Forest*, a poem in praise of the values of liberty and civilization – English liberty and civilization that is, for, apart from the odd, jejune pastoral expression of hope that the "freed Indians" would eventually be able to "woo their sable loves" in the liberty and civilization of "their native groves", there is no hint of the real barbarity of the "Asiento" monopoly. In 1720, Pope, like Swift, was busily investing capital in the South Sea Company in the hope of a quick killing.[32]

The profits to be made from slavery, then, conditioned or compromised the literary expression of both pro-commerce and anti-slavery writers. As C.A. Moore puts it, "The conscience of the public was so blinded to the moral issue by the widespread participation in dividends that it was very difficult to bring independent judgement or sentiment to bear upon the subject."[33] The dilemma over the slave trade – the recognition of its immorality, and yet at the same time its profitability – was one aspect of the general dilemma of the age in its attempt to reconcile the moral with the economic. "Religion is one thing, trade is another" – it is this separation between the two, or, as Anderson puts it, "the withdrawal of economic affairs from the jurisdiction of morality", which posed crucial, central problems at the time to many writers on economic matters. These problems lay at the very core of Britain's commercial existence; indeed, they provoked questions about the country's very survival as a world power. Davenant, for instance, recognized the evils resulting from trade, but also its "necessity" in terms of Britain's continued supremacy over its rivals and competitors:

> Trade, without doubt, is in its nature a pernicious thing: it brings in that Wealth which introduces Luxury; it gives a rise to Fraud and Avarice, and extinguishes Virtue and Simplicity of Manners; it depraves a People and makes for that Corruption which never fails to end in Slavery, Foreign or Domestick. *Licurgus*, in the most perfect Model of Government that was ever fram'd, did banish it from his Commonwealth. But, the Posture and Condition of other Countries consider'd, 'tis become with us a necessary Evil.

Some fifty years later, John Brown came up against the same hurdle; he rails against the luxury and immorality created by the wealth from commerce, but realizes that to discourage or curtail such commerce would lead to national decline, with rival countries overtaking Britain in economic and military might. "Thus are we fallen into a kind of Dilemma", Brown muses, uncertain of the solution.[34] The dilemma was also faced by some pro-slavery writers, particularly on the issue of baptizing and Christianizing blacks. Slave-owners, one apologist pointed out in 1730,[35] were reluctant to educate their slaves to the Christian gospel because of the economic costs. The slaves would have to be given time off work to attend Bible classes, which would mean a loss of production. This would be "too great an Invasion on the property of the Masters". If, for instance, the writer calculates, a planter were to allow one-fifth of his total collection of one hundred slaves to be educated once a fortnight in the gospel, and estimating that each slave made a six-pence profit per day for his owner, then the owner would lose a whole £13 *per annum* – £65 *per annum* if he let *all* his blacks be educated. To educate all the hundred thousand blacks in the West Indies would cost a massive sum of £65,000. As to the morality of the slave trade itself, the writer does not deny that "Millions of Lives it destroys", but stresses that it is still "absolutely necessary" for reasons of national supremacy – Britain, France, Spain, Holland and Portugal are all involved in the slave trade, and, "were any of them to break it off on the Topick of Unlawfulness, they would soon lose their Share in the Profits arising from it, which is hardly to be expected from them unless their Neighbours could be prevail'd to drop theirs too".[36] Because of this international competition, the writer concludes, it is unlikely that the slave trade will decline, unless God personally intervenes! God of course did not intervene, but the black slaves themselves did. Whenever opportunity presented itself they revolted – in the slave factories on the West African coast, onboard the slave ships taking them to the colonies, and on the plantations. These revolts, and the bloodletting and barbarities they unleashed, made more of an impact on the dismantling of slavery than the poems issued by English writers. The sword was mightier than the pen: the irrationality of whites, their refusal to be persuaded by reasoned and moral arguments, forced blacks into violent behaviour. This legacy of the "criminalization" of blacks is, according to contemporary opinion, still a distinguishing feature of the racial encounter between blacks and whites. As Joe Harte, a black British political campaigner put it, in writing about the Brixton riots of 1981, "Our community the world over resents the burden imposed on us by white society to dramatize our grievances before they are met."[37]

CHAPTER 2

On Not Being Milton: Nigger Talk in England Today
(1990)

I

IT'S HARD TO PUT TWO words together in creole without swearing. Words are spat out from the mouth like live squibs, not pronounced with elocution. English diction is cut up, and this adds to the abruptness of the language: *what*, for instance, becomes *wha* (as in *whack*), the splintering making the language more barbaric. Soft vowel sounds are habitually converted: the English tend to be polite in *war*, whereas the creole *warre* produces an appropriate snarling sound; *scorn* becomes *scaan*, *water wata*, and so on.

In 1984 I published a first collection of poems entitled *Slave Song*, written in a Caribbean creole and dealing with the Romance of the Cane, meaning the perverse eroticism of black labour and the fantasy of domination, bondage and sadomasochism. The British Empire, as the Thistlewood Diaries show, was as much a pornographic as an economic project.[1] The subject demanded a language capable of describing both a lyrical and a corrosive sexuality. The creole language is angry, crude and energetic. The canecutter chopping away at the crop burst out in a spate of obscene words, a natural gush from the gut.

In the preface to *Slave Song* I speak of the brokenness of the language, which reflects the brokenness and suffering of its original users. Its potential as a naturally tragic language is there in its brokenness and rawness, which is like the rawness of a wound. If one has learnt and used Queen's English for some years, the return to creole is painful, almost nauseous, for the language is uncomfortably raw. One has to shed one's protective sheath of abstracts and let the tongue move freely in blood again.

In writing *Slave Song* I had no Caribbean literary models to imitate, since I knew none. Apart from my early childhood in Guyana, I was brought up in England and no Caribbean literature was taught in schools. So I was wholly ignorant of the creole poetry of Edward Burns. What, in fact, triggered *Slave Song* were the years I spent as an undergraduate at Cambridge reading English literature. There occurred my discovery of the "gaudy and inane phraseology" of much of eighteenth-century poetry, the wrapping of stark experiences in a napkin of poetic diction. Take James Grainger's poem *The Sugar-Cane*, for instance, in which the toil of plantation life is erased or converted into pastoral. Instead of "overseer", Grainger uses the term "Master Swain"; instead of "slaves", "assistant planters". The black condition is further embellished by calling the slaves "Afric's sable progeny". Grainger's poem is a classic example in English poetry of the refusal to call a spade a spade. Then there were all those antislavery pieces in a highfalutin Miltonic rhetoric and cadence, in which the poets used the black experience merely as a vehicle for lofty, moral pronouncements on good and evil. Or Coleridge's Greek ode against slavery, which won him the Browne Gold Medal at Cambridge: the African here is subject to the exercise of classical erudition.

The real discovery for me, however, was of medieval alliterative verse. Reading *Sir Gawain and the Green Knight* was a startling moment. The sheer, naked energy and brutality of the language, its "thew & sinew", reminded me immediately of the creole of my childhood. John of Trevisa, a fourteenth-century translator, described the alliterative poetry of the North of England as "harsh, piercing and formless". This quality of lawlessness and the primarily oral form of delivery bore a curious resemblance to Guyanese creole. I began to see, albeit naively, the ancient divide between north and south in Britain, the Gawain poet standing in opposition to Chaucer in terms of a native idiom versus an educated, relaxed poetic line tending towards the form of the iambic pentameter. The north/south divide is, of course, evocative of the divide between the so-called Caribbean periphery and the metropolitan centre of London. London is supposed to provide the models of Standard English, and we in the Caribbean our dialect versions.

The comparison between England and the modern Caribbean is not altogether fanciful, for in a sense we West Indians live in the Middle Ages in terms of rudimentary material resources. The British Empire was, after all, a feudal structure with robber barons and serfs. Transportation by horse, mule or canoe, peasant farming, manual labour, villages lying in patches of land encircled by bush in the way that dense forest lay just outside English castle walls – these features and others of Guyana's countryside conjure up medieval life. And if, as Johan Huizinga states in *The Waning of the Middle Ages*, the sound of church bells dominated the air of England, so too in Guyana is religion a vital, noisy force. And out of this matrix of spirit and earth is born a language that is both lyrical and barbaric. But the very unsystematic and unscientific nature of the language which is a source of strength to writers like me is cause for summary dismissal or parody for others. Peter Porter, for instance, speaks dismissively of the "difficulty" of understanding creole; presumably Porter has no time for Shakespeare or Joyce either. In *Slave Song*, in anticipation of such automatic responses, I clothed the creole poems in an elaborate set of "notes" and "translations" as an act of counter-parody, in the way that Eliot annotated his *Waste Land* supposedly for the benefit of his lazier readers. The more common English response to creole, however, is to be found from Alan Coren's pen. Coren, in 1975, published the second volume of the collected thoughts of Idi Amin, which had been appearing in *Punch* magazine for some months. In the introduction Amin is made to reveal the burden of words:

> One trouble wid de bes' seller business: you gittin' boun' to de wheel o' fire. No sooner you dishin' out one giant masterpiece to de gobblin' pubberlic, the comin' round yo' premises an' hammerin' on de door fo' de nex'. "Come on out, John Milton!" de mob yellin', "We know you' in there! We just' finishin' de *Parachute Lost* an' we twiddlin' de thums, wot about di year's jumbo pome you lazy bum?"
>
> It hardly surprisin' E.N. Fleming packin' up de Jane Bond racket an' turnin' to de penicillin business. Dam sight easier, scrapin' de mold off bread an' floggin' it up de chemist than bashin' de fingers flat day an' nights on de Olivetti an' wonderin' where you' next' plot comin' f'om.
>
> Natcherly, de same happenin' wid de present writer. Las' year, de astoundin' fust book hittin' de shops, an' befo' anyone know wot happenin' de made fans smashin' down de premises o' W.H. Smith an' carryin' de amazin' tomes off by de crate! De pubberlisher rushin' out four impressions in four munce, an' still de cravin' not

satisfied. "It no good", de pubberlisher informin' me. "Only one way to shut de slaverin' buggers' gobs, yo' majesty: you havin' to cobble together another great milestone in de history o' literature, how about Wensdy week?"

So here I sittin', shovin' de affairs o' state on one side, an' puttin' together a noo volume o' de famous weekly bulletins f'om downtown Kampala. Hub o' de Universe.[2]

Two ancient images of black people emerge from Coren's pen. Firstly, the sense that they are scientifically illiterate. This idea can be traced back to seventeenth- and eighteenth-century European writings which describe African societies as being devoid of intellectual capacities. ("No ingenious manufacture amongst them, no arts, no sciences", as David Hume declared.) They squat in mud huts and gnaw bones. They know neither compass nor telescope. European literature is littered with blacks like Man Friday, who falls to earth to worship Crusoe's magical gun, or the savage in Conrad's steamship who acted as fireman:

> He was an improved specimen; he could fire up a vertical boiler. He was there below me, and, upon my word, to look at him was as edifying as seeing a dog in a parody of breeches and a feather hat, walking on his hind-legs. A few months of training had done for a really fine chap. He squinted at the steam-gauge and at the water-gauge with an evident effort of intrepidity – and he had filed teeth, too, the poor devil, and the wool of his pate shaved into queer patterns, and three ornamental scars on each of his cheeks. He ought to have been clapping his hands and stamping his feet on the bank, instead of which he was hard at work, a thrall to strange witchcraft, full of improving knowledge. He was useful because he had been instructed; and what he knew was this – that should the water in that transparent thing disappear, the evil spirit inside the boiler would get angry through the greatness of his thirst, and take a terrible vengeance. So he sweated and fired up and watched the glass fearfully (with an impromptu charm, made of rags, tied to his arm, and a piece of polished bone, as big as a watch, stuck flat-ways through his lower lip), while the wooded banks slipped past us slowly, the short noise was left behind, the interminable miles of silence – and we crept on, towards Kurtz.[3]

Secondly, the sense that they are linguistically illiterate. Just as they are ignorant of the rules of scientific formulae, so they are ignorant of the rules of grammar. Their language is mere broken, stupid utterance. Again this view of black expression is firmly entrenched in European conceptualization. In seventeenth-century travel literature and anthropological writings, the bestiality of the natives is reflected in their language. Sir Thomas Herbert, in 1634, suggested that Africans and apes mated with each other, the evidence for this being that African speech sounded "more like that of Apes than Men . . . their language is rather apishly than articulately founded".[4] Many passages focus on the monstrosity of their organs of speech as well as their organs of propagation. Whilst John Ogilby (1670) writes about the "large propagators" sported by the men of Guinea, and Richard Jobson (1623) on male Mandingoes' being "furnished with such members as are after a sort burdensome unto them", William Strachey (1612) focuses on their "great big lips and wide mouths".[5] Thick lips and monstrously misshapen mouths, sometimes, as in the case of the anthropophagi, located in their chests, indicated an inability to make proper speech. When we find eloquent and civilized blacks in English literature of the period, as in the case of Mrs Aphra Behn's Oroonoko, their physical features are more European than African: "His mouth, the finest shaped that could be seen; far from those great turn'd lips which are so natural to the rest of the Negroes."[6]

In the eighteenth century, which was the Age of Slavery as well as the Age of the Dictionary, such attitudes to Africans were sustained, the link between barbarism and lack of speech made explicit. Volume 389 of the *Spectator*, from May 1712, described Hottentots as "Barbarians, who are in every respect scarce one degree above Brutes, having no language among them but a confused Gabble, which is neither well understood by themselves or others". Given the centrality of the Word in eighteenth-century English civilization (Pope's "What oft was thought, but ne'er so well expressed"; Hogarth's *Conversation Pieces*; Steel's *Tatler*; Johnson's *Dictionary*), the apparent wordlessness of the Africans was deemed to be incontrovertible evidence of their barbarism.

The equation between African and animal, sustained by the issue of language, which gave moral validity to the slave trade, continued in the nineteenth century, the Age of Imperialism and Anthropometrics. Africans' skulls, lips, teeth and mouths were scrupulously measured by leading white scientists to reveal black cultural and moral primitivism and therefore the necessity of continuing colonial rule. Science underpinned the imperial process. It was also quite obvious, however, that Africans had language, and this posed a problem to white conceptualization since language was an undeniable *human* characteristic. Professor Bernth Lindfors has illustrated the problem by reference to the case of the San people of South Africa, a group of who were brought to Britain between 1846 and 1850 to be displayed at circuses and fairgrounds.[7] The speech of the San visitors was their most noticeable feature: 70 per cent of it consisted of a set of implosive consonants, commonly called "clicks", which were absent from the English phonological system. Lindfors states that "the number and variety of these click consonants, complicated still further by subtle vowel colourings and significant variations in tone make it, from the phonetic point of view, among the world's most complex languages". To the Victorians, however, hardly interested in such analysis, San speech merely sounded like animal noises. The *Liverpool Chronicle* reported that "the language resembles more the cluck of turkeys than the speech of human beings" (5 December 1846), and the *Era* described the language as "wholly incomprehensible, for nobody can interpret it . . . The words are made up of coughs and clucks, such as a man uses to his nag. Anything more uncivilised can scarcely be conceived" (6 June 1847). Even when admission of the humanity of the San people was grudgingly conceded, the classics of white literature were raised against them: the *Observer* printed that "their distinguishing characteristic as men is their use of language, but besides that, they have little in common . . . with that race of beings which boasts of a Newton and a Milton" (21 June 1847). The science of Newton and the literature of Milton are sufficient to put black people in their place. Idi Amin's (Alan Coren's) reference to Milton is not a loose one. Milton's ornate, highly structured, Latinate expressions, so unattractive to modern tastes influenced by Eliot and Yeats, are still the exemplars of English civilization, against which the barbaric, broken utterances of black people are judged.

II

In January 1978 Margaret Thatcher made a speech broadcast on prime-time television which reinforced the notions of "otherness" so prevalent in British writings on blacks. It was rhetoric which decimated the neo-fascist National Front party as an electoral force by winning the far-right of the Tory party:

> If we went on as we are, then by the end of the century there would be four million people of the New Commonwealth or Pakistan here. Now that is an awful lot and I think it means that people are really rather afraid that this country might be swamped by people with a different culture. And you know, the British character has done so much for democracy, for law, and done so much throughout the world, that if there is a fear that it might be swamped, people are going to react and be rather hostile to those coming in.

Her pronouncement, however, was very outdated, for the native British some four decades earlier had already exhibited "rather hostile" (note how the upper-class term "rather" softens the sinisterness of "hostile" and "afraid") behaviour towards fellow black citizens. In September 1948, two months after the first boatload of post-war West Indian immigrants arrived on the SS *Empire Windrush*, race riots broke out in the streets of England. A decade later, in 1958, anti-black riots erupted in Nottingham and in the Notting Hill area of London, with gangs of white teenagers engaged in "nigger hunting", the working-class version of fox-hunting. In the next decade onwards, communal violence based on Catholic–Protestant/Irish–English hostilities became a daily feature of British life. The killings of civilians, policemen, soldiers, politicians and one member of the Royal Family dominated television screens. In the eighties, race riots in Bristol, Liverpool and London (the old slave ports) led the police to use plastic bullets for the first time on the British mainland. Today, even Home Office statistics reveal that the number of physical racial attacks on black people runs into the thousands annually, while the night-time burning down of homes is a routine experience for some immigrant communities. When E.P. Thompson declared that "England is the last colony of the British Empire", it was to such neo-colonial violence and communal strife that he was referring.

One of the many ways in which young British blacks have resisted white domination is in the creation of a patois evolved from the West Indian creole of their parents. The poetry that has emerged from the black communities is expressed in the language of this patois, and one of its greatest exponents is Linton Kwesi Johnson:

> Shock-black bubble-doun-beat bouncing
> rock-wise tumble-doun sound music:

> foot-drop find drum, blood story,
> bass history is a moving
>   is a hurting black story.
>
>   (Johnson, "Reggae Sounds", lines 1–5)[8]

Johnson's poetry is recited to music from a reggae band. The paraphernalia of sound systems, amplifiers, speakers, microphones, electric guitars and the rest which dominates the stage and accompanies what one critic has dismissed as "jungle-talk" is a deliberate "misuse" of white technology. "Sound systems", essential to "dub-poetry", are often homemade contraptions, cannibalized parts of diverse machines reordered for black expression. This de/reconstruction is in itself an assertive statement, a denial of the charge of black incapacity to understand technology. The mass-produced technology is remade for self-use in the way that the patois is a "private" reordering of "standard" English. The deliberate exploitation of high-tech devices to serve black "jungle-talk" is a reversal of colonial history. Caliban is tearing up the pages of Prospero's magic book and re-pasting it in his own order, by his own method, and for his own purpose.

    A feature of black British poetry is a sheer delight in the rhythm and sound of language that survives technology, and this joyousness is revealed in poems like Mikey Smith's "R-ooTs" (the line "lawwwwwwd", as Edward Brathwaite says, sounding like the exhaust roar of a motorcycle) or in the writings of Jimi Rand. There is a deliberate celebration of the "primitive" consciousness of sound in Smith's "Nock-Nock":

> Me was fas asleep in me bed
> wen a nock come pun me door,
> bright and early, fore day morning
> before dawn bruk.
> Nock nock – nock nock,
> badoombadoom nock nock
> badoombadoom nock nock
> badoombadoom nock badoom nock.
> Who dat: a who dat nock?[9]
>
>   (Smith, "Nock-Nock", lines 1–9)

The deliberate wearing of the "primitive" label is even more explicit in Smith's "Nigger Talk" poem:

> Funky talk
> Nitty gritty grass-root talk
> Dat's wha I da talk
> Cause de talk is togedder talk,
> Like right on, out-a-sight, kind-a-too-much.
> Ya hip to it yet?
> Ya dig de funky way to talk
> Talk talk?
> Dis na white talk;
> Na white talk dis.
> It is coon, nignog samba wog talk.[10]
>
> (Smith, "Nigger Talk")

The use of language is inextricably bound up with a sense of being black. Hence John Agard's poem "Listen Mr Oxford Don" is conscious of the way creole suffers from the charge of being surly and indecent ("Mugging de Queen's English"), and Agard links this literary indictment to attitudes in the wide society where blacks are accused of a host of criminal activities:

> Dem accuse me of assault
> On de Oxford dictionary /
> Imagine a concise peaceful man like me /
> Dem want me serve time
> For inciting rhyme to riot
> So mek dem send one big word after me
> i ent serving no jail sentence
> I slashing suffix in self-defence
> I bashing future wit present tense
> and if necessary
> I making de Queen's English accessory / to
> my offence[11]
>
> (Agard, "Listen Mr Oxford Don", lines 22–26, 33–39)

Johnson, Agard and others are reacting against the "rational structure and comprehensible language" which Robert Conquest saw as a distinguishing feature of the Movement poets and which still afflicts contemporary English verse. The charge that Alvarez levelled against the Movement – the disease of gentility – is still relevant today. Andrew Motion, for instance, can visit Anne Frank's room and, on emerging, conclude that all Anne Frank wanted was to

> leave as simply
> as I do, and walk at ease
> up dusty tree-lined avenues, or watch
> a silent barge come clear of bridges
> settling their reflections in the blue canal.[12]
>
> (Motion, "Anne Frank Huis", lines 21–25)

There is glibness and gentility here, disguised as understatement but really amounting to a kind of obscenity. As Michael Hulse has commented, "to go as a tourist to a house which, like many similar houses in Amsterdam, focussed human hope and suffering, and then to parade the delicacy of one's response, savours somewhat of an opportunism that is slightly obscene". The quiet understatement of Motion's response to human tragedy is as obscene as Conrad's heated, insistent rhetoric ("It was the stillness of an implacable force brooding over an inscrutable intention", etc.): both belong to a tradition of colonizing the experience of others for the gratification of their own literary sensibilities.

The pressure of the same racism that destroyed Anne Frank and the encounter with the thuggery that lurks beneath the polite surface of English life and letters force black writers into poetry that is disturbing and passionate. The play of the light of memory upon pine furniture, touching vignettes of domestic life, elegiac recollections of dead relatives, wonderment at the zigzag fall of an autumnal leaf – none of these typical contemporary English poetic concerns are of special relevance to them. They participate in a West Indian literary tradition which seeks to subvert English canons by the use of lived nigger themes in lived nigger language. Their strategies of "rants, rudeness, and rhymes" look back half a century to the West Indian struggle to establish "black" expression. In March 1931 a new Trinidadian journal, *The Beacon*, attempted to instigate a movement for "local" literature, encouraging writing that was authentic to the West Indian landscape and to the daily speech of its inhabitants. "We fail utterly to understand", an editorial of January/February 1932 commented on the quality of short stories received for publication, "why anyone should want to see Trinidad as a miniature Paradise, where gravediggers speak like English M.P.'s". Emphasis was placed on the use of creole, and on a realistic description of West Indian life, for political and aesthetic reasons. To write in creole was to validate the experience of black people against the contempt and dehumanizing dismissal by white people. Celebration of blackness necessitated celebration of black language, for how could black writers be true to their blackness using the language of their colonial masters? The aesthetic argument was bound up with this political argument, and involved an appreciation of the energy, vitality and expressiveness of creole, an argument that Edward Brathwaite has rehearsed in his book *The History of the Voice* (1984). For Brathwaite, the challenge to West Indian poets was how to shatter the frame of the iambic pentameter which had prevailed in English poetry from the time of Chaucer onwards. The form of the pentameter is not appropriate to a West Indian environment: "The hurricane does not roar in pentameters. And that's the problem: how do you get a rhythm which approximates the *natural* experience, the *environmental* experience?"[3] The use of creole, or Nation language, as he terms it, involves recognition of the vitality of the oral tradition surviving from Africa, the earthiness of proverbial folk speech, and energy and power of gestures which accompany oral delivery, and the insistence of the drumbeat to which the living voice responds.

England today is the largest West Indian island after Jamaica and Trinidad – there are over half a million of us here – and our generation is confronted by the same issues that Brathwaite and other writers faced in their time. If a writer was to be recognized, the pressure then was to imitate slavishly the expressions of the Mother Country. Hence the vague Miltonic cadence of Walter Mac M. Lawrence, one of our early Guyanese writers, in describing, quite inappropriately, the native thunder of the Kaiteur Falls:

> And falling in splendour sheer down from the heights
> that should gladden the heart of our eagle to scan,
> That lend to the towering forest beside thee the semblance
> of shrubs trimmed and tended by man –
> That viewed from the brink where the vast, amber volume
> that once was a stream cataracts into three,

> Impart to the foothills surrounding the maelstrom beneath
> Thee that rage as this troublous sea.[14]

Brathwaite and others eventually rescued us from this cascade of nonsense sounds. The pressure now is also towards mimicry. Either you drop the epithet "black" and think of yourself as a "writer" (a few of us foolishly embrace this position, desirous of the status of "writing" and knowing that "black" is blighted) – that is, you cease dwelling on the nigger/tribal/nationalistic theme, you cease *folking* up the literature and you become "universal" – or else you perish in the backwater of small presses, you don't get published by the "quality" presses and you don't receive the corresponding patronage of media-hype. This is how the threat against us is presented. Alison Daiches, summarizing these issues, puts them in a historical context: the pressure is to become a mulatto and house-nigger (Ariel) rather than stay a field-nigger (Caliban).[15]

I cannot feel or write poetry like a white man, however, much less serve him. And, to become mulatto, black people literally have to be fucked (and fucked up) first – which brings us back to the pornography of Empire. I feel that I am different, not wholly, but sufficiently for me to want to contemplate that which is other in me, that which owes its life to particular rituals of ancestry. I know that the concept of "otherness" is the fuel of white racism and dominates current political discourse, from Enoch Powell's "rivers of blood" speech ("In these great numbers blacks are, and remain, alien here. With the growth of concentrated numbers, their alienness grows not by choice but by necessity"), to Margaret Thatcher's "swamped by people of a different culture". I also know that the concept of "otherness" pervades English literature, from Desdemona's fatal attraction to the body of alien experience in preference to the familiarity of her own culture to Marlow's obsession with the thought that Africans are in one sense alien but in a more terrible sense the very capacities within Europeans for the gratification of indecent pleasures. But these are not my problems; I'm glad to be peculiar, to modify the phrase. I'd prefer to be simply peculiar and to get on with it, to live and write accordingly, but gladness is a forced response against the weight of insults, a throwing off of white men's burdens.

As to "universality", let Achebe have the last word, even if in the most stylish of English:

In the nature of things the work of a Western writer is automatically informed by universality. It is only others who must strain to achieve it. So-and-so's work is universal; he has truly arrived! As though universality were some distant bend in the road which you may take if you travel out far enough in the direction of Europe or America, if you put adequate distance between yourself and your home. I should like to see the word "universal" banned altogether from discussion of African literature until such a time as people cease to use it as a synonym for the narrow, self-serving parochialism of Europe, until their horizon extends to include all the world.[16]

CHAPTER 3

On Cultural Diversity
(1991)

I AM SITTING QUIETLY AT Frankfurt airport's departure lounge, waiting for my British Airways plane to London. There are about fourteen other passengers. I am reading Salman Rushdie's exciting new essay, "Minority Literatures in a Multi-Cultural Society", in a book called *Displaced Persons*. The book, published in Denmark by an Australian Press (Dangaroo), is a collection of prose and poetry, some of it delivered at a symposium in Stockholm hosted by the Royal Academy of Sweden in 1986. The writers include a Jamaican living on the coast of Sussex, a Trinidadian living in Canada, a Canadian of Dutch parents, a Romanian of Greek parents who lived in Australia and a Pakistani who worked in Birmingham.

By a miracle of timing, a hand touches my shoulder exactly as I alight on this line in Rushdie's essay: "it has been an important aspect of what it means to be a work of art that the work will cross frontiers". The line is so compelling that I have to reread it. When I look up, two heavily armed German guards are standing over me. They address me in German, and while I don't understand a word of their inquiry, I reach automatically into my bag and hand over my passport. I immediately resume reading the Rushdie essay with a sense of elation and expectation: the generous and humane prose is arguing a dangerous case — that the business of the writer is to break through the confines of narrowness, whether it be the political narrowness of nationalism or the cultural narrowness of localism or the imaginative narrowness of social realism or even the existential narrowness of reality itself:

Defence of walls which are erected around the culture can have the effect of crushing the literature inside it as well as keeping hostile forces out. This internal marginalisation also seeks implicitly to control the writer's choice of subject matter. He must choose to write about the great public issues, that is to say there is pressure to write politically, or he is not important, not, if I may use the term, pure. The use of ideas of homogeneity and purity by the majority white culture can easily create such mirror images in the beleaguered minority groups . . . I remember when I was twenty-one and beginning to write – I was in Pakistan then, having just left the University. I found it more or less impossible to write there because of the existence of total censorship. My problem with censorship was not so much ideological, although it was there too; it was more that I could never get a straight response to my work. I could never properly evaluate what I was doing . . . I came back to England to try to overcome this problem, and although I would agree that England is by no means Paradise, the situation there did not seem to me to be comparable to the one I had left.

How was he to foresee the hatred soon to be unleashed against him by British-based Pakistanis? And how was I to understand the German interrogation that followed?

The guards take away my British passport and return after ten minutes or so. They signal that I must get up and follow them. I am led to an immigration desk. "How long, what you do Germany?" the man asks in broken English, scanning my passport.

I pause, wondering whether to answer him in my native creole. ("Three, four day me bin ya" – on reflection, sounding partly German.) Instead, I put on my best official English and inform him that I had been invited to read poetry at a Commonwealth Literature Festival organized by some distinguished German Professors at Berlin and Frankfurt.

"What you do England?" he wants to know, his polite smile masking an aggressiveness.

I reply that I am based at Wolfson College, Oxford. As soon as I utter the name of the college, its Jewishness makes me feel uncomfortable. I remember my Hindu roots with a sudden sense of relief. I throw my mind back to the Second World War, trying to figure out whether the Germans had any grudges against Hindus. I can't think of any. Instead, the word "Aryan" and the figure of the Swastika, shared by both Germans and Indians, enter my mind forcibly and remain there throughout the interrogation.

"What 'PLN. Zealand'?" he asks, pointing to the entry in the passport under "Place of Birth". "You New Zealand? Maori?"

"No, it's Plantation Zealand," I tell him. "It's a sugar plantation in Guyana, which the Dutch used to own until the British conquered them."

A few of the passengers stare in my direction, making me feel foolish and guilty. The possession of a British passport by a Guyanese born of Indian parents in an old Dutch slave plantation was obvious cause for scepticism. And they would doubt *me* rather than the colonial history which created my condition.

"Which year you leave Ghana?" he continues.

"Not *Ghana*. Ghana is in Africa. I come from *Guyana*, in the West Indies, or rather the coast of South America."

Although a country on the continent of South America, Guyana shares an identical history with the West Indies, a history of British colonization, slavery and indentureship, and is considered a West Indian island. It is, in a sense, an island, being the only English-speaking country in South America. To have to explain all this rich cultural diversity to an immigration officer would be intolerable.

"Spell," he orders, and I write GUYANA in bold letters on a piece of paper. He looks at it and is perplexed.

"On top of Brazil, next to Venezuela," I offer, hoping that the names of these bigger, more familiar countries will convince him that my little Guyana actually exists.

A few days before I had stood before the Berlin Wall, filled with a sense of the stupidity of Europeans and suddenly feeling proud that I came from a country of under a million people that had never fought a war, had never contributed substantially to the world economy or to world history, and had never boasted of this or that scientific or technological invention. Its insignificance was its significance. But not now, standing before a hostile immigration officer. The feeling of pride becomes one of guilt and shame, and so the word "Jonestown" escapes from my mouth automatically.

"What?"

"Jonestown," I repeat, slowly and emphatically.

It makes no sense to him either. A few years previously, nine hundred black American men, women and children belonging to a Christian cult led by a white American had committed suicide in the green jungles of Guyana. The news was flashed around the world, Hollywood rushed out a film, a few cheap paperbacks appeared and Guyana was put on the world's map for a few months. Other obscenities in other countries replaced ours and the world soon forgot us.

He picks up the phone, spells GUYANA to the person at the other end and waits. Several minutes later, he receives a reply. He turns to me and asks, "Which Guyana?"

"Just Guyana," I say, confused for a moment, before my sense of geography returns. "British Guyana."

The South American coast had been colonized by different Europeans, so that there became a French Guiana, a Dutch Guiana, and a British Guiana. Travel among the three parts, in which the native Amerindians had roamed freely for centuries, then became a physical and bureaucratic nightmare.

Half an hour elapses. British Airways makes its final call. I am growing desperate, but the immigration officer is cool. The phone rings at last, he speaks into it, listens, speaks again and puts it down. "What papers you carry, other identification?"

I willingly fish out a letter from the University of Berlin, inviting me to Germany. He looks at it briefly and hands it back, as if it could easily be a forgery. British Airways calls for remaining passengers to board immediately. I am getting angry. I rummage through my wallet, show him my university card and British Library card. He pays no attention to them. I show him my American Express credit card, the only other piece of plastic in my wallet bearing my name. His mood changes, as in the television advertisement. He takes it from me, inspects it carefully.

"You from Sri Lanka?" he asks. The question suddenly explains everything. Sri Lankans, fleeing from a civil war, were entering Britain without visas, or with forged British passports. Airlines which brought them in were being fined. I looked like a Sri Lankan, small-built and dark-skinned. (I *was* in all probability a Sri Lankan; my forefathers shipped from the south of India in the middle of the nineteenth century to Guyana.)

"No, I am not a Sri Lankan," I reply. He takes my word for it, gives me back my passport and American Express card, and points to the British Airways gate. I rush towards the plane, only to be delayed at the security point by one of the original guards. Methodically and maliciously he goes through my bag. "C-a-s-s-e-t-t-e," I say slowly, as if teaching language to a child or a barbarian, as he looks puzzlingly at a tape of calypso. He picks up a box and looks into it. "C-o-n-d-o-m-s," I inform him.

When I eventually enter the plane, it is my misfortune to be wedged between two white youths. If either of them speaks to me or if their elbows touch mine by accident I swear I will kill them.

"Cultural diversity" can be a cosy term, evolved out of a blend of European postcolonial guilt and enlightenment,to justify tolerance of our presence in the metropolis. Justification is sought by the white intelligentsia, because deep down they know that a sizeable segment of the British people of a certain generation, those about forty, say, would prefer it if we went away and never came back.

How we got to Britain in the first place still puzzles and upsets most of these people; as Salman Rushdie once said, the British don't know their history because most of it took place overseas. Rushdie was being wicked, though, for you can't be scornful of the British for not knowing – most of them in their involvement with Empire merely followed orders and took on the scraps of prejudice handed down by their social and intellectual superiors.

They didn't make the Empire (the politicians, merchants, poets, intellectuals and the like did this); they only made the Empire work. And they worked for the Empire without knowing what it was, what it meant, what it would lead to (immigration to the motherland, for a start). They were happy to feel superior to the rest of the world – who wouldn't, especially when there was little personal gain from the Empire? At the height of the extremely profitable (for whom?) slave trade, the mortality rate of white sailors on board ship was sometimes higher than that of slaves. All they had were intangibles fed to them by their superiors, the belief that they were an economically, culturally, intellectually and theologically superior race, the Master Race. They were even made to fight the Germans in two World Wars to settle the point.

The West Indians who arrived in British cities after the Second World War were brought here to serve the Master Race, on buses, trains, in restaurants and hospitals. Before long, however, some of the children of the Master Race were dancing to reggae and steel band, shopping for plantains in Brixton market, and mingling with West Indians in pubs, meeting houses and bedrooms. This seeming disruption of the master–servant relationship came about quickly. The West Indians soon lost their awe for the Motherland (an awe bred into them through a colonial education which asserted the glory of British customs, manners, history and language), when they quickly realized the levels of basic ignorance in the society. Samuel Selvon, who worked as a toilet cleaner in London bars while writing novels, spoke of the "abysmal darkness" he encountered in England:

> This was the country whose geography and history and literature I had been educated upon long before I knew that Port-of-Spain was the capital of Trinidad. So why did they ask questions like if the people lived in trees, are there many lions, tigers, and elephants and, of course, *our* language! Where did you learn . . . ? The stories – the actualities – are manifest, but I'll only say this: not Buckingham Palace, not the West End or the Tower of London or the glitter of Piccadilly Circus, not even white men performing menial labour as porters or road-sweepers, not the fact that there were so many whites who could not read or write, struck me as forcibly, or rather impressionably, as this appalling ignorance about my part of the world, when I had been led to believe that I was coming to the fountain-head of knowledge. Though I was from a small island that might be flicked off the map like a speck of dirt from a jacket, I felt ten feet tall.

The British, as described by Selvon, were ignorant of the way their economic appetites refashioned the personalities of the Africans and Indians shipped to the West Indies. They were unaware of the trauma of loss (especially of ancestral languages, which still afflicts the living West Indian). They were unaware of how West Indians created anew out of this void, how they took on the English language, altered it so that it could bear the weight of their personal and communal experiences in the shape of a novel by V.S. Naipaul or a poem by Derek Walcott. Or how they took the quintessentially English game of cricket, mastering its conventions but also inventing new stroke-play (Kanhai's sweep shot) or forms of spin (Valentine and Ramadhin) to delight British spectators.

Unlettered as many of them were, the West Indians who arrived in the

1940s were a highly complex people, containing traces and amalgams of Africa, India and Europe, survival skills nurtured over centuries, a huge curiosity for the world outside their islands, and a desire to give and take and be generous in the New World of Britain. The best aspect of West Indians is this willingness to take, transform and give back. We only pelt stones or start fires when the British seek to wall us in, cut us off, from the possibilities of social and cultural exchange, social and cultural growth. The main lesson that the British can learn from West Indians is how to give and take. When Naipaul wrote in *The Middle Passage* that "nothing was created in the West Indies" he was pointing to the absence of British gifts to the place. They built a few fortifications, a few neo-Palladian mansions, a few churches, a few schools and little else. When they gave, they did so sparingly and out of self-interest. Shakespeare, Milton and Newton were made accessible to a select few who were to be fashioned into mimic men, slavishly obeying the dictates of the metropolis.

The greater self-confidence brought about by the loss of awe at things British enabled West Indian migrants quickly to put down their cultural baggage. Black-led churches, reggae bands, restaurants, publishing houses, bookshops and community centres sprang up, many of which survive today, in spite of financial difficulties and attempted vandalism by hostile white people.

The city, by its very nature, seemed to encourage West Indian culture to take root. Mandeville's enduring image of the hive to describe London betokens the city's capacity to allow for the growth of new cells. Brixton and other parts of south London became such cells. West Indians who moved in soon refashioned them into Jamaican or Barbadian villages (as far as possible), complete with bars selling Red Stripe beer and grocery stores selling coconuts, patties and pepper sauce. They also gave new names to places, altering English words in the progress: Bayswater became "The Water" (or, more correctly, "de wata"); Notting Hill Gate became "The Gate". Every Easter they organized a huge carnival, just like back home. They put on masks and costumes and road-marched behind floats ringing with steel band music. Hundreds of thousands of white people came for the spectacle, music and spicy food.

A city packs people in. They live on top of each other, alongside each other, sideways to each other. The city is a hive in this sense, but there are no inevitable passageways between one cell and another. And this has been the problem for West Indian culture in London – the white people who come to the West Indian cells for a while, to attend a carnival or to taste curried goat, return afterwards to their own cells. They don't spend long enough in the West Indian cells to appreciate the syntax, metre, chords, daubs, noises and smells created in them.

And they don't invite West Indians to visit *their* cells (called universities, banks, concert halls, theatres, arts councils, art galleries, Houses of Parliament, television studios) for a prolonged period either, or in any great numbers. The city is culturally diverse, but there is little cross-fertilization of cultures taking place. White people remain incarcerated in their own cells, afraid to venture out in case they are mugged by West Indians.

It has also been so in the Metropolis. Black people arrived in London in significant numbers two centuries ago as servants to the British aristocratic and mercantile classes. These black immigrants were the most culturally diverse and widely travelled people in the world. Some were born in Africa and then shipped to the West Indies, perhaps to several islands, then sometimes to America before being brought to Britain. They set up cells in parts of London, like St Giles; those not employed in households hustled a living by street, fairground or circus entertainments. As long as they remained colourful entertainers, they were tolerated by the populace. Those with economic or educational ambition were liable to be shipped back to the West Indies and sold into slavery. A few, like Olaudah Equiano and Ignatius Sancho, were befriended by enlightened white people, who gave them access to schools and books. It was only when the Anti-Slavery Movement got into full swing at the end of the eighteenth century that public sympathy for the plight of black people grew substantially.

The black presence was only barely tolerated. Influential voices kept calling for stricter immigration controls and for deportation of those already settled in Britain. Philip Thicknesse, writing in the 1770s, complained that "London abounds with an incredible number of these black men . . . a mixture of negro blood with the natives of this country is big with great and mighty mischief . . . if they are to live among us, they ought by some severe law to be compelled to marry only among themselves".[1] In the 1970s Enoch Powell was saying the same thing, albeit with more eloquence and classical erudition ("mischief" was also one of his favourite words, cropping up in speech after speech on the immigration/repatriation theme). As to the need for cultural purity, Margaret Thatcher's infamous speech on the "swamping" of Britain by immigrant cultures finds echoes in dozens of eighteenth- and nineteenth-century pronouncements: "'Tis said there is a great number of Blacks come daily into this city, so that 'tis thought in a short Time, if they be not suppress'd, the City will swarm with them" (*Daily Journal*, April 1723).

In the anniversary year of Columbus's journey to the Americas, and the subsequent profound alteration of boundaries and cultures, Britain will enter into an integrated Europe. Over time, Britain's own cultural boundaries will be altered and the Old World will become a New World. The New World values in Britain will not be those derived from its West Indian citizens, but from white Europeans. We'll all be eating more pizzas, downing more lager, spraying more French perfumes, driving more German cars and exchanging more footballers. My limited and symbolic experience of European immigration controls makes me fear that British blacks, the original New World folk, will be largely excluded from the new New World jamboree. Our calypso, reggae, creole poetry, art of cricket and the like, already only of minority interest in Britain, will compete for attention against German folk songs, dissident writings of eastern Europe, the French passion for cycling, and so on. If 1492 created us, 1992 could possibly kill us. Perhaps West Indians will eventually slip their cultural moorings and get lost in the swamps of New World Europe. Or perhaps we will be able to adapt, modify and enrich our culture in the new environments. Perhaps new excitements will arise when we encounter the Dutch blacks, the French blacks, the German blacks, and discover what we share that transcends colonial boundaries.

CHAPTER 4

Teaching West Indian Literature in Britain (1997)

I

THE WEST INDIES, IN THE words of Nobel Laureate Derek Walcott, is "the world's most accessible fuck".[1] Not surprisingly, courses on the region's culture are considered "sexy"; they are swamped by eighteen- to twenty-one-year-old white undergraduates who come seeking excitements other than the intellectual. Some have black lovers, or have smoked marijuana. All have danced to Bob Marley. The richer ones have lain under the sun of Barbados. Speaking generally, they attend West Indian Literature classes because they find their own culture jaded, lacking frisson and danger. To be a West Indian Literature student is to be cool, hip and sub-cultural, like the subject of their enquiry, the blacks who inhabit the ghettos of Kingston or Brixton.

The teacher's business is to disabuse them of their expectations and to police their enthusiasms. The teacher is kill-joy. The teacher instructs them to read the unreadable, to speak the unspeakable: postcolonial and postmodernist theory. The student in an early class on Sam Selvon who exclaimed, "But Trinidad is such a *vibrant* place, all that music and rhythm and sand and simple speech. Whoever would want to live in England!", by the end of the course speaks of West Indian culture in sombre, terrorist terms – it subverts canons, it interrogates the great tradition, it challenges the direct authority of the dominant, it contests the ideological hegemony of cultural precepts, it mugs the Queen's English. At the end of the day, West Indian culture equals mugging, in spite of the highfalutin rhetoric. And its students' initial innocence has been lost to the more mature pleasures of mastering the techno-chip jargon of theory.

The fault is partly ours. We are West Indian teachers in single numbers inhabiting the margins of the Western academy. Our jobs are not necessarily created out of the academy's desire to enlarge and enrich its humanities curriculum by being more fully representative of humanity, but out of post-imperial guilt, or the social pressure exerted by street-blacks. Our centres are handouts, forms of welfare cheques. The Centre for Caribbean Studies at the University of Warwick, the first of its kind at a British university, was, after all, created in the wake of the Brixton and Toxteth riots, and the American invasion of Grenada. The West Indies, in the words of George Lamming, is "a unique experiment", characterized by fantastic survivals, hybridities and amalgamations.[2] Through immigration, multicultural societies emerged – a complex mixture of Amerindians, Africans, Asians and Europeans living together with the varied legacies left by Spanish, English, French and Dutch colonizers, and now within the shadow of the United States. There is scarcely an ideology in the Third World that does not have a Caribbean provenance, the most striking expression of which is perhaps the Cuban revolution.[3] The Western academy, however, remains to be convinced of the intellectual potential of "Caribbean studies". Hence the marginal status reflected in marginal and precarious funding.

The survival and career enhancement of the marginal and tokenistic West Indian scholar in the Western academy depends on mastery of the Western idiom. The same goes for other "Third World" scholars in their own countries. As the Indian academic, Meenakshi Mukherjee puts it, "a generation ago, when I began to study literature as an academic discipline, I submitted to the central ideologies of power in the literary and intellectual domain which at that time were Anglo-American in origin and male in outlook". European critical traditions have since displaced the Anglo-American, but the problem remains that validation is the business and privilege of the "Centre". Thus the radical ideas of a critic like Edward Said have had to "pass through the Centre . . . in order to return to the periphery". If, as Mukherjee argues, the most crucial terms and concepts of the new critical discourse are "historically linked with certain phases of literary development in Europe", then their inapplicability to "Third World" literature should be evident. Yet the West Indian teacher, with a minor and vulnerable status in the Western academy, knows with what his bread is buttered. And it's French butter. Instead of devising a West Indian poetic in which to read West Indian literature, the teacher reaches for brand names and market leaders – Lacan, Derrida et al. The result is, as Mukherjee states memorably, "mime and ventriloquism".[4]

The writers have done what they can to sneer at the new theoreticians, none more brilliantly than Derek Walcott in arguing for chaos, paradox and non-sense as sources of creativity:

> A lot of dead fish have beached on the sand. Most of the fish are French fish, and off their pages there is the reek of the fishmonger's hands. I have a horror, not of that stink, but of the intellectual veneration of rot, because from the far off reek which I get from the stalls of the academy, there is now a school of fishermen as well as schools of fish, and these fishmongers are interested in examining the disembowelled entrails of poetry, of marketing its guts and its surrounding conversation of flies. When French poetry dies the dead fish of French criticism is sold to the suckers. "Moby Dick is nothing but words, and what are words, and what do I mean when I say Moby Dick, and if I say Moby Dick what exactly do I mean?" It convinces one that Onan was a Frenchman, but no amount of masturbation can induce the Muse... I cannot think because I refuse to, unlike Descartes. I have always put Descartes *behind* the horse.[5]

Walcott's is an ancient Romanticist charge against the critic who is "murdering to dissect". Wole Soyinka's charge is more contemporary; it is against the atomic white light of theory which threatens abstraction and annihilation: "We have been blandly invited to submit ourselves to a second epoch of colonisation – this time by a universal–humanoid abstraction defined and conducted by individuals whose theories and prescriptions are derived from the apprehension of *their* world and *their* history, *their* social neuroses and *their* value systems. It is time, clearly, to respond to this new threat."[6] The challenge to the West Indian teacher then, within the Western academy, is to abandon Western critical theory as being inappropriate to an understanding of West Indian literature, and to take the consequences in terms of career, or in terms of being seen to be unfashionable or intellectually backward. The

West Indian teacher will then have to offer for analysis a set of propositions about the history and culture of the region – a particular region, *derived from the body of creative writing itself*. The primacy of the writing must be restored, otherwise the centuries-old struggle for self-expression will be denied. The work of Pauline Melville, to cite but one writer arbitrarily, emerged from the plundering and silencing of her Amerindian ancestors. We can either be alert to her writing – its specific body of ideas, its specific form and texture – or we can drown her living voice – and the voices of the past – in a chorus of *their* (French, Anglo-American) techno-speak. And if we are to quarrel with Pauline Melville's ideas or craft, then that disputation is best served by positioning another West Indian literary work against hers. The books should speak with each other, the task of the teacher being to host the dialogue. The criteria for literary judgement should be derived from the works themselves and not from Plato and his footnoters.

II

The problem with postmodernist theories is that they tend to dismiss "presence" as a kind of metaphysical conceit and valorize "absence", "aporia" and "kenosis". Such approaches may be suited to an exploration of such a novel as *Flaubert's Parrot*, but they should be anathema to students of literature written by blacks. Take Olaudah Equiano, for instance, the eighteenth-century African–British writer, whose central concern was with textual presence – placing himself before the audience, asserting his humanity ("Am I not a man and a brother?") at the height of the slave trade, the philosophical justification of which was the designation of blacks as a species of lower primates. Post-Structuralism thinks of literature as a dance of the pen. For Equiano, it was anything but. Writing, for him, was a deadly serious business. It was bound up with his own personal salvation as well as with the Abolitionist cause. As a slave in the Americas, his mastery of the English language saved him from beatings and brutalization, since he could argue eloquently against violence and injustice, quoting biblical precepts to his Christian persecutors. When he published his autobiography in Britain in 1789, he lived by its revenues, travelling all over Britain reading from it and, in the process, selling thousands of copies to a new market of readers – the Abolitionists. Equiano had found a niche in the market for books, and out of his blackness he created a text which exploited that niche and became, literally, a best-seller. Equiano made such a fortune from the sale of his book that he became a moneylender, his clients being white Englishmen! The wide currency of the book, as well as its literary merit, ensured that it became a potent weapon in the hands of Abolitionists.

A postmodern, historical approach, which for good measure also kills off the author, is patently inappropriate to a reading of Equiano. Deconstruction, for instance, mocks the notion of referentiality and representation. It sunders the link between word and world. In the words of Sukhdev Sandhu, "This is most pernicious. Equiano emerged from and wrote of social milieux which he knew about with a kind of painful intensity. To say that his book stems from a particular period and body of social circumstances is not to deprecate its literary qualities, but to make the point that you cannot fully appreciate his work without a firm grasp of the social and historical materiality that underpins it."[7]

To illustrate, I quote in full a story Equiano tells of a venture in which he was involved, with a fellow slave, both of them sailors on ships trading among the Caribbean islands:

> and at our sailing he had brought his little all for a venture, which consisted of six bits' worth of limes and oranges in a bag. I had also my whole stock, which was about twelve bits' worth of the same kind of goods, separate in two bags, for we had heard these fruits sold well in that island. When we came there, in some little convenient time he and I went ashore with our fruits to sell them, but we had scarcely landed when we were met by two white men, who presently took our three bags from us. We could not at first guess what they meant to do, and for some time we thought they were jesting with us, but they too soon let us know otherwise, for they took our ventures immediately to a house hard by, and adjoining the fort, while we followed all the way begging of them to give us our fruits, but in vain. They not only refused to return them, but swore at us and threatened if we did not immediately depart they would flog us well. We told them these three bags were all we were worth in the world, and that we brought them with us to sell when we came from Montserrat, and showed them the vessel. But this was rather against us, as they now saw we were strangers as well as slaves. They still therefore swore and desired us to be gone, and even took sticks to beat us, while we, seeing they meant what they said,

went off in the greatest confusion and despair. Thus in the very minute of gaining more by three times than I ever did by any venture in my life before, was I deprived of every farthing I was worth. An insupportable misfortune! But how to help ourselves we knew not. In our consternation we went to the commanding officer of the fort and told him how we had been served by some of his people, but obtained not the least redress: he answered our complaints only by a volley of imprecations against us, and immediately took a horse-whip in order to chastise us, so that we were obliged to turn out much faster than we came in. I now, in the agony of distress and indignation, wished that the ire of God in his forked lightning might transfix these cruel oppressors among the dead. Still however we persevered, went back again to the house, and begged and besought them again and again for our fruits, till at last some other people that were in the house asked if we would be contented if they kept one bag and gave us the other two. We seeing no remedy whatever, consented to this, and they, observing one bag to have both kinds of fruit in it, which belonged to my companion, kept that; and the other two, which were mine, they gave us back. As soon as I got them I ran as fast as I could, and got the first negro man I could to help me off; my companion, however, stayed a little longer to plead; he told them the bag they had was his, and likewise all that he was worth in the world, but this was of no avail and he was obliged to return without it. The poor old man, wringing his hands, cried bitterly for his loss, and indeed he then did look up to God on high, which so moved me with pity for him that I gave him early one-third of my fruits. We then proceeded to the markets to sell them, and Providence was more favourable to us than we could have expected, for we sold our fruits uncommonly well; I got mine for about thirty-seven bits. Such a surprising reverse of fortune in so short a space of time seemed like a dream to me, and proved no small encouragement for me to trust the Lord in any situation.[8]

Over the years, in teaching this passage, I have stressed the following:

- The pathos, consciously created by alliteration, rhythm and repetition, designed to appeal to an age of sentimentality ("we told them that these three bags were all we were worth in the world").
- The story's conscious mimicry of the structure of biblical parables (including a powerful moral ending), designed to appeal to an age of religious seriousness.
- The emotional and symbolic power of the goods of oranges and limes (as

opposed to meats, which Equiano would have also traded in), in line with the tastes of an age of romanticism.
- The careful and rational arguments ("we told them . . . we showed them") Equiano uses to regain his goods, appealing to an age of enlightenment.
- The deft shifts of linguistic registers, revealing something of Equiano's command of narrative in an age of narrative. (The line "An insupportable misfortune! But how to help ourselves we knew not" moves from the rhetorical flourish to quick, pragmatic monosyllables, recalling Robinson Crusoe's apostrophe to money. The shift from the rhetorical to the realistic is repeated later, with Equiano's voice swelling to Old Testament proportions to damn the cheats – "the ire of God in his forked lightning" – then quickly returning to earth with "still however we persevered".)
- The exceedingly polite and literary turn of phrases, revealing Equiano's adoption of the mask of an eighteenth-century gentleman, in an age of slavery which sought to prove the inferiority of blacks by reference to their inability to arrive at language. ("He answered our complaint only by a volley of imprecations against us, and immediately took a horse-whip in order to chastise us, so that we were obliged to turn out much faster than we came in.")

Other linguistic strategies in this brief passage include the questioning of the moral authority of whites to rule and subjugate. The use of the religious world "chastise", for instance ("took up a horse-whip in order to chastise us"), evokes a topsy-turvy world in which the sinner is confused with the sinned-against. The white man plays God when he is mere thief and wielder of a callous whip. The world turned upside-down is of course the "moral" of Equiano's tale ("such a surprising reversal of fortune in so short a space of time"), as it was of many eighteenth-century pieces of white writing, but in Equiano's case the trope is deeply painful since it originates not from the philosophical imagination but from the weals on his black skin. The "moral" of Equiano's tale may read like an ordinary piece of Christian wisdom, but its consciously conventional tone disguises a profound "existentialist" sorrow at the day-to-day experience of black people: its uncertainties, aborted hopes and cruel vicissitudes. As a slave, Equiano knew the condition of non-being: he knew that *being*, in the context of an age of commerce, depended on owning *something*, and on making it subject to his will (hence the measuring of his life according to the worth of his oranges and limes, and his freedom to dispose of *his* goods). Equiano saved £40 and purchased his own freedom. He bought his own life, then sold it in the form of an autobiographical publication, making a massive profit out of the "existentialist" transaction. The "moral" of his tale, "to trust the Lord in any situation", is massively ironic when we consider the commercial meaning of the word "trust". In God he trusts; everyone else must pay him cash.

I teach Equiano as an artful storyteller and writer, one who is always conscious of the moods and trends of his age, and who exploits these for the sake of money-making and for the liberation of his fellow blacks. The exploited becomes the exploiter, with a moral and ethical purpose, thereby undermining the very foundations of eighteenth-century commerce: the bifurcation between ethics and business, expressed in the eighteenth-century dictum "religion is one thing, trade another", was the very rationale for slavery.[9] Above all I teach Equiano as an eighteenth-century travel writer, one who knew the "tricks" of contemporary travel writing, its mixture of money-making, exotic adventure and Christian zeal; one who mimicked the "tricks" so as to expose their hollowness and hypocrisy.

Such approaches to Equiano are very different from those of some of my white students who impose upon the writer their own second-hand theories, thereby trivializing the literary genius of the man. Hence the student who took a pseudo-psychoanalytic view, describing Equiano's longing for his mother (from whom he was separated as a boy, and enslaved) as an Oedipal concern, and argued that the oranges represented Equiano's testicles, and that their theft symbolized the persistent emasculation of the black by white supremacists since the seventeenth century. Westerners whose idea of liberation is the arousal of the clitoris, and who meditate upon their genitalia for the meaning of emancipation, obviously have utterly different perspectives and lifestyles from Equiano and the mass of his descendants. By all means, they should wank over their own texts, but to do so over ours is to repeat the sexual patterns of slavery in which the black could be violated in silence (the silence of the Letter of the Law), word and world severed in a manner prophetic of postmodern theories.

III

How to avoid Western theory, which will exoticize, capture and Calibanize the black subject, is the challenge before the West Indian teacher in Britain. Suspicion of Western theory must go hand-in-hand with a re-conceptualization of the nature of West Indianness, one which foregrounds the existence of cultures only partially affected by contact with the European. Teachers of Caribbean studies in Britain still tend to focus on the ways Britain had an impact on the economy, social and kinship institutions, and psyche of African slaves and their descendants. The prevalent view still is that the region was made (or, to use Walcott's imagery, *laid*) by Britain. In other words, we are mulattos and mimic men and women; we play cricket, but with sufficient exuberance and flair to make us a little distinctive; we speak English, but with sufficient grammatical oddities to justify our different colour. Little attention is paid to the myriad ways in which Africans altered British manners and thinking, even in the era of slavery. The creative impact of African languages, philosophies and cultural practices on the day-to-day lives of white masters and overseers is hardly understood. No one denies the massive erasure of African cultures in the era of slavery, but few investigate and document the ways in which the British became "Africanized" in the process. Caribbeanists remain habituated to reading colonial history as a one-way traffic of values, in which British culture supplanted and superseded that of the African while remaining "unadulterated" by anything African. The Western academy also appears unable to read non-Western Caribbean traditions in their total or partial survivals, preferring to focus instead on the Western effort to eradicate these traditions. As a result, notions of colonizer/colonized, centre/periphery, and so on, continue to dominate descriptions of the historic relationships between British and West Indian cultures.

Of Caribbean intellectuals, it is the Guyanese painter Aubrey Williams who is most explicit in his championing of the non-Columbian values of the region. He confesses that, as a result of his working in Europe, with a European education, the images of his canvas are inevitably "glossed over with European angst, European psychology, European everything because I am still a captured individual".[10] He is also trapped in the materiality of Europe in that he has used canvases and oils; he cannot "go back" to grinding pigments and using fats. And yet his whole life's struggle, as a Guyanese of Amerindian, African, Indian and European ancestry, has been to banish the European aspect from his art. He concludes on a confused note of defiance and despair, "All my life I have been trying to get rid of it, but I don't know whether I can. If we can get rid of it in ourselves it will be a great achievement. I don't think that getting rid of economic structures, or changing them, is enough. We have to find new values, new directions, which we can now do only with the coming generations. Not so much with ourselves." Williams's position is open to the charge that it evokes the very notions of ethnic purity and essentialism which underpinned the imperial project and which wreaked such havoc upon the very pre-Columbian peoples who inspire his art. I think, however, that Williams simply wanted a downgrading of the role of Europe in our making, in favour of a greater recognition of our native resources, the communities of native values which survived in spite of the conquistadors, planters and missionaries.

I would suggest that one of the ways of fulfilling Williams's quest for "new values and new directions" in the region is by engagement with what is oldest in the region, namely our Amerindian cultures. In Guyana we have many such living cultures – Wai Wai, Macusi, Arawak, Carib – but Western Caribbeanists know next to nothing of Amerindian languages, oral and written expressions, myths, religions, art, music, diet, political economy, gender relations and so on. Evidence of the wilful neglect of Amerindian cultures is stark: I know of no anthology of West Indian oral and written literature (and there are many, produced by such specialist publishers as Longman and Heinemann) which includes a single Amerindian poem, chant, song, prayer or proverb. There is, correspondingly, a total ignoring of Amerindian ideas in books that purport to deal with the intellectual traditions in the region. There is not even a footnote in such books, explaining the absence. The simple fact is that the scholars who produce such texts – which form the basis of teaching Caribbean studies in the Western academies – have rarely travelled into the interior to meet Amerindians, never mind studied their languages and cultures. To do so demands effort – the effort to *know* the subject. The dismal truth is that Caribbeanists are still very much timid external observers of the cultures of the region. Herskovitz's injunction that they should "get down from their verandas" and live among the peoples they study falls on deaf ears. If the region has always been prey to piracy and quick plunder, today it endures new pirates from the metropolis – people who make quick visits, observe hastily and in fright of the native presence, then return to pronounce with authority in the centres in Britain.

The Amerindians, the most invisible of West Indian peoples, are paradoxically signposts of the future. What distinguishes their existence is the absence of recognition of boundaries. They carry no passports, seek no visas and observe none of the territorial imperatives and protocols of the colonial legacy. They have no sense of centre or periphery. Maps, colonial in conception, which demarcate the land, are alien to them. Amerindians cross over at will to Venezuela and Brazil, irrespective of the fact that the landmass was divided up by the Portuguese, the Spanish and the British. Similarly, their sense of time is not linear and periodic but circular and continuous.[11] They are postmodern in the movements of their own lives without the bureaucracy of theory to inform them of the fact, or to validate their condition.

Another way of realizing Williams's desire for originality rooted in native form and native content is to attend to Asian cultures, another neglected aspect of Caribbean studies. Among immigrants to the region, Indians have proved to be the most resilient to Christian conversion. H.P.V. Bronkhurst, the nineteenth-century Methodist missionary, confessed to utter frustration at the stubbornness of Indian beliefs: "In preaching to the coolies, whether in sugar estates, in the yards, villages and publicly, in large numbers or privately in their houses, we meet with endless objections brought before us again and again."[12] So successful were they in resisting colonial brainwashing that today, one hundred fifty-five years after their first arrival, Indian cultures, centring on the mosque and Hindu temple, flourish in Guyana and Trinidad, in original and creolized forms. The resistance to Christianity was, of course, never total, and in addition Indian cultures were open to change within the slowly dissolving framework of tradition.

In a recent essay on the influence of Indian classical and folk music on the making of West Indian literature, Sasenarine Persaud, a Guyanese writer, has this to say of Sam Selvon: "Sam Selvon's work is not without the influence of these rhythms and closer examination may well show that much of his often touted calypso rhythms are actually the rhythms of chowtals or taans."[13] Persaud invites us to listen to the orality of Selvon's narrative with more subtlety and greater awareness of Indian songs, song-games, tales, proverbs, riddles, charms, oaths and jokes which constitute a distinctive Indo-Caribbean orality. Needless to say, critics of Sam Selvon have wholly ignored this dimension to his writing. Persaud proceeds to reveal how a West Indian novel can be Indian in structure and technique by reference to one of his own works, in which the division into three sections and varying length of each section correspond to the three rhythms of the classical Indian raag, with the reversal of rhythms informed by the yogic view that there is no beginning and no end, just cycles to and from pure consciousness. The exploration of the nature of memory, which constitutes Persaud's fiction, also has a distinctive Indian motive. The nature of memory is a central Afro-Caribbean concern, given the metropolitan efforts to erase the Africanness of the African and the counter efforts of writers like Equiano to remember the dismembered body of the past by the fusion of the living imagination and scholarly recovery of data. Persaud's project differs in that he is not concerned with the materiality of history within a particular time span. Persaud is concerned with the "essence of the reality of re-incarnation, which is memory. If the individual can sit down and train the consciousness to retrieve what the consciousness has recorded, then he can see past, present and future. This is the essence of yoga."[14]

I would venture that Persaud's essay, if developed and magnified, can offer completely new ways of reading certain works by West Indian writers, of Indian origin or otherwise. The critical terminology used, derived from Sanskrit literature and Indian classical and folk music, is refreshingly different from the jargon critics use today, which is almost entirely derived from the West. If we are to deconstruct West Indian fictions, then let us attempt to use vocabulary and concepts derived from Indian aesthetics that are native and alive and present, because they are still being used in everyday and ritualistic life by a substantial proportion of our Indo-Caribbean peoples. If we learn the vocabulary and the cultures that create and sustain that vocabulary, we may well find surprising correspondences with the Western concepts which we take on board with such ready mimicry. Why are we, for instance, so engrossed with Paul de Man's rejection of a metaphysics of presence, when closer to home we have critics and priests who also reject the notion of origin, but from a native yogic philosophy? And if that yogic philosophy, which speaks of seamlessness, contradicts the Afro-Caribbean search for specific roots and origins, how can we embrace that contradiction to forge a sense of national unity? Such Caribbean questions are possibly beyond solution by the use of European conceptualizations, as Aubrey Williams intimated.

Since 1838 we have had in the West Indies a body of texts of staggering physical bulk and philosophical dimensions, which have been almost completely ignored by Caribbeanists. I refer to the Hindu epics. The *Aeneid* of Virgil runs to twelve thousand lines, the *Iliad* of Homer to double that number; the *Ramayana* rolls on to a hundred thousand lines, while the *Mahabharata* quadruples that sum; the *Vedas*, when collected, form eleven huge Octavo volumes, while the *Puranas* extend to two million lines. I mention *quantity* so as to highlight the fact that the act of ignoring these texts is an act of monumental bias. These native texts are available, they have existed in English translations for decades, and are regularly performed on stage and village grounds by the common people (as Derek Walcott reminded us in his reference to the Ramlila Festivals at the opening of his 1992 Nobel Prize speech).

The *Ramayana*, narrated, sung and dramatized by Indo-Caribbeans from the days of indentureship to today, was important for several reasons. The story of banishment, exile and displacement, and perilous new encounters among strange tribes, the story of a fall from grace into a prison-house of misery, served as an allegory of the experience of indentureship. We don't have to keep imposing a Homeric grid on native life, or agonize over Western theories of tragedy, to express the character of our West Indian historical and individual selves. Exile and homecoming are the *Ramayana*'s themes.

The *Ramayana* ends with the rule of Rama, the Golden Age, or Ram Raj, the Age of Light. The absence of poverty, petty jealousies, diseases, hunger and death was, of course, the antithesis of life in the nineteenth-century United Provinces and Bihar, from where Indo-Caribbeans originated, as well as the life that awaited them in colonial plantations. Scholars like Clem Seecharan have argued that the shame of the actual past, and the guilt of severing family ties and abandoning traditional duties in fleeing to the colonial plantation, encouraged Indians to forget their specific origins. What replaced the sense of history was a sense of the *Ramayana*, and as direct contact with India diminished with time, it was the *Ramayana* which represented India to the descendents of indentured workers: "It was an India that was as opulent, magical and epic as the fables of the *Ramayana*; a land on the brink of a

Golden Age (a view strengthened, incidentally, in the 1940s, when India fought for and won independence from Britain; the second colony to do so)."[15] In other words, India existed in the realm of the imagination and, as a result, the image of India was susceptible to manipulations in order to fit specific exigencies. India (the past) was made and remade with the same freedom with which the *Ramayana* was constructed – the *Ramayana* having no single authorship but being a product of writings and rewritings, accretions and transformations. The *Ramayana* existed in different versions, and not merely as a printed text. The *Ramayana* had an oral existence – for the common people, it existed as stories and songs and dramatic performances which could be altered according to the nature of the audience or the nature of the performances or the nature of the landscape and environment, or simply the contingencies of the moment. If we want to identify postmodernism in the West Indies, we can look at the ancient *Ramayana* and to its reception and enactments in the region. The coolie, wielding his cutlass before the cane on the nineteenth-century plantation, was, in a peculiar way, at the cutting edge of theory.

To conclude, to teach West Indian Literature in the Western academy will be a flawed and partial exercise *until* the Amerindian and the East Indian, with their particular cultural and philosophical dimensions, are placed at the centre of our considerations. To do so will involve recognition that West Indian peoples are not merely creatures of Britain, forged by British cultural values. It will involve, therefore, redefinition of the character of the West Indian, with emphasis on the cultural values and practices that survived British colonization. Caribbeanists will have to be retrained, at the very least in terms of learning Sanskrit, Hindi or an Amerindian language. A concomitant redefinition of Britishness will emerge inevitably, one that recognizes Britain's historic inability to penetrate "other" cultures, and one that qualifies the belief that still prevails, about the crumbling of "native" cultures before Britain's superior imperial might.

Selected Bibliography

Appiah, K.A. "Is the Post- in Postmodernism the Post- in Post-Colonial?" *Critical Enquiry* 17 (Winter 1991): 336–57.
Ashcroft, Bill, Gareth Griffiths and Helen Tiffin. *The Empire Writes Back: Theory and Practice in Post-Colonial Literatures*. London: Routledge, 1989.
———. *The Post-Colonial Studies Reader*. London: Routledge, 1995.
Baker, Francis, Peter Hulme and Margaret Iversen, eds. *Colonial Discourse/Postcolonial Theory*. Manchester: Manchester University Press, 1994.
Baugh, E. *Critics on Caribbean Literature*. New York: St. Martin's, 1978.
Chrisman, Laura, and Patrick Williams, eds. *Colonial Discourse and Postcolonial Theory: A Reader*. London: Harvester, 1993.
Cudjoe, S.R., ed. *Caribbean Women Writers*. Cambridge, MA: University of Massachusetts Press, 1990.
Dabydeen, D., ed. *The Black Presence in English Literature*. Manchester: Manchester University Press, 1985.
Dabydeen, D., and B. Samaroo, eds. *India in the Caribbean*. London: Hansib, 1988.
Dirlik, Arif. "The Postcolonial Aura: Third World Criticism in the Age of Global Capitalism". *Critical Inquiry* 20 (Winter 1994): 329–56.
Fanon, Franz. *Black Skin, White Masks*. 1952. Reprint, London: Pluto, 1986.
———. *The Wretched of the Earth*. 1963. Reprint, London: MacGibbon and Gee, 1965.
Gilroy, Paul. *The Black Atlantic: Modernity and Double Consciousness*. London: Verso, 1993.
James, C.L.R. *Spheres of Existence*. London: Alison and Busby, 1980.
King, B., ed. *West Indian Literature*. London: Macmillan, 1979.
Lazarus, Neil. "Disavowing Decolonisation: Fanon, Nationalism and the Problematic of Representation in Current Theories of Colonial Discourse". *Researches in African Literatures* 24, no. 4 (Winter 1993): 69–98.
Maes-Jelinek, H. *Wilson Harris, the Uncompromising Imagination*. Sydney: Dangaroo, 1991.
Miyoshi, Maso. "A Borderless World? From Colonialism to Transnationalism and the Decline of the Nation State". *Critical Inquiry* 19 (Summer 1993): 726–51.
Mohanty, Chandra. "Under Western Eyes: Feminist Scholarship and Colonial Discourse". *Feminist Review* 30 (Autumn 1988): 61–88.
Mudimbe, V.Y. *The Invention of Africa*. London: Currey, 1988.
O'Callaghan, E. *Woman Version*. London: Macmillan, 1993.
Ramchand, K. *The West Indian Novel and its Background*. Revised edition. London: Heinemann, 1983.

Rao, Venkat. "Self-formations: Speculations on the Question of Post-Coloniality". *Wasafiri* (Spring 1991): 7–10.
Said, Edward. *Orientalism*. London: Routledge, 1978.
———. *Culture and Imperialism*. London: Chatto and Windus, 1993.
Tiffin, Helen. "Postcolonialism, Postmodernism and Rehabilitation of Postcolonial History". *Journal of Commonwealth Literature* 23, no. 1 (1988): 169–81.

CHAPTER 5

From Care to Cambridge
(1998)

I WAS SENT TO ENGLAND in 1969 to join my father, who, several years earlier, had divorced my mother in Guyana and emigrated in the hope of finding work in London. He had been a cruel man to her and the childhood memory of his selfishness influenced my relationship with him in England. I disliked and feared him the instant he collected me at Heathrow. He was a short, pot-bellied, dark-skinned East Indian. I had not seen him since early childhood. I was now thirteen. He shook my hand wordlessly at the airport. We headed for a place called Balham, mostly in silence.

He had married again, to a red-skinned Guyanese – a move up for him in the chain of being, given the relationship between status and shades of colour in the Caribbean. She was jealous of me on behalf of the four children she had borne for him. I was a threat to her family, a part of her husband's past she naturally resented. I felt sorry for her, and at the same time puzzled by her weakness in tolerating the excesses of my father.

Looking back after eighteen years, I suppose I was too severe in my hostility to him. He had come to England in the 1960s as an ambitious immigrant, had scraped together a few paper qualifications by long study at night school, and had gradually acquired nice possessions like a house and car. His aggressive material and sexual greed was motivated by insecurity. Being a mere boy, I did not understand his own trauma. It was only much later that I discovered that he had once spent a few months in Brixton jail on a charge of fraud. I believe he forged some papers to get some money. The experience was deeply shameful to him; he had never allowed anyone to visit him in Brixton jail. And he never spoke of it afterwards.

London was bewildering. There was the marvellous novelty of brick houses joined end to end, snow, eating with a knife and fork, deep red apples, wearing a school blazer with shirt and tie, and buses to ride on. The white people were frightening, to begin with. On the second evening, I ventured outdoors to view the street and was overtaken by a middle-aged white man wrapped in a winter overcoat; his skin, in the streetlamp light, took on a ghostly, grey appearance. I have never been so terrified in England as I was that night by the sight of that pale image of death.

School was exhilarating. The white boys swore in a shocking way, every other phrase being "fuck your mother". They also seemed academically dull for white people. They disliked the Asian boys because we (although Indo-West Indian, I was quickly re-categorised as a "Paki") were far better at the subjects than they were. I took particular delight in beating them at English. What was enjoyable about the English school was the relative lack of competitiveness and the more liberal environment. In Guyana, education was the only means of escaping from the mud, and city school places were few, so the boys were deeply selfish and competitive, refusing to share ideas or information or books. The teachers there beat us to learn, and parents beat us at home whenever the term school reports came in. Some of us became adept at cramming and cheating so as to survive. England, however, was wonderfully relaxed, being more luxurious than Guyana, but yet many of the English youth were extremely ignorant. They showed little curiosity about the world outside England, but were quick to invent derogatory names to call foreigners. A small percentage of them possessed a humane spirit which marked them out. These boys appeared to be in advance of any of my schoolmates in Guyana. Although just thirteen or fourteen, they read novels, and some wrote poetry or composed songs which they played on musical instruments. They were generous of spirit, ready to share (indeed, encourage) ideas and make friends. The oddest group were the black British children, who were not only dull but surly with it. I had been accustomed in Guyana to highly motivated schoolfellows, Afro- and Indo-Guyanese, who worked hard to be top of the class. The brightest boys in my school in Guyana, those whom I looked up to almost in awe, were Afro-Guyanese. In England, however, the British-born blacks were startlingly dull and deemed by the teachers to be aggressive troublemakers. There was obviously something wrong with England itself which created the gap between the achievement of the West Indian and the black British child.

A series of resentments and disagreements ended with my stepmother's packing my clothes one night and telling me to leave right away. My father, unsure about what to do, counted out thirty £1 notes and said he was sorry things didn't work out. I was about fifteen, so Social Services was called in as soon as I reported to school the next morning. I had spent the first night in clichéd fashion on a park bench in Tooting, stuffed with pound-notes, defiant and at the same time anxious about what to do next.

I spent the next three years in Care, when, in 1974, I went up to Cambridge, where I became not so much a *displaced* as a *misplaced* person. It was a most uncomfortable experience. I simply didn't have the money that social life in Cambridge demanded. A basic Cambridge accoutrement such as a dinner jacket or suit was beyond my means. This was 1974: the student revolts of the 1960s had died totally, and the undergraduates had reverted back to rugby matches, wine-tasting parties and the wearing of monocles. Had I gone to Cambridge in the 1960s, I would have been at home in its environment of studied under-privilege and working-class solidarity. Nor was there money for the obligatory grand tours to Europe that undergraduates made during the "vacs". At the beginning of each term the undergraduates would be greeting each other with cries of "How were your vacs, old boy?" (truly), and the tedious pattern of intellectual tourism would follow. Being a West Indian, and barring finances, I had no desire whatever to see Europe. England was our destination, and England was enough. I imagined that Europe would be more or less the same as England – shops, art galleries, motorways and even more white people. It was only in the mid 1980s that I made my first venture into Europe – to Spain, which turned out to be remarkably like back home in its peasantry, "colonial" architecture and tropical climate – and only because the trip was being paid for by the British Council. I was going to a Commonwealth Literature Conference in Spain as the poet representing Britain, travelling first class for the first and last time in my life, and with a most generous hotel and spending allowance. I read some creole poems at the Conference, about the barefooted folk of Guyana, then flew back in style to England.

During the so-called vacs I would escape from Cambridge to bedsits in

Tooting or Clapham South, and to the safe retreat of the nearest dole office. It was a relief to be surrounded by black people again, and ordinary houses, after the gorgeous human and architectural ambience of Cambridge. The experience of being in Care even took on an almost romantic glow. True, I was always desperately short of money while in Care, but I had developed a fine strategy of survival based on a mixture of study and theft. The study involved a devouring interest in books of history and literature; the theft was a means of acquiring the books. It was not a widespread or habitual crime, and my secret removal of books from various public libraries would not have bankrupted these institutions. Of course I stole food as well, when supplies were severely low, sometimes from Sainsbury's, but more often from the Asian shop at the top of my road. I preferred to patronize the latter because the shopkeeper was a nice man in a turban and over the months I had struck up a vague friendship with him, talking about cricket or India or illegal immigration or the weather. He practised his English by these long conversations and I was happy to help out. I felt sure that if he had caught me walking out of his shop with tins of sardines or jars of marmite he would not have called the police. Sainsbury's was another matter. I also stole the odd sum of money, and I once broke into the coin-meter in my room and in an adjoining room in the bedsits where I lived. These years in Care were a mixture of the sordid and the streetwise, perhaps more the former than the latter, and yet they deepened my sense of human values. Although poor, the people of South London were not always mean and closed. There were many deeds of kindness from various Asian people, to whom I will always be grateful. Their deprivation bred a kind of adolescent idealism in me, so that *things*, edible and desirable as they were, didn't ultimately matter. What mattered were ideas, which things merely facilitated. I had become so foolishly moral that when I broke into the first coin-meter I actually left in the empty coin-box an I.O.U. scribbled on a piece of paper, with my initials.

    I went up to Cambridge at the age of eighteen to read English Literature, but really wanted to become a priest. I spent three unhappy years there, never going to the lectures or seminars. In my three years I went to two lectures altogether, the first to see what they were like, the second to impress a visiting girlfriend by taking her to a lecture on art. The first occasion was painful: a balding, loathsome lecturer in robes spat out eighteenth-century philosophy for an hour, his talk full of insulting asides about his colleagues at the University. I felt deeply stupid, since I could follow neither the topic nor the gossip; terrified, too, engulfed by a horde of white youth who obviously understood the lecture, since they were scribbling away vigorously in their notepads.

I retreated to the university library, where I spent many exhilarating hours of solitary reading and researching. I dwelt mostly on Hardy, Lawrence, Strindberg and medieval poetry, reading practically all I could, including the very obscure books (Hardy's play for mummers, for example, more or less forgotten by all). Hardy's peasant people and country fatalism reminded me, sentimentally, of back home, and I liked, too, the fact that he was scorned socially by eminent gentlemen like Sir John Galsworthy for having muddy boots. Lawrence was a rebellious outsider who made it to the top out of hunger and contempt. He was passionate and imaginative, and his celebration of pre-Columbian consciousness was despised by clever, necktied establishment figures like Eliot and Wyndham Lewis. Strindberg's dramas were shrieking, delirious, yet deeply idealistic, imbued with obsessions about inviolable purity which were strangely Hindu. Finally, medieval poetry. Reading *Sir Gawain* was a startling moment. The sheer energy and nakedness of the dialect instantly recalled the "pre-civilized" language of Guyanese creole. By total immersion in this "Western" literature, I was able to sense its universal roots, or at least its borrowings from our cultures, and read them through Guyanese eyes. When I read Sam Selvon's novels for the first time two years later, I could hear Chaucer's chuckle in every passage.

In the summer of my second year at Cambridge, I borrowed some money and returned home to Guyana. My stepfather was apparently dying of liver problems (he had been an alcoholic for twenty years or so), so I had to go home, as the eldest son, to sort things out. Home, in fact, was not the whole of Guyana, but a small, wooden town therein, audaciously named New Amsterdam. No one outside of New Amsterdam knows or cares about the existence of the place (it has a population of fourteen thousand or so), but it was a town which bred writers of international reputation like Edgar Mittelholzer and Wilson Harris. Guyana from the air was a vast, green spread scored by lines of rivers. From the protected cabin of the airplane it looked a pleasant enough landscape. As the plane swerved and lowered towards the tarmac, I recalled the sense of dread that most Guyanese feel about the jungle that is our abode. Most of the country is bush. We live on a thin strip of coastland, with the impenetrable bush behind us and the roaring Atlantic before us. On a clear day you can see nowhere. We are an island not only in our own country but in a continent – an island not in terms of geography, but in being the only English-speaking country in South America. Prospero's magic was wondrous. When I was a boy I had read a newspaper story of some New Amsterdam men who had ventured deep into the bush in search of gold. A few months later, one stumbled out, half-starved and babbling. The rest had either been bitten by snakes or struck down by diseases and accidents. They had found nothing, but the one man was determined to come out alive to speak the truth. He made the headlines and the story was carried for weeks. The story reminded me of the Tarzan films which so enraptured us in our boyhood, packed into the pit of the Globe cinema, a cinema appropriately named since it offered one of the few chances of viewing the world outside of New Amsterdam. The cinema was located, also appropriately, at the edge of the mouth of the Berbice River, which flowed out into the ocean beyond.

It was the same river I had to cross on my first homecoming. The steamer, left over from the days of British rule, careened from one riverbank to the next, loaded with old Morris Oxford passenger cars and market goods. A crippled man smelling of rum dragged himself along the aisles. He sang Hindi songs and shoved his hand at the passengers. A little girl, barely five, followed him with an alms box in which I placed a few coins in remembrance of our shared Indianness.

Coolie Mother[1]

Jasmattie live in bruk –
Down hut big like Bata shoe-box,
Beat clothes, weed yard, chop wood, feed fowl
For this body and that body and every blasted body,
Fetch water, all day fetch water like if the whole –
Whole slow-flowing Canje river God create
Just for *she* one own bucket.

Till she foot-bottom crack and she hand cut-up
And curse swarm from she mouth like red-ants

And she cough blood on the ground but mash it in:
Because Jasmattie heart hard, she mind set hard

To hustle save she one-one slow penny
Because one-one dutty make dam cross the Canje
And she son Harilall *got* to go school in Georgetown,
Must wear clean starch pants, or they go laugh at he,
Strap leather on he foot, and he *must* read book,
Learn talk proper, take exam, go to England university,
Not turn out like he rum-sucker chamar* dadee.

*Chamar – low-caste.

Coolie Son
(The Toilet Attendant Writes Home)

Taana boy, how you do:
How Shanti stay? And Sukhoo?
Mosquito still a-bite all-you?
Juncha dead true-true?
Mala bruk-foot set? Food deh foh eat yet?

England nice, snow and dem ting,
A land dey say fit for a king,
Iceapple plenty on de tree and bird a-sing –
Is de beginning of what dey call "The Spring".

And I eating enough for all a-we
And reading book bad bad.

But is what make Matam wife fall sick
And Sonnel cow suck dry wid tick?

Soon, I go turn lawya or dacta,
But, just now, passage money run out
So I tek lil wuk –
I is a Deputy Sanitary Inspecta,
Big-big office boy! Tie round me neck!
Brand new uniform, one big bunch keys!
If Ma can see me now how she go please . . . .

Catching Crabs

Ruby and me stalking savannah
Crab season with cutlass and sack like big folk.
Hiding behind stones or clumps of bush
Crabs locked knee-deep in mud mating
And Ruby seven years old feeling strange at the sex
And me horrified to pick them up
Plunge them into the darkness of bag,
So all day we scout to catch the lonesome ones
Who don't mind cooking because they got no prospect
Of family, and squelching through the mud,
Cutlass clearing bush at our feet,
We come home tired slow, weighed down with plenty
Which Ma throw live into boiling pot piece-piece.
Tonight we'll have one big happy curry feed,
We'll test out who teeth and jaw strongest,
Who will grow up to be the biggest,
Or who will make most terrible cannibal.

We leave behind a mess of bones and shell
And come to England and America
Where Ruby hustles in a New York tenement
And me writing poetry at Cambridge.
Death long catch Ma, the house boarded up
Breeding wasps, woodlice in its dark-sack belly:
I am afraid to walk through weed yard,
Reach the door, prise open, look,
In case the pot still bubbles magical
On the fireside, and I see Ma
Working a ladle, slow-
Limbed, crustacean-old, alone,
In case the woodsmoke and curry steam
Burn my child-eye and make it scry.

CHAPTER 6

On Samaroo's *Tempus Est*: The Earliest Colonial Rewriting of Shakespeare's *The Tempest*
(2000)

THE TEMPEST IS WITHOUT DOUBT the most rewritten and reinvented of Shakespeare's works, inspiring plays, poems, novels, paintings and films, as well as a considerable body of socio-political essays from all corners of the globe. The very openness of the work invites speculation, even of the most bizarre kind. As scholars like Mark van Doren declare, "*The Tempest* is a composition about which we had better not be too knowing"; its meanings are not "self-evident", but are subject to a variety of interpretations, contradictory to the point of confusion, of which "even the wildest is more or less plausible". The instability of the text involves its very origination, since the date of its writing is unknown. Its literary and historical sources present us with another mystery. Ovid, Mandeville and Montaigne are commonly cited by critics, but so are seventeenth-century travelogues or ephemera such as Silvester Jourdan's *A Discovery of the Barmudas*. The authenticity of the text itself is open to question. Its first publication in 1623 was supervised by a blind printer, William Jaggard, who employed three compositors of differing carelessness. They worked from a manuscript prepared by the legal scrivener Ralph Crane, who probably worked from Shakespeare's rough draft or a copy of Shakespeare's rough draft – no one knows for sure – the receding of the original work creating space for error as well as conscious tampering. Crane is said to have tidied up Shakespeare's manuscript, assuming it was indeed Shakespeare's manuscript. He divided the punctuation according to his own style of expression. He may well have meddled with the metre of the play. Speeches may have been taken out of the mouth of one character and given to another. For example, Miranda's savage outburst against Caliban in act 1, scene 2, calling him "abhorred slave", accusing him of gabbing "like / A thing most brutish" and of belonging to a "vile race", quite rightly struck critics as not quite in keeping with the fragrance of her character, but sounding more like the cursing of a cheated and revengeful harlot. So, for two hundred fifty years, editors gave Prospero the violent speech to preserve Miranda's linguistic virginity. Even a single letter of a word changed by Crane or the blind printer could alter perceptions of the play in a profound way. The editors of the New Arden edition point to the controversy over Ferdinand's exclamation in act 4, scene 1:

> Let me live here ever;
> So rare a wonder'd father and a wise
> Makes this place Paradise.

Ferdinand's eulogy to Prospero typifies the overwhelming male orientation of the play. In 1709 Nicholas Rowe published an edition of *The Tempest* which changed "wise" to "wife" ("Let me live here ever; / So rare a wonder'd father and a wife / Makes this place Paradise"). Feminists were understandably supportive of the substitution of "f" for "s" – wife for wise – since Ferdinand then appears to acknowledge Miranda's presence and power. It was argued that the "apparent long 's' was actually a broken 'f' which remained intact in the first few impressions but subsequently lost half of its crossbar". So, apart from zealous editors, blind printers and slack compositors, the meaning of *The Tempest* was possibly affected by weak or base metal. The apparent lack of justification, as it were, in Shakespeare's text, has paradoxically *justified* myriad interpretations of the play. Artists from the seventeenth century onwards have been so fervent in their spin-doctoring of its contents that even Prospero would have been rendered speechless by their labour. I will add my own ingredients to this alchemical cauldron by suggesting a green and New-Age aspect, but before I do I will rehearse some previous transmutations.

Firstly, feminist criticism, which asks questions about the prehistory of the drama, stories which lie outside Prospero's commanding narrative, stories about women. Who is Claribel, apart from being the daughter of the King of

Naples and the wife of the King of Tunis? Who is Prospero's wife, equally dismissed from the text in Prospero's grudging one-liner to Miranda: "Thy mother was a piece of virtue, and / She said thou wast my daughter." And Sycorax, Caliban's mother, who is killed off before the play begins and subsequently remembered by Prospero in a few utterances? Sycorax is described variously as swine, bitch, hag, vile witch. This trinity of dimmed and muted women are given voice and presence in the fiction and poetry of Marina Warner, Hilda Doolittle and others. Marina Warner also fleshes out Sycorax's literary forebears in the figures of Circe and Medea, in the process intimating the ways in which Prospero is mired in an ugly and obsessive sexuality, his puritanical rant masking unspeakable desire and unspeakable experience. The possibility of a union between Prospero and Sycorax, who then gave birth to Caliban, sheds new light upon Prospero's fanatical protection of his daughter, as well as on Prospero's recoil from Caliban as from his darker self. In Suniti Namjoshi's poetry, Caliban is female and enjoys a lesbian relationship with Miranda outside of Prospero's conception. In Sarah Murphy's novel *The Measure of Miranda*, a young Canadian Miranda blows up a Central American dictator on seeing photographs of tortures he had sanctioned, and she dies in the process. Gender politics, power politics, Third World politics, the politics of human rights, and the politics of revolutionary suicide engage with each other in ways unforeseen by Prospero, never mind Shakespeare, but which have significance today in terms of the assassination of Rajiv Gandhi by a Tamil woman or the activities of General Pinochet's squads of rapists.

The gendering of *The Tempest* runs parallel with interpretations of the play as an allegory of class conflict. In Derek Jarman's film, Caliban is, in the words of one reviewer, "a bald North-country prole", unwilling to accept any system of social subordination. As Chantal Zabus notes, "in his revisitation of Victorian England, Jarman gives Caliban the trimmings of an Edwardian butler". His underclass companions, Stephano and Trinculo, are dressed in a cook's and a sailor's outfit: "The butler, the cook and sailor represent lower-class male occupations and as such hint at the exploited classes of British society." The Caribbean writer Sydney Doby shares Jarman's class concerns. In her novella *Prospero's Bay*, published in 1999, the scene is a tourist hotel in Jamaica, the management of which is riddled with class hostility. The black manager, an Ariel character, frets over paperwork, punctuality and polish, distancing himself from the black hotel staff, whom he sees as semi-literate, unskilled and disposable labour. Proud of his certificate in Hotel Management from the Polytechnic of Tooting, London, his contempt for the working class extends to the white tourists of lesser breed. His two-year scholarly sojourn in England, funded by the British Council, has made him an expert in sniffing out the aristocrat who is modest, self-effacing and quietly-mannered, from the Johnny-come-lately with his designer-label loudness of appearance, and from white trash who are on all-inclusive package holidays and so eat and drink like fevered swine. A system of discreet apartheid separates the various English classes within the space of the hotel, and much of the humour and menace of the work comes from the incongruities that are revealed when one class accidentally enters the space of the other. The Prospero character, the owner of the hotel, is an Englishman whose incessant self-promotion and boasting of social influence have a certain poignancy, masking self-hatred and inferiority. He is of a lower middle-class south London origin: through prolonged study he was granted a place to read Pure Mathematics at one of the poorer Oxbridge colleges. His Oxbridge life is a series of social humiliations which eventually erode his confidence in the pursuit of pure scientific knowledge, so he settles for the practical and becomes an accountant and entrepreneur. Ownership of a hotel in the colonial outpost of Jamaica is his way of fleeing a class-ridden England. In Jamaica he can lord it not over the natives, who play no part in his pained psyche, but over the hotel clientele from places like Barnsley and Huddersfield.

Both Jarman and Doby deliberately ignore any racial colouring of the play, but, in the latter part of the twentieth century, postcolonial criticism has dominated interpretations of *The Tempest*, with Caliban giving full vent to the grievances of empire. Prospero has come to symbolize the tyrannical European whose technology of printing press and compass and gun has unleashed havoc in native communities, and whose calculating rationality has denied the intuitive processes by which the distance between self and other can be bridged. Caliban becomes the field Negro, the canecutter, the eternal labourer, dispossessed of island and of native culture and who is trapped in retaliatory behaviour. Ariel symbolizes the mulatto or house-Negro, the new breed of West Indian given a degree of authority and policing over his fellow blacks in the imperial system of divide and rule. Miranda is the European virgin who has to be protected against heathen invasion, against native lust. She is the site of struggles between the colonizer and the colonized. If she is lost to the colonized, the whole of European civilization crumbles. Postcolonial renderings of the play highlight what is now a generally accepted view of the economics of empire, from the scholarship of Eric Williams onwards, that the trade in slaves and slave-produced commodities underpinned Western economic and cultural development. British places like Bristol and Liverpool, once fishing villages, became thriving cities and some of the world's greatest seaports because of the business of slavery. Britain's great commercial systems in banking and insurance arose to service the slave trade. In the realm of culture, the eighteenth-century taste for neo-Palladian and neo-Gothic architecture was enabled by the revenues from slavery. The Beckford family, which built Fonthill as a monumental display of both styles, made their pile from the Caribbean, from Caliban's uncouth and Philistine labour. The new merchant and commercial classes gentrified themselves by building mansions stocked with Old Masters – or Black Masters, as they were called in the eighteenth century, because of the accumulation of grime. So the owners of Black Masters were also the owners of black slaves. At the time, the word "patron" had a dual meaning – supporter of the arts, but also possessor of slaves. Jonathan Swift's vicious attack on the Prospero-type prefigures the tone of much postcolonial writing. In *Gulliver's Travels* he works himself into a froth when contemplating Empire: "Ships are sent with the first opportunity, the natives driven out or destroyed, their princes tortured to discover their gold; a free license given to all acts of inhumanity and lust, the earth reeking with the blood of its inhabitants: and this execrable crew of butchers employed in so pious an expedition, is a *modern colony* sent to convert and civilize an idolatrous and barbarous people." The deepest mood of postcolonial writing, however, is not righteous and retaliatory anger but a song of redemption. *The Tempest*, as with *Othello* and *Titus Andronicus*, may have given expression to a horror of miscegenation, but some postcolonial writers have sought a reconciliation between master and slave by dreaming of an ideal love between Caliban and Miranda.

I want now to move to an eco-critical reading of *The Tempest*, one suggested by what is apparently the earliest colonial rewriting of the play, by a hitherto unknown East Indian Guyanese called Samaroo, who in 1929 published a bizarre document called *Tempus Est*, audaciously subtitled "the final version". I can speak of Samaroo and the formal properties of his writing later, but first let me abstract from *Tempus Est* some of his green ideas, even though I run the risk, by such abstraction, of simplifying his surrealistic composition. *Tempus Est* has three concerns relevant to Shakespeare's play. Firstly, a huge clearing has been made in the Amazonian rainforest of Demerara, and it is on this devastated spot and island of desolation that Samaroo sets the Shakespearean scenes. Prospero is neither man nor woman, white nor black, Christian nor pagan. He is a living economy of bones arranged in a hieroglyph which reads itself aloud, each utterance about gain and loss and compounded interest giving life to demonic machines which, inspired by the power of his rhetoric, set about gang-raping and then mutilating the forest. The forest is named Miranda, but when she appears in a violated state, she is the very picture of Lavinia from *Titus Andronicus*, "ravished, her hands cut off, and her tongue cut out". The sounds and sweet airs of the forest have been reduced to Miranda's ghastly whine as she gives birth to Caliban, who is a bionic creature, partly living tissue, partly mechanical cog, the friction and fury between the two parts crippling the thing, not just physically but in terms of its broken utterances. Caliban's sole instinct and craving is to mate with Miranda and to cannibalize Prospero, a wondrous instance of the eco-oedipal, the greening of sexual psychology. The total absence of sexual feeling in the characters, as well as Prospero's various reincarnations, suggests that Samaroo is concerned with the cold-hearted and yet incandescent greed that degrades an environment. Apart from being bones arranged in symbols of addition and multiplication, Prospero is in another scene a gigantic purse, the lips of which form speech that is a glossolalia of newly minted words.

Prospero's attitude to nature is one that would have been familiar to Samaroo, whose landscape was being deforested and converted into sugar plantations. Samaroo appears to elaborate upon Shakespeare's stage business – for example, in act 1, scene 2, when Caliban is ordered to fetch fuel, or when Ferdinand states in act 3, scene 1, "I must remove / Some thousands of these logs, and pile them up, / Upon a sore injunction" – by suggesting that Prospero's rulership of the island is bound up with its exploitation and eventual deforestation. Prospero's attitude towards nature is enshrined in the documentation of empire. In Aphra Behn's novel *Oroonoko* (1688), the Amazonian rainforest is Edenic not in terms of a pristine beauty but because it is a natural resource ripe for commodification by European settlers: "The shades are perpetual, the trees bearing at once all degrees of leaves and fruit . . . the very wood of all these trees have an intrinsic value above common timber, so they are, when cut, of different colours, glorious to behold, and bear a price considerable . . . Besides this they yield rich balms, and gums."

English literature openly encouraged and made use of the commercial exploitation of nature: commerce and industry had caught the literary imagination of the period and represented the progressive hope of the future. Robinson Crusoe is, of course, the most memorable and enduring embodiment of the practical. There is nothing romantic or spiritual in Crusoe's attitude towards nature or towards the landscape of the island. His view is quite simple: if it moves, shoot it, skin it, eat it or cut it down and hack a boat out of it. Crusoe submits all life to economic judgement. His ledger-book mentality extends to the killing of natives as he makes a neat inventory of his victims:

> 3 killed at our first shot from the tree.
> 2 killed at the next shot.
> 2 killed by Friday in the boat.
> 2 killed by ditto, of those at first wounded.
> 1 killed by ditto, in the wood.
> 3 killed by the Spaniard.
> 4 killed, being found dropped here and there of their wounds, or killed by Friday in his chase of them.
> 4 escaped in the boat, whereof one wounded if not dead.
> ———
> 21 in all.[1]

In Samaroo's *Tempus Est*, the emphasis is not so much on the destruction of native life, which is assumed, but on wanton cruelty to animals. In yet another incarnation, Prospero is situated in a library of dead animals, which he studies obsessively for signs of life. His cell is packed with an assortment of butterflies, insects, birds and fish neatly pinned to boards or set in boxes, and all annotated not in terms of their species or their aesthetic qualities but by the date they were caught, the method of killing, whether by poisoning or spearing or starvation, and their market value to collectors of exotica. Money is a factor in Prospero's treatment of wildlife, but this obsessive scrutiny of his bounty for signs of life suggests a fascination with killing for the sake of killing, for the mystery of killing. Prospero's behaviour is evocative of the most bizarre and inexplicable aspect of the colonial encounter, which was the impulse to destroy even when seized by awe at the appearance of native life. In 1586 an English adventurer, John Sarracoll, and a company of soldiers landed in Sierra Leone and entered a small town, which astonished them. Sarracoll wrote, "We found their houses in the streets so finely and cleanly kept that it was an admiration to us all, for neither in the houses nor streets was so much dust to be found as would fill an eggshell." Then something quite inexplicable happened. The soldiers, for no apparent reason, set fire to the town and it was erased within fifteen minutes. The critic Stephen Greenblatt has unearthed other examples of European astonishment suddenly converted into the desire to kill. The Spanish explorer Bernal Diaz, in the 1520s, came upon the city of Mexico and was amazed at its palaces and gardens. Diaz wrote, "I stood looking at it and thought that never in the world would there be discovered other lands such as these. Gazing on such wonderful sights we did not know what to say or whether what appeared before us was real." Diaz and his men then set about destroying the place utterly. The simultaneity of awe and the urge to kill can never be fully understood, and perhaps it lies in Prospero's statement about Caliban: "This thing of darkness I / Acknowledge mine." Three hundred years later, in Conrad's *Heart of Darkness*, comes Marlow's monumental confession of the meaning of his Congo experiences:

> We were wanderers on prehistoric earth, on an earth that wore the aspect of an unknown planet . . . we were travelling in the night of first ages, of those ages that are gone, leaving hardly a sign – and no memories. . . .
>
> The earth seemed unearthly . . . and the men were – No, they were not inhuman . . . They howled and leaped, and spun, and made horrid faces; but what thrilled you was just the thought of their humanity – like yours – the thought of your remote kinship with this wild and passionate uproar.[2]

In other words, Africans are identified as mirror-images or twins of Europeans, and the sudden revelation of kinship evokes immediate horror and an overwhelming urge for repulsion and distancing. It is not a matter of killing the father figure but of killing the twin. Such horror of oneself is the horror of the existence of the multiple self, and Samaroo's originality, in 1929, was to intuit Prospero's need to kill animals as Prospero's need to deny kinship between the human and the non-human. He rationalizes division by killing and price-tagging nature. Elaborating on act 4, scene 1 of *The Tempest*, when Caliban and his companions are hunted by dogs – "Let them be hunted soundly," Prospero commands, putting the horn to his mouth – Samaroo identifies Prospero with any number of European adventurers or planters, for whom the hunting of runaway slaves was inseparable from the hunting of animals. I isolate the person of Charles Waterton, who in 1903 wandered through Guyana marvelling at the diverse forms of wildlife while peppering them with bullets. Take the sloth. Waterton's otherwise prosaic narrative soars to poetic heights when describing this animal: "The hair is flat which puts you in mind of grass withered by wintry blast." Such fascinating contemplation of an equatorial kinship with the northern hemisphere is swiftly ended by the killing and stuffing of the sloth. Waterton laments the absence of a wild spirit in England, for its forests have been cut down, its rude creatures made extinct. Guyana is paradise, but only in terms of the Rambo-esque opportunities to wrestle with alligators and boa constrictors and recalcitrant natives. Waterton is certain of his supreme position in the chain of being, a system of subordination ordained by God. His faith in hierarchy is, as Chris Campbell argues, part of the intellectual heritage of Great Britain. His account of his hunting prowess in Guyana looks back to the work of the eighteenth-century writer William Somerville. In Somerville's poem *The Chase*, hunting is divinely ordained, symbolic of the division among God, man and beasts:

> Hence great the distance 'twixt the beasts that perish
> And God's bright image, man's immortal race.
> The brute creation are his property
> Subservient to his will, and for him made.
>
> (Somerville, *The Chase*, book 4, lines 7–10)

Somerville evokes the science of Isaac Newton to give rational underpinning to the theology of the chain of being. The orderly heavens reflect the orderly class-system of England, a system in which hunting is the exclusive prerogative of the upper class.

From orb to orb, where Newton leads the way;
And view with piercing eyes the grand machine,
World above worlds; subservient to his voice,
Who, veil'd in clouded mystery, alone
Gives light to all.

(Somerville, *The Chase*, book 4, lines 519–23)

Newton is central to an understanding of Samaroo's text. In the process of a long diatribe against nature in creole, Hindi and Latin, Prospero gradually takes shape and comes to life as Shiva, the Hindu destroyer of the universe. The word is a curse made flesh, or rather the cursed word is fleshed into a machine called Prospero–Shiva, literally armed with axes, which sets about not clearing the trees but hollowing them out, degutting them, and leaving them standing in a ghostly settlement called New Tongue, which is the creole pronunciation of New Town. In the colonial period there were innumerable new settlements innocuously called New Town, but Samaroo's naming is significant because Prospero–Shiva's diatribe is sprinkled with half quotations and misquotations from William Blake: "not a grain of sand, not a wild flower left, but I will not wipe from my eye / nor seashore, nor palm of hand nor herb nor fountain nor rill, but to my wile." This couplet is a mishmash of Blake's famous lines, "To see a World in a Grain of Sand, / And a Heaven in a Wild Flower, / Hold Infinity in the palm of your hand, / And Eternity in an hour", which are intimately linked with other lines from Blake which are central to his vision of man's kinship with nature and the cosmos:

> each grain of sand
> every stone on the land
> each rock and each hill
> each fountain and rill
> each herb and each tree
> mountain, hill, earth and sea
> cloud, meteor and star
> are men seen afar.

(Blake, from letter to Thomas Butts, lines 25–32)

The conscious is grounded in and integrated with the unconscious, the interior and the outward worlds penetrate each other, centres and peripheries coalesce in the marriage of heaven and earth. Blake contrasts the alchemical imagination with what he calls Newton's "single vision", which is conventional perception within the material world. As Michael Mitchell writes, "single vision" is the privileging and separating of the conscious from the unconscious, "a process which gives birth to division, categorisation, measurement". Revelry becomes levelling, labelling. Logos becomes technologos: hence Samaroo's creation of the Prospero–Shiva machine. Its couplet, which rhymes "eye" and "wile" ("not a grain of sand, not a wild flower left, that I will not wipe from my *eye* / nor seashore nor palm of hand nor herb nor fountain nor rill, but to my *wile*") conveys the authoritarianism of technology. "Wile" echoes "will" – previous words like "hill" and "rill" encourage the pun. So the two end words of the couplet are "eye will", words which are ominous in their suggestion of dictatorship. But Samaroo resists the rhyming logic of the diction of his couplet by choosing not "will" but "wile", as if to expose technology as artifice and trickery which hollows out nature, which takes the word out of flesh. And the "eye" of the couplet again refers to Blake's association of science and single vision. The miraculously complex and living eye is reduced to "I", to ego and singularity and separation and inequality. Blake's argument with Newton is that you "believe a lie / when you see with, not through, the eye"; "may God us keep / from single vision and Newton's sleep." In Samaroo's text, Prospero's penultimate incarnation is as a gilded monocle laid out in grass to catch the sun's rays and ignite the forest. Single vision yokes heaven and earth, but catastrophically. The gilded monocle is a whimsical reference to the vision or single vision of El Dorado which drew settlers to the green landscape of Guyana. In 1929 Samaroo could see, *through* his own eyes, the consequences of such greed, which were deforestation and ecocide.

Prospero's final incarnation, not surprisingly, and perhaps disappointingly, given the originality of Samaroo's mind, is as a paper-making machine. Trees are mangled and turned into pulp, which is then turned into square pieces of paper, monotonously lined. An empty glove traces endless obscene words on the paper, words like root, vein, waterfall, rock, spirit, sky, culminating in the closing line of the Latin mass, which is also the last line of Samaroo's text: "*ite, missa est*" – Go, it has been finished. But Samaroo creolizes the Latin to "*ite, massa est*" – in other words, "massa day done," meaning, though, not the end of tyranny but the achievement and fulfilment of single vision which is the final crucifixion of the spirit. Samaroo's pessimism about mechanization is a Guyanese counterpart to the Surrealist movement formulated in Europe in the 1920s. World War I, which saw the monstrous appearance of warplane and tank, heightened protest against the purely scientific and materialist worldview. Surrealism sought to discover a preternatural spirit in the seemingly inanimate, to see into the life of things. The language and imagery of the unconscious, manifested in dreams and in inexplicable psychic states, offered clues to a reality above and within the surface reality.

The twenties' anxiety about the machine has even greater force today, especially after Hiroshima and Auschwitz. The New Age movement is one expression of that anxiety, though it is possibly fatuous to speak of a movement, given the variety of New Age beliefs and practices, from UFO-spotting to aromatherapy. At depth, however, the New Age movement rejects dualism, that is, the separation between mind and matter, humanity and nature, humanity and God. Secondly, it rejects a reductionism which fragments the whole into separate parts. It denies that the whole of reality is merely the sum of its separate parts. Its holistic and organic concepts are prefigured in Samaroo's text, which pays homage to *The Tempest* and yokes Shakespeare's play to early twentieth-century concerns about the environment which are even more urgent today.

Let me end by quoting two writers who share Samaroo's concerns and who, in different ways, link ecology to the language of poetry, to modes of seeing and expressing the world that deny reductionism and commodification. Firstly, Ted Hughes's condemnation of the muting of the song of the earth: "While the mice in the field are listening to the universe, and moving in the body of nature, where every living cell is sacred to every other, and all are interdependent, the developer is peering at the field through a visor, and behind him stands a whole army of madman's ideas, and shareholders, impatient to cash in the world." Finally, the Caribbean poet Aimé Césaire:

> Poetic cognition is born in the great silence of scientific knowledge. Through reflection, observation, experimentation, man, bewildered by the data confronting him, finally dominates them. Henceforth he knows how to guide himself through the forest of phenomena. He knows how to use the world, but that does not make him King of the World. Image of the World. Yes. Science can offer him an Image of the World but briefly and superficially. Scientific knowledge enumerates, measures, clas-

sifies and kills. To acquire it man has sacrificed everything: his desires, fears, feelings and psychological complexes.

Ted Hughes and Aimé Césaire – poet of the North, poet of the South; poet at the centre, poet at the margin – and so we can foolishly extend the dance of binaries, the dance of death, except that both, in the face of ecological disaster, asserted the primacy of the imagination over race, class, gender, nationality and ideology. Both were, first and foremost, poets struggling to achieve a language appropriate to the living fabric of landscape, a metre and cadence and diction to name and hallow the landscape. Elsewhere were scientific formulae, economic fabulation, deforestation – in short, the *prosaic*.

Acknowledgements

This is a revised version of a lecture commissioned by the BBC as part of its "Shakespeare for the Millennium" series. The BBC has asked the editors to point out that transcripts of the other talks in the series are available online on the BBC Radio 3 website (http://www.bbc.co.uk/radio3).

Selected Bibliography

Bate, Jonathan. *The Song of the Earth*. London: Picador, 2000.
Branch, Michael P., Scott Slovic and Daniel Patterson, eds. *Reading the Earth: New Directions in the Study of Literature and the Environment*. Moscow, ID: University of Idaho Press, 1988.
Hodge, Jessica, ed. *The Tempest*. Arden Shakespeare Edition 3. Andover: Thomson Learning, 1999.
Hulme, Peter, and William H. Sherman, eds. *The Tempest and its Travels*. London: Reaktion, 2000.
James, David G. *The Dream of Prospero*. Oxford: Clarendon Press, 1967.
Lie, Nadia, and Theo D'haen, eds. *Constellation Caliban: Figurations of a Character*. Amsterdam: Rodopi, 1997.
Palmer, D.J., ed. *Shakespeare: The Tempest: A Casebook*. Basingstoke: Macmillan, 1968.
Vaughan, Alden T., and Virginia M. Vaughan. *Shakespeare's Caliban: A Cultural History*. Cambridge: Cambridge University Press, 1991.

CHAPTER 7

Hogarth and the Canecutters
(2000)

I

I CAME TO CALIBAN IN the 1980s, not through Caribbean reinventions of the play but through William Hogarth's painting *A Scene from the Tempest*.[1] It was, and still is, perhaps the most neglected of Hogarth's major paintings, receiving a few cursory lines from art historians and next to nothing from Shakespeare scholars. Given the compartmentalization of the study of the humanities in the West, the silence of the latter is understandable. That of the former is inexplicable. Typical of the refusal to look at the painting is Mary Webster's one-liner, which ignores content altogether to make a vacuous comment on style: "Hogarth has given himself a greater freedom of invention, which the smoother, more free-flowing paint accentuates."[2] Lawrence Gowing ignores both content and style, giving the barest of information, then immediately looks away to someone else's art: "The picture shows, Act 1, Scene 2. Shakespeare provided a source for history painting. The subject was later adapted, probably by Hayman, for one of the decorations in the Princes' Pavilion at Vauxhall."[3] Even Ronald Paulson, whose work on Hogarth amounts to monumental scholarship, turns a blind eye to the painting, and makes a cursory comment on its "Conversation Piece" structure.[4]

Hogarth is a masterful painter of the ugly, grotesque and deformed, and Caliban is his first and finest specimen of beast. Caliban's emergence onto Hogarth's stage is utterly dramatic, his earth-coloured skin glowing against a gloomy background, lit up by desire as much as by the rich, red drapery of Miranda's chair. He is half-man, half-fish, his feet webbed, his legs leprous with scales. The growth on his shoulder, like clipped or embryonic wings, suggests an inability to fly, an enslavement to the weight of his flesh. He is indeed gross in the proportions of his massive arms and legs, his swollen belly and his huge hands, one of which is clenched in rage. That he is a creature from the bowels of the earth is suggested by the snake – ancient Christian icon of sin – knotted around his burden of sticks. His evil and retaliatory nature is symbolized crudely in the white dove he stamps on, preventing it from flying. Caliban's warped intellect is indicated by the swelling on his forehead, which no doubt mirrors the swelling underneath his loincloth. Mary Webster is right in one respect: Caliban's loincloth is a masterpiece of freeflowing brushstrokes, revealing his capacity for copious ejaculation. The size and shape of the loincloth are a measure of Caliban's monstrous sexuality.

Meanwhile, a cherubic Ariel flies effortlessly, serenading Prospero, Ferdinand and Miranda. If Caliban's hands curl in hatred or reach threateningly for a stick, Ariel's pluck gently at a lute's strings. If Caliban is a gargoyle, a figure from Gothic art, then Prospero, Ferdinand and Miranda are his neoclassical opposites. Ferdinand clasps his hands and bows gracefully before Miranda as before the Virgin Mary. Prospero is the picture of a venerable magus or prophet or patriarch. The wand he holds delicately contrasts with Caliban's rough-hewn, phallic sticks. If Caliban is the exposed nerve of lust, the others are fully and decorously clothed. On their side of the picture lie Prospero's book, its pages open at philosophical and scientific formulations, and an armillary sphere. Neither Prospero, Ferdinand nor Miranda speaks – their delicate lips are closed – for they communicate through Ariel's heavenly music. Caliban's mouth is open, exposing broken teeth and the capacity for howling and cursing.

And yet they have no vivid life; there is no drama to their presence. They could have stepped out of any of a thousand Renaissance paintings of the Holy Family. Any competent artist could have painted them, copying previous models. Not so Caliban. He bears the stamp of Hogarth's originality, which is his mastery of the degraded form. (Hogarth's only obvious nod to the past is in Caliban's Rubenesque belly.) Lewd and cackling whores, vomiting drunks and the like excited Hogarth's imagination. He despised grand, historical art and religious paintings, with their abstractions and well-lit, stiffly formal figures. Caliban is an extreme and mythological version of the low-life specimens he later painted, those who actually lived in the dark spaces of brothels and gaming houses. The dribble escaping Caliban's mouth is Hogarth's own relishing of his self-made creature. "This thing of darkness I / Acknowledge mine", he is saying, with open fervour. Hogarth's sympathy for Caliban is suggested in the coloration of his skin. A conventionally religious light falls on the Virgin–Miranda, but Caliban is lit in a complex way. The monotony of Miranda's porcelain whiteness contrasts with the rich, terracotta texturing of Caliban's skin. The effect of richness is created by hints of golden hues. His deformed forehead, for instance, gleams like a nugget of gold. The scales on his leg are like chipped and loosened gold leaf. The gilded tassel hanging from the gilded shoulder of Miranda's chair (or throne) echoes Caliban's colour. Caliban is primeval earth, but seamed with gold, such as Raleigh hoped to discover in Guiana.

As to Caliban's lack of intellect, his inability to fly, the faggot he bears explains all. He is simply weighed down by Prospero's cruelty. On reflection, the crushed dove, its wings splayed in aborted flight, signals Caliban's own condition. Caliban stamps upon the dove, not in a gesture of innate cruelty, but to signify (since he has none of Prospero's language in which to address Prospero) the crushing force of Europe.

Caliban's capacity for fine feeling, such as evoked by Ariel's lute, is suggested in his prominent and exaggerated ear, the duct of which is echoed in the shape of his exposed navel and in the shape of the aperture made by his clenched hand:

> Be not afeard, the isle is full of noises,
> Sounds, and sweet airs, that give delight and hurt not.
> Sometimes a thousand twangling instruments
> Will hum about mine ears; and sometime voices,
> That if I then had wak'd after long sleep,
> Will make me sleep again . . .
>
> (Shakespeare, *The Tempest*, III.ii.133–38)

It is Caliban who is open-eared to Ariel's celestial music, even as enslavement to Prospero makes him open-mouthed in protest and pain (as in the beak of the squashed dove).

Prospero and Ferdinand are, by contrast, closed to the redemptive possibilities of music, even as it is being played to them, and for them. Hogarth, famous for the most careful deployment of detail, covers over their ears with thick hair. Only Miranda's ear is noticeably exposed, and in this Hogarth makes a subtle connection between her and Caliban. Her ear is tilted in Caliban's direction, as if the two are connected by Ariel's gentle music but also by Caliban's anguished cry. Ronald Paulson asserts that "if Miranda is the protagonist, Hogarth has arranged the composition to emphasise the contrast between her true lover and her pseudo-lover Caliban, who weaves fantasies of raping her, and the structure of choice is here a true and not a parody [sic] one, since all indications point to Miranda's making the proper judgement."[5] Paulson is wrong. On close inspection, all indications point to Miranda's suspension of judgement. In moral terms, Miranda is equidistant between Ferdinand and Caliban, but a trick of perspective makes her appear, in spatial terms, closer to Caliban. Her gesture in holding up her hand in protest is as much aimed at Ferdinand as it is at Caliban: her thumb beckons towards Ferdinand but her little finger points towards Caliban. Her other hand fumbles and spills the liquid being fed to the (Christian) lamb, the spillage echoing in pointed detail the escape of spittle from Caliban's mouth. Typically, spillage in Hogarth's art signifies sexual desire: here, Miranda is as aroused by Ferdinand's presence as Caliban is aroused by hers. Miranda's ambivalent sexuality is suggested in the detail of her exposed ankle and feet (her gown is deliberately upturned), which endow her with a certain coquetry. Such nakedness, echoed in her half-exposed breast, allies her with Caliban as it distances her from her garbed suitor. Her feet are pointed in the direction of Ferdinand as if out of heightened desire, even as her hand protests such desire. Miranda, then, is not the bland or conventional Virgin she appears to be, but Hogarth endows her with an ambivalent character. Caliban is the embodiment of her sexual desire. She is an "open book", unlike Prospero's book, which lies open at her feet but which paradoxically contains knowledge of how to imprison and enslave. On reflection, Prospero's elegant wand is more sinister than Caliban's crude sticks. Miranda is caught between a honey-tongued Prospero fingering his wand and a Caliban wielding curse and cudgel. The structure of the painting makes no neat divisions among Caliban, Prospero, Ferdinand, Miranda and Ariel. Spatially they are distributed within the painting in a series of overlapping structures. The upright triangle of Ariel,

Ferdinand and Miranda overlaps the upturned triangle of Ariel, Miranda and Caliban, as well as the upturned triangle of Prospero, Miranda and Caliban, and such patterning reflects Hogarth's sense of the complex moral connections among the various characters.

II

My preliminary comments should suggest that a complete dissertation can be written on the painting, relating it to the iconography of Caliban in European, Latin American and Caribbean art. My doctoral dissertation on William Hogarth (University College, London, 1982), made the briefest of comment on the *Tempest* painting. I limited myself to making a connection between Caliban and the black man in Hogarth's *Marriage à la Mode*. At the time of my doctoral dissertation I was writing poems that were eventually published in two collections, *Slave Song* (1984) and *Coolie Odyssey* (1987). My response to Hogarth's *Tempest*, unspoken in the dissertation, was fleshed out in poetry. Why? I don't know, but perhaps it was a youthful feeling, excited by too much reading of the Romantics, that academic prose "murders to dissect" and that Hogarth's complex art demanded poetic utterance.

What my poetry does is to echo the moral ambivalence in his painting by presenting the mistress of the plantation as being simultaneously virginal and voracious. In "The Canecutters' Song" she watches the nakedness and ardour of the canecutters, repelled and seduced by their squalor. In "Nightmare" she is terrorized by the dream of rape and ritual humiliation, yet "wet she awake, cuss de daybreak"; that is, she curses the *aubade* tradition which imprisons her in virtuousness. Of course, I have been soundly whipped by male and female critics (Benita Parry foremost!) for seeming to say that women secretly want to be possessed and mutilated in the mud.[6] By and large I have taken my chastisement silently, since to yelp is to apologize for what I have written, and I am genuinely unsure as to whether there are grounds for apology. The deeper vision in *Slave Song* and *Coolie Odyssey* is of the possibility of tenderness between Miranda and Caliban, between the oppressor's daughter and the broken slave (see "Miranda" on the page following). Here the sun is Prospero, the tyrant enlightenment, the incandescence of the branding iron.

As to the canecutters, I depict them as foul-mouthed, aggressively obscene, wielding their cocks like cutlasses. And yet they are no more than Hogarth's squashed dove, expressions of stunted and frustrated love. Their true desire is not to rape Miranda and people the isle with mulatto monsters, but simply the freedom to dream of the possibilities of romance (that is, love and poetry):

> White hooman walk tru de field fo watch we canecutta,
> Tall, straight, straang-limb,
> Hair sprinkle in de wind like gold-duss,
> Lang lace frack loose on she bady like bamboo-flag.
> An flesh mo dan hibiscus early maan, white an saaf an wet
> Flowering in she panty.[7]

What I wanted my canecutters to do was to aspire to and arrive at lyrical words, their final emancipation from Prospero's definition of them as grunting brutes and people without a literature.

Miranda[8]

> His black bony peasant body
> Stalk of blighted cane
> In dry earth.
>
> I will blot out the tyrant sun
> Cleanse you in the raincloud of my body
> In the secrecy of night set you supple and erect.
>
> And wiped him with the moist cloth of her tongue
> Like a new mother licking clean its calf
> And hugged milk from her breast to his cracked mouth.
>
> That when he woke he cried to dream again
> Of the scent of her maternity
> The dream of the moon of her deep spacious eye
>
> Sea-blue and bountiful
> Beyond supplication or conquest
> A frail slave vessel wracked upon a mere pebble of her promise.
> And the sun resumed its cruelty
> And the sun shook with imperial glee
> At the fantasy.

CHAPTER 8

West Indian Writers in Britain
(2000, with 2010 postscript)

MANY PEOPLE TODAY, WORLDWIDE, remember exactly what they were doing when John F. Kennedy was assassinated in Dallas. I remember distinctly where I was when I read my first West Indian novel, Naipaul's *Miguel Street*. I was in our house in New Amsterdam, British Guiana. I was eleven. Although the house was normally crowded (there were nine of us at the time) I remember a solitude in which Naipaul's novel was the sole presence. And the overwhelming pleasure I felt in the presence of the novel resulted from recognition of myself and my surroundings, as if for the first time. Here were characters that behaved and spoke like our own people, and they were in the pages of a book which our schoolteacher had instructed the class to read: a book therefore that had authority. Before *Miguel Street* there were dozens of Nancy Drew and Hardy Boys novels, comic books, Aesop, Charles Lamb's *Tales from Shakespeare*, children's versions of Greek and Roman myths, Ladybird histories of great scientists, artists, explorers and generals (for our humble public library was stocked with a fine sample of English and American publications). Like other children, I read as much as I could: there was no television in the country, and the library occupied as central a place in childhood as the cricket field and the cinema. The books from England and America were enchanting, but it was the enchantment of a world outside of Guyana, an immeasurably bigger and more heroic world which I knew – as colonial children did – I would encounter one day as an emigrant or student. The experience of reading Naipaul was entirely different. It was about me – all of us – struggling to achieve, but failing in sad and comic ways. The failure was not dismal – like the Africans in the Tarzan films – but poignant, showing us to be people of ambition and humility. We were small people, but we had human qualities.

Later in life, I can see incipient, if not open, contempt in *Miguel Street* for the West Indian character, but as a boy I felt only pathos, possibly because the pathos of the novel was not unlike that in the Bombay film melodramas which Indo-Guyanese grew up on. The Bombay films were also about small people mired in poverty and adversity, hustling to survive or to triumph over their circumstances by marrying the rich lawyer's daughter or into the upper castes, or gaining a place at university and a subsequent powerful profession.

The Indian dimension to Naipaul's writing and character has stayed with me, inevitably, since I am of Indian origin. The novels I've written so far are forms of wrestling with Naipaul, the revered and despised Indian, and the revered and despised father figure. My childhood in Guyana was marked by a sense of Indian inferiority. We had a measure of political power, but in a fragile way. Most of us were subsistence farmers. The rich Indian businessmen and professionals were as alien to us as the urbane and sophisticated Afro-Guyanese who seemed to run the country. The politicians were mostly black, and in our illiteracy we were vulnerable to their superior knowledge of the Law as well as to their superior physical build. Apart from politically inspired race riots in the early 1960s, rarely did black people behave badly towards us. Quite the opposite: I (and many of my generation in New Amsterdam, of differing ethnic groups) owe my early educational ambitions to one Mr Spencer, a local Afro-Guyanese teacher who, in his day, was celebrated for his outstanding care of his pupils. But the Spencers of the world seemed unusual: although there was little or no overt violence done to us, we lived in a mood of subdued fear of our black neighbours and fellow citizens, who outnumbered us considerably in New Amsterdam.

These were the impressions of boyhood – a sense of actual or imagined bullying by black people – which account for the prominence of Indians like the politician Cheddi Jagan and the cricketer Rohan Kanhai in my mind. They were powerful men who were acknowledged leaders in their fields. So was Naipaul, the writer of a book which was a classroom set text.

The subsequent wrestling with Naipaul is partly owed to my desire to explore what I most revere and despise in the Indo-Caribbean. In my first novel, *The Intended*, I explore black–Indian tensions in Guyana and in Britain, in the person of an unnamed Indo-Guyanese character who vacillates between self-contempt and outrage at black failure. Halfway through the novel I realized that it was an imagined biography (and possibly, travesty) of a young "Naipaul" wanting the values of Oxford, which are set against a valueless black world. In the second novel, *Disappearance*, a Naipaulian rationality, detachment and ironic manner are represented in the figure of the engineer. In the latest novel, *Counting House*, the central character is called Vidia, and I try to understand his sense of sexual inability as well as his obsession with money. Needless to say, all these characters may well be versions of myself rather than of Naipaul, and I will happily engage with any allegation that I am merely "wearing the mask of Naipaul" to secret my own failings and excesses. The point I wish to make, however, is that Naipaul has had a profound and direct impact on West Indian writers of my generation. We no longer "write back" to Conrad and Defoe, but to the likes of Naipaul, and in so doing, we create a sense of a living literary tradition which is distinctly West Indian. Those who came in the boats in the 1940s onwards, equipped with little but their imaginations, "fathered" West Indian literature and "fathered" works by subsequent generations. The (en)gendering of the literature is now being examined by scholars like Evelyn O'Callaghan, Carolyn Cooper and Ramabai Espinet, who point to our ignorance of the seminal works of Una Marson, Rajkumari Singh and Louise Bennett. The re-issuing of women's writings introduces the contemporary West Indian writer to an even more varied body of ancestral voices.

Ancestral voices can, however, be tyrannical. Selvon and Harris may have written in the freedom of knowing that they came from largely unrecorded backgrounds. The landscape and the people of the West Indies were there to be written about almost for the first time. This sense of freedom would have held certain terrors, but what terror can compare to the one which I, and others, face today: the terror of the genius of the ancestral voices? I cannot write about the sea without reference to Walcott. I cannot write about the Guyanese rainforest without reference to Wilson Harris. I cannot write about an Indian childhood, or about peasantry, without reference to Sam Selvon. Tradition is a splendid idea, but it can stifle individual talent.

My personal ambition is to try to live up to the literary standards set by the earlier writers. "Audience" for me does not reside in the criticisms of

British readers, although I am grateful for these, shamelessly so when the responses are positive. I really don't mind being a victim of any British appetite for the exotic, if it means that I can get some royalties here and there. As to the British guilt for the Empire which translates into book-buying and prize-giving, I'll gladly jostle in the queue for handouts and reparations. (I've even contemplated writing a sombre novel on slavery to cash in on white angst.) I can only recognize myself as a "proper" writer, however, when Harris or Walcott or Brathwaite or Naipaul has a kind and genuine word to say about anything I have published. I live in dread of their critical utterances. In other words, I am not just conscious of previous Caribbean literature, but also the processes by which it came about, and my position in it.

In 1992, on the 500th Anniversary of Christopher Columbus's adventure in the West Indies, Derek Walcott was awarded the Nobel Prize for Literature. St Lucia is a dot on the world's map. Without modern navigational technology, the British Airways pilot could so easily miss the island and fly on to the continent of South America. Columbus himself had taken the wrong turn, and instead of reaching his expected destination of India, he had arrived at another place, which he titled West India, christening its natives Indians.

As the plane descends to land in St Lucia you see a few fields of scrawny sugarcane, some untidy allotments, goats in untended fields, and patches of housing. Naipaulian images of an unfinished society come to mind, but these are qualified when you recall the creativity of the St Lucian, a creativity that can be measured by the fact that, in the last forty years, St Lucia has given the world two Nobel Prize winners. In the 1960s Arthur Lewis was given the Prize for Economics: imagine winning the Nobel Prize for Economics coming from a country with no economy to speak of, indeed, when whatever economy you inhabited was in total control and possession of the British, since you were of colonial status. Derek Walcott was the second St Lucian to be honoured by the world, and the dot of his island had the powerful status of a full stop at the end of a sentence. It gave definition to a sentence by closing it, in this case the Columbian phase, or phrase, of our existence, which sentenced indigenous peoples to extermination, but which also saw the survival, adaptation and creative transformation of African and Asian cultures in the region, in spite of three centuries of slavery and indentureship. Walcott once said that, at the beginning of his poetic career, he couldn't mention the word "mango" in his poetry for fear of confusing and alienating English publisher and English reader alike. By 1992, Walcott was able to name his landscape and define the culture of the region.

Walcott's *Omeros* is dedicated to "shipmates in the craft", the craft not being only the craft of poetry but also the slave and coolie boats which brought us to the Caribbean from the days of Elizabeth I, and eventually landed us in England in the days of Elizabeth II. After the Second World War, West Indians were recruited to Britain to help rebuild its fabric, to work in hospitals, factories, and railway and bus depots. Among the mass of workers arriving on the boats were a few prospective writers, people of Walcott's generation. There were James Berry and Edward Brathwaite, Sam Selvon and George Lamming, Andrew Salkey and Michael Anthony, Stuart Hall and V.S. Naipaul, Jan Carew and Wilson Harris, an all-male line-up. These early writers, coming in different boats and from different islands, shared Walcott's passion to name self and to name landscape. The Trinidadian Sam Selvon said, "I believe that the West Indian novelist had, among his major responsibilities, that of making his country and his people known accurately to the rest of the world", the "rest of the world" in his day being, of course, England. Roger Mais, a Jamaican novelist, wrote that his purpose in writing was to reveal something of "the dreadful conditions of the Jamaican working classes". His contemporary Vic Reid said that his project was to describe "the kindliness, humour and beauty of my people". When V.S. Naipaul began to publish, C.L.R. James wrote to him to congratulate him for "showing the English what stuff we are made of".

Literary efforts at self-definition and self-description coincided with agitation for Independence and decolonization. Some writers, like Martin Carter and Roger Mais, were jailed in the Caribbean for opposition to Britain, and their poetry and fiction were nourished by political and prison experiences. Others, like C.L.R. James, wrote fiction, history and political philosophy, and worked closely with up-and-coming anti-colonial politicians like Jomo Kenyatta and Kwame Nkrumah for "the liquidation of colonialism and imperialism". The few West Indian cultural organizations that sprung up in Britain in the 1950s had political affiliations. James Berry, secretary of the African and Caribbean Social and Cultural Centre in Paddington, said that his group "could not help being political". Norman Manley, a leader of the Jamaican

Independence movement, was one of several visiting speakers: "Everybody who came over who was important, came and talked". Cultural groups such as Berry's, while organizing poetry-writing workshops and the like, also issued political leaflets or participated in letter-writing campaigns to British parliamentarians.

Most of the writers who emerged in the 1950s, however, had no direct personal involvement in political movements. They came to write poetry and fiction, not political tracts. They confessed a passionate and obsessive ambition to write works of the imagination, and none more so than the Guyanese Edgar Mittelholzer. Mittelholzer uses the language of war in describing the efforts to write and be published:

> In my imagination the whole thing had taken on the flavour of a military campaign. I was a general at the head of an army, and the objectives were clearly defined. The enemy was Life-cum-editors-and-publishers-in-London. I must hurl the whole weight of my war-machine against their defences, infiltrate here, infiltrate there, and then, in one big offensive, batter away at the inner fortifications until victory was achieved. The acceptance of a short short-story by a weekly paper would constitute a mere infiltration; the same would apply to an article. But a full-length story accepted by one of the monthly magazines, like *The Strand*, *Pearson's* or *The Royal* would be a major breakthrough. Final victory would be represented by the acceptance of a novel by a publisher.

Mittelholzer wrote furiously and copiously, and posted from British Guiana several stories to English magazines, only to receive rejection slips and the return of his manuscripts under separate cover. The more he was repulsed, the more fanatical he became, penning stories for speedy despatch to the metropolis:

> Every time I looked in the newspaper and saw that a ship was due from England, I had to steel myself for an enemy onslaught. When I heard the postman dismount from his bicycle at the gateway, I knew it was Zero Hour. The bulky envelopes meant another repulse. Disheartening, but that was war. Attack again. Back went the manuscripts to other editors. Sometimes three or four went off at the same time, for I never stopped writing in the intervals of waiting to hear about those dispatched. No one guessed what a grim struggle was being waged. I presented a blank face to the outside world. I went to ice-cream matinees ... and danced as though I were a

carefree young man not yet settled in any special occupation. Only I could hear the artillery booming in the background, sometimes drowning out the wailing of the saxophone and the cling-clang of the piano.

Mittelholzer had to leave Guyana and travel to England to fulfil his ambition for a writing career. In the colonies there were no publishing houses or distribution systems. The few magazines that existed – magazines like *Bim* in Barbados, started in 1942, or *Kyk-over-al* in Guyana, started in 1945 – had scant readership, and paid nothing to contributors. Their quality was also uneven. Mittelholzer says bluntly, "The local papers were of no interest to me so far as my main objective was concerned. Their standards were too low." To be a writer you had to be validated by the centre, by being on the lists of a London publisher. To remain in the Caribbean was to languish in obscurity, and indeed to court self-annihilation. Sam Selvon says he could easily have dissipated his life in beach-parties, rum-drinking and middle-class flirtations:

> I went to London because I was becoming convinced that, had I stayed in Trinidad, I would have succumbed to the apathy which lured people into accepting their situation and social and cultural circumstances. I wanted to confront the challenge of mainstream culture, or what had been presented to me as such at school. I needed not only the intellectual stimulation but the possibility of being published, heard; the possibility of making a living by writing as I did for the BBC. Only in London did my life find its purpose.

Finally, it has to be said, too, that the writer in the West Indies was seen to be a kind of lunatic, one with no prospects of a decent house, a decent marriage and a decent situation in society. Why did one want to write when the thing to do was to become a lawyer or doctor or civil servant? V.S. Naipaul's character B. Wordsworth, in the novel *Miguel Street*, is a tragicomic portrait of a would-be writer. B. Wordsworth – "B" stands for "black" – is seen as an idler and an eccentric, one who will get nowhere with his life because of his unworldly literary ambitions. In any case, being black, Trinidadian society automatically believes him to be lacking in talent; his ambitions therefore are seen to be even more ludicrous. He is doomed to rejection and penury:

> He pulled out a printed sheet from his hip-pocket and said, "On this paper is the grandest poem about mothers and I am going to sell it to you at a bargain price. For four cents".

> I went inside and I said, "Ma, you want to buy a piece of poetry for four cents?"
> My mother said, "Tell that blasted man to haul his tail away from my yard, you hear".
> I said to B. Wordsworth, "My mother say she ain't have four cents".
> B. Wordsworth said, "It is the poet's tragedy".

In addition, Naipaul is saying that B. Wordsworth, by remaining in Trinidad, is doomed to mimicry. The master-script is English, and the colonial writer is shackled to it, perceiving and describing his tropical, equatorial landscape in English romanticist images – of vales and meadows, rills and purling streams. Colonial brainwashing – the processes by which the Ethiopian is washed white – means that only such images are acceptable to the Trinidadian reader as authoritative, as "proper" literature. To find a native voice, the would-be writer has to emigrate away from colonial expectations.

And so the writers boarded the SS *Empire Windrush* and later boats, equipped with little except fierce ambition, individual talent and, in the case of Sam Selvon and George Lamming, a shared "Imperial" typewriter. Both Selvon and Lamming had had some literary experience: Selvon was a sub-editor of the *Trinidad Guardian*'s magazine supplement, and Lamming had acted as an agent for the Barbadian cultural journal *Bim*. Both were in the process of writing their first novels, and the boat trip to England allowed both some time to continue their work. Selvon talks of how Lamming would come to his cabin to borrow the typewriter, which he loaned him reluctantly. Lamming would then conveniently forget to return the typewriter, or else would lock himself in his cabin and refuse to come out. Selvon would curse him in vivid Caribbean language and threaten to break down the door and choke him. The squabbling over the typewriter continued when they arrived in London and shared accommodations in a men's hostel, until Lamming bought his own second-hand machine. Ten years after the journey, Lamming wrote lyrically about Selvon's boat-novel, depicting him as a solitary, romanticist figure:

> Selvon and I, like members of some secret society, were always together. But this comradeship turned to a strange reticence during the last few days of the journey. Sam had taken to walking alone in the more remote parts of the ship. Sometimes he would be seen working in odd corners: a small grey typewriter on his knees and long black locks of hair fallen forward, almost screening him from view. He would

go up on the deck if no one was there. He would take refuge in the dormitory whenever it was empty.

Note the detailed recollection of the typewriter as being small and grey. The truth was probably that Selvon was not seeking the solitude of poets but merely trying to put distance between himself and Lamming. Such then, were the humble origins of two outstanding seminal Caribbean novels, George Lamming's *In the Castle of My Skin*, published by Michael Joseph in 1953, and Sam Selvon's *A Brighter Sun*, published the year before by Alan Wingate.

Anne Walmsley, in her comprehensive study of the Caribbean Artists' Movement in Britain between 1966 and 1972, writes that

> would-be writers arriving in Britain from the Caribbean in the 1950s found a range of opportunities and encouragement open to them, especially if they lived in London. Book publishing was experiencing somewhat of a post-war boom; small, young publishing houses were eager to bring out work by fresh, vigorous new voices from far corners of the Commonwealth, especially those who used English with the fluency, individuality and verve of West Indians. Publishers found a ready market for books about these writers' tropical home environment and society, despite their containing much implicit, and, especially in the work of Lamming, explicit criticism of colonialism. Books which reflected the new phenomenon of West Indians making their home in London also found an audience.

Sam Selvon himself spoke of the "wonderment and accolade that greeted the boom of Caribbean literature and art in Britain in the early fifties". Undoubtedly there is much truth in such statements. Between 1952 and 1958, Selvon, Lamming, John Hearne, Mittelholzer, Naipaul and Andrew Salkey published, among them, twenty novels, so we can assume that their publishers found sales to be satisfactory. Lamming won the Somerset Maugham Award in 1957 and Naipaul won it in 1959. Naipaul had also received, in 1957, the John Llewellyn Rhys Memorial Prize. Andrew Salkey received the Thomas Helmore Prize in 1955, and Sam Selvon was given a travelling scholarship by the Society of Authors in 1958. Such honours are a measure of the favourable reception accorded to West Indian writers in the 1950s, though it has to be said that the experience of the mass of West Indians was very different: anti-black riots in 1953, and racial disturbances throughout the fifties, made West Indians feel decidedly unwelcome in Britain.

The BBC's *Caribbean Voices* programme was the main platform for readings by West Indian writers and for discussion of their work. Being on the programme signified that the writer had arrived, and this sense of arrival was consolidated by the receipt of a BBC cheque for one's literary contribution. Sam Selvon talks of being awed by his first BBC cheque. The cheque, he says, was printed on thick, textured paper, which gave it imperial authority, and it was made out, not in plebeian pounds sterling, but in gentlemanly guineas. Although the irony of being paid in currency, the title of which derived from the slave trade, was not lost on writers like Lamming and Selvon, the descendents of slaves, nevertheless they received it gladly. Selvon confesses to being dead broke, but carrying his cheque around for days before cashing it, so as to experience the privilege of being a writer, one so designated and anointed by the BBC.

Caribbean Voices, however, was aimed at a West Indian audience in the West Indies, and it is doubtful whether it made any significant impact on promoting Caribbean writing among a British readership. The programme, after all, was broadcast from London on a Sunday evening, at 2315 GMT, when only the unemployed or the insomniac was awake in Britain, the rest of the population retiring early in preparation for Monday morning work. The timing of the broadcast was solely because the West Indies were some eight hours behind GMT. It was the British newspaper and magazine which brought West Indian literature to the attention of the British, not the BBC's *Caribbean Voices* programme. All the major journals – the *Times, Times Literary Supplement, Manchester Guardian, Spectator, New Statesman* and *London Magazine* – reviewed West Indian writing on an immediate and regular basis. American journals readily available in Britain, like the *New York Times Book Review* and the *New Yorker*, also gave coverage to the emerging literature.

The most sensitive and intelligent of the British reviewers was undoubtedly Francis Wyndham, the distinguished editor, critic and prose writer. Wyndham reviewed regularly for the leading literary periodicals, and later became editor of *Queen* magazine and assistant editor of the *Sunday Times* magazine. He was instrumental in rediscovering Jean Rhys, who had totally disappeared from the British literary scene, and promoting a reassessment of her work. His championing of the technical genius of Jean Rhys is his greatest contribution to the appreciation of West Indian literature. His reviews avoided the pitfalls of exotica and newness, drawing attention instead to the varied formal qualities of the writing. Take, for example, his review of Sam Selvon's collection of short stories, *Ways of Sunlight* (*Times*, April 1953):

> The reviewer of novels is always, and sometimes rather desperately, on the look-out for anything which might be called a "trend": it was, for example, a purely journalistic expedient which saddled the "redbrick" writers with an inaccurate label and an unintended social significance. Can something be made of the fact that many of the most interesting post-war French books are by North Africans, while in the English literary scene of the fifties West Indian writers play an increasingly prominent part? Something, perhaps, about colonial vigour providing a necessary stimulus to decadent metropolitan culture? Better not try; even to refer to a West Indian "school" is misleading, as the only merit these writers share is their independence of each other, an artistic variety which reflects the racial variety of their islands' populations. A school implies the existence of a master; here we have a collection of prefects, catholic enough to include the over-wrought eroticism of Edgar Mittelholzer, the Maugham-like narrative efficiency of John Hearne, the deceptive simplicity of V.S. Naipaul's ironic comedies, the rich, poetic loquacity of George Lamming, the limpid lyricism of Samuel Selvon.

He does not praise Selvon in a patronizing way. Indeed, he states boldly that "Selvon's talent is not ideally suited to the novel" but to the short story. When he does speak highly of Selvon he does so with intelligence and restraint, again drawing attention to the writing as *writing*, rather than as black exotica: "Those told in dialect have an irresistible charm, owing as much to the author's technical subtlety as to the unfamiliar delights of the language." Today's critics, motivated by race, class and/or gender agendas, who treat literature as mere illustration of sociology, who promote or damn so-called black or Third-World literature on ideological content, would find Wyndham's emphasis on *quality* and *form* to be rather quaint and colonial. Since all authors are dead or redundant, according to prevailing theory, such critics would dismiss as irrelevant the fact that writers like Selvon were in agreement with Wyndham's approach. Selvon resented reviews that relished his so-called primitive and innocent dialect, not appreciating the extraordinary effort he made as a writer to *conceal* the artfulness of his creole so as to make it appear naturalistic. Later in life Selvon wrote persuasively of the ways in which he shaped and transformed creole to make it both lyrical and lucid to the English ear. He wanted to be appreciated as a language alchemist, and for the creolization of the form of the English novel.

Compared to Francis Wyndham, most early reviews were riddled with errors or motivated by ideology. Maurice Richardson's review of Selvon's novel *An Island Is a World* (1955) in the *New Statesman* (23 April 1955) gets Selvon's Indian ancestry completely wrong by stating, with utter and authoritative assurance, that Indo-Caribbeans are of Malayan origin. This betrays, at best, intellectual laziness on the part of Richardson; at worst an imperial mindset that cannot discriminate among various subject peoples. Richardson is condescending about the anti-colonial mood of the novel: "Mr. Selvon carries, perhaps inevitably, a few chips on his shoulders." Although the review speaks positively of Selvon's "genuine talent" and recognizes a "Caribbean upsurge" of fiction writing, it lacks all conviction; when Richardson states that Selvon "can give the impression of a character in the turn of a phrase", he is merely resorting to cliché. Given that Richardson knows nothing about Trinidad, his statement that Selvon "handles the Trinidadian way of speech brilliantly" is self-consciously excessive in its praise, indicative (arguably) of the imperial habit of "benevolence" to the native more than of critical integrity. In any case, the "Trinidadian way of speech", having very low status as far as Richardson is concerned (we suspect), can have adjectives like "brilliant", "outstanding", "excellent" or whatever heaped upon it, and yet remain a dunghill. True taste only emerges from an appreciation of the Queen's English, in the presence of which critics like Richardson are discerning in their use of adjectives.

The anonymous reviewer of Selvon's *Lonely Londoners* (1956) in the *Times* (6 December 1956) behaves differently from Richardson. Instead of gentlemanly condescension to the writing, here is cautious outrage at its political incorrectness. "Mr Selvon is an intellectual born in Trinidad but of Indian parentage", the review begins, innocuously enough it seems. The following sentences, however, expose the reviewer's agenda: "Nevertheless, he does not seem quite the right person to present the case for West Indian immigrants to Britain. Indeed, by presenting the average Caribbean as foul-mouthed, promiscuous and simple-minded, he does them some disservice." Apart from responding simplistically to Selvon's characters, one's objection to the review is its presumption that Selvon's art should serve good race relations or some similar socio-political cause. In other words, because Selvon is "black", he should be community relations officer first, and artist second. The opening sentence is now capable of being distressed: Selvon is an "intellectual", and as such should know better than to present the natives as "natives". He is, however, "an intellectual born in Trinidad", so his shortcomings perhaps have to do with his colonial origin. If he is not quite an intellectual, neither is he quite a West Indian: he was "born a Trinidadian *but* of Indian parentage". Not being quite an intellectual nor quite a West Indian means that he is not "quite the right person" to describe immigrant life in London. Needless to say, all of this would have come as a surprise to Selvon, who was totally creolized and who *never* thought of himself, nor wanted to be thought of, as an intellectual. Once again we may have here the case of the white man describing the "native" in ways unfamiliar to the "native"; and the white man who determines which native is best qualified to speak on behalf of the natives.

The reviewer, however, is not a trenchant imperialist. Note the caution and hesitancy of his opening remarks, indicated by words like "but", "not quite" and "nevertheless". And even when he feels bold enough to press his charge, starting with the word "indeed", he is not totally convinced of his correctness; hence he states that Selvon's portrayal of West Indians does them "*some* disservice". Not *total* "disservice", for perhaps the "average Caribbean" *is* largely "foul-mouthed, promiscuous and simple-minded".

The reviewer suddenly changes tack by acknowledging in the following paragraph that *The Lonely Londoners*, however, is "primarily a poetic novel, not a social document", but there is no commitment to making the case for Selvon's artistry. He pronounces on Selvon's "effective" use of dialect, but even so, adds an immediate qualification: "effective, if self-conscious, use of dialect". Before getting totally mired in hesitancy, he then brings the review to a swift end.

Ifs and buts are not part of the vocabulary of Isabel Quigly, who reviewed Selvon's *An Island Is a World* for the *Spectator* on 15 April 1955. She is adamant about what she really, really wants, and finds Selvon a limp and impotent disappointment. She regrets "how closely the cast of an intelligent young West Indian's mind seems to resemble that of a young European; how, apart from the conscious passages of description and local colour, this novel might just as well have been written by an Englishman". Quigly really, really wants Selvon to be a black caged and ferocious beast, but he is instead, for her, a disappointing King Kong: "It is absurd to complain that Mr. Selvon has got away, as undoubtedly he has, from his island; absurd to expect the vision of a primitive from one who is at least half sophisticated. But Mr. Selvon at this stage has lost the directness of the one before acquiring the complexity of the other, a common occurrence in a world where the eye of innocence is given spectacles at the earliest age and in the remotest places."

Such lament for lost primitivism recurs in many other reviews by different hands, in different guises. Words like "primitive" (sometimes disguised as "naturalistic"), "charm" and "childlike" are common, even as the reviewers take up politically correct positions against colonial exploitation. With the notable exception of Francis Wyndham, reviewers sought in West Indian fiction what was apparently absent in post-war Britain: colour, gaiety, innocence, virility. Such poignant desire for the characteristics of the Noble Savage ensured that West Indian writing was eagerly received by the literati, even as the real thing – the nigger – was being hunted down and hounded out of the neighbourhood.

Periodic explosions of racial violence conditioned the literature of the 1970s and 1980s, the character of which is best illustrated in the poetry of Linton Kwesi Johnson. Johnson practically exploded on the scene in 1975 with the publication of his first collection, *Dread, Beat and Blood*. Johnson had learned from his Jamaican-based predecessor, Kamau Brathwaite, who had already legitimized the exploding of English literary form. Arguing against the pentameter, the standard line of English poetry, and for a native black aesthetic, for a poetic line that approximated to the landscape of the Caribbean, Brathwaite had declared, "The hurricane does not roar in pentameters." In other words, Edward Long's linearity and aesthetic of logic was inappropriate to Caribbean expression. (In his 1774 *History of Jamaica*, he declared that West Indians couldn't think straight – nor, for that matter, shoot straight – and were without the faculty of logic: "Their corporeal sensations are in general of the grotesque frame; they will rarely miss a standing object, but they have no notion of shooting birds on the wing, nor can they project a straight line, nor lay a substance square with another.")

Johnson's imagery is of broken glass and tumbled-down tenements, the violence and futility of the landscape conveyed in a doom-laden reggae beat. If the earlier writers paid homage to the canonical texts of English literature by rewriting them, Johnson simply tears up the master-scripts, or dubs them out of existence. Such radical posturing, however, masks an understandably fragile self-confidence, or at least a nervousness, for the language Johnson uses is an uneasy amalgam of Jamaican English, black British patois and white urban slang – uneasy because it had never been used before for literary purposes. The young Johnson is naturally nervous with this newly minted language: hence, for instance, the often forced modifications of English diction, the smearing of words beyond visual or aural recognition, the effect being not a subtle alteration of the meaning of words (Eliot's definition of the effects of poetry at its best), but an appearance of illiteracy. But such "illiteracy" is valorized by Johnson out of an embarrassment of being associated with the Queen's English, and with English texts. His is an attempt to create a black English that is alienated from its metropolitan source and which contains little or no echo or allusion whatsoever to white texts. Johnson's poetry is also a partial attempt to break with the West Indian past, break with its ancient creoles used so lyrically and with such veneration by Derek Walcott and Sam Selvon; break, too, with the confidence and unselfconsciousness with which West Indian writers, products of a sound colonial education, engaged with Western texts from Homer to Eliot. Johnson is asserting the birth of a new creature, the black British, seeking to be orphaned from its colonized past so as best to engage militantly and with pristine energy with a hostile present.

Much of the writing of the 1970s and 1980s is bitter, angry and retaliatory. The wilful attempt to cleanse itself of all-white influences and references so as to assert a particularized black British identity has been seen by some critics as replicating the very totalitarian and essentialist project it sought to protest against. Wilson Harris used the term "ontic tautology" in bemoaning such writings. And, as V.S. Naipaul repeatedly says to Paul Theroux, "You can't beat literature out of a tribal drum", and that was what, arguably, the more frenzied, less talented followers of Johnson were attempting to do. The writing was in danger of being enslaved to the linearity of social realism. Blackness was in danger of becoming a fetish, a privileged scar. The Mope syndrome – a term used by the Irish historian Liam Kennedy – that is, "the most oppressed people ever" syndrome, was leading to literary paralysis or to uncreative outbreaks of patois. And a more or less terrified or embarrassed white intelligentsia either ignored the writing in the review pages of their journals or else overdosed on guilt and handed out laurels and little prizes indiscriminately. (I too jostled in the queue for literary reparations and handouts.)

Emancipation from this new system of slavery came spectacularly with the publication of Steve Martin's novel *Incomparable World* in 1995. Steve Martin is a young black person of Jamaican origin whose only stated career is as a former worker in the post office, his only contact with English letters before the appearance of his novel. Some commentators have criticized the early pages of the novel as being excessively adjectival, the common weakness of first novels, but perhaps also a sad reflection on the publishing industry, which is reluctant to edit writing by black British authors for fear of offending racial sensibilities or for fear of curbing the so-called exotica of such writers. But the triumph of Martin's novel is manifold: firstly, in its discovery of eighteenth-century Britain, a time when black people were, for the first time, very visible in British society, to such an extent that some commentators thought of them as a threat to the purity of the race. Martin's novel revels in the low life of the eighteenth century and the knavery of blacks bent on survival. The novel reeks of piss-pots and gutters sluggish with dead puppies, and syphilitic sores, powdered harlots and gin-soaked copulation. As Chris Campbell puts it, the story is "overlaid with delightful visions of Swiftean squalor and stench". Martin greedily absorbs Hogarth's and Cruikshank's images of bawdiness, Gay's and Swift's and Pope's pictures of the dirt and vitality of the city. Like these artists, Martin relishes the foulness and idealism of eighteenth-century life to such an extent that the novel's concerns about racism are eventually eclipsed by the sheer joy – *jouissance* – in writing the dungeon of thieves or the smoke-filled coffeehouse or the pathos of whores in a devious brothel or the carnival spectacles of Southwark Fair. In other words, ideology is eclipsed by the artistic challenge of writing the texture of a period of British society normally deemed devoid of blacks and, therefore, alien space to someone like Martin.

Secondly, writing the eighteenth century means the astonishing discovery of eighteenth-century black British texts – astonishing, because no one would have expected it at the height of the slave trade. In 1788 John Newton described the interior of a slave ship thus: "The slaves lie in two rows, one above the other, on each side of the ship, close to each other, like books upon a shelf. I have known [them to be] so close, that the shelf would not easily contain one more." African slaves like Olaudah Equiano, Ignatius Sancho, Ukawsaw Gronniosaw, Ottobah Cugoano and Phyllis Wheatley all published books – autobiographies in prose and verse – in English between 1770 and 1789. Black people had moved from being packed like books upon a shelf to being the makers of English books. And it is this emancipation into the English word and into the form of the English epistle or the English travelogue or the English novel that Martin celebrates unselfconsciously. If Linton Kwesi Johnson was queasy about any association with English letters, Martin positively revels in the challenge of mimicking Equiano's eighteenth-century mimicking of English expression. This is partly Homi Bhaba's idea of mimicry as subversion, but also mimicry as homage to Equiano's genius in mastering the idioms and literary forms of the eighteenth-century English, so as to best appeal to the nation for the emancipation of blacks. But even such ideology in Equiano is finally subsumed to the sheer challenge of literary composition. Equiano had cast his story as part Homeric epic, part picaresque fiction, part pulpit sermon, part exotic travelogue, part burlesque, part economic tract, with the unstable narrative replicating the complex life of someone removed as a child from his family, culture, language and landscape, catapulted into new world of plantation slavery, then, after a series of stupendous accidents and adventures, ending up in England as an Afro-Saxon gent, wig, cravat, library and all.

Ignatius Sancho, another African and Equiano's contemporary in England, wrote of himself, "You have here a kind of medley, a heterogeneous ill-spent Hetroclite [abnormal, irregular] (worse) an eccentric sort of a–a–; in short, it is a true Negro calibash of ill-sorted, undigested chaotic matter." In other words, Edward Long's linearity was an impoverished concept, wholly irrelevant to the complex movements and vicissitudes of an African's life in eighteenth-century white societies. Equiano and Sancho embraced the abnormal, the irregular, the unstable, the eccentric, the absent, the unspoken, the boundary-less, the cross-cultural; they were postmodern long before the theory came into being. In writing to Equiano and Sancho, Martin is acknowledging black settlement in this country, including literary settlement, that is three centuries old; Martin sees his novel not as a product of individual talent but of a tradition of black British writing inaugurated by the likes of Equiano and Sancho (both of whom are characters in his novel). No longer is there the need for the retaliatory gesture of writing back to *Robinson Crusoe* or *The Tempest*; instead Martin engages with Sancho and Equiano, who had already challenged the brutish images of blacks in English literature and who had emancipated themselves from racist ideology by mastery of the craft of writing. They had written themselves out of slavery, as he, Martin, will write himself out of the predicament of present-day Britain.

Finally, the irreverent tone of Martin's narrative, the multiplicity of comic devices, the frequent self-parodying and the refusal to valorize, amount to challenges to the writing of slavery. Before Martin, most writers – black and white – were sombre, reverential and ponderous when dealing with slavery. In presenting "general properties and large appearance" – Samuel Johnson's criteria for good literature – they had in fact produced work of predictable ideology and predictable pathos. Martin's mischievous humour liberates the slaves from the baracoons of dull, worthy narratives, and raises questions, more familiar in Jewish circles, about the representation of historic tragedies which still afflict the living. Fruitful comparison can be made between Martin's approach to slavery and Benigni's to the Holocaust, in his film *Life Is Beautiful*. Slavery and the Holocaust were two different tragedies altogether, but the representation of them provokes similar questions in terms of the shaping of humorous art out of the mess of unbearable pain. Is Martin making light of human suffering in terms of the levity of his prose? Or is he making light of human suffering in a different sense, illuminating the hold of the slave ship to reveal a horror which can only be expressed in its negative, which is comedy – humour being the inevitable expression of that which cannot be comprehended, which cannot be made meaningful, subject to reason, to a linear explanation. In raising such questions, it seems to me that black British writing is striving for liberation not only from ethnic categorization, from expectations of drumbeat or ghetto blast, but, more crucially, liberation from the logic of suffering or the logic of disability which was Edward Long's original point.

Just before he left Britain in 1978, Sam Selvon urged that "we have now to start thinking in terms of world literature, of contribution universally rather than merely with protest novels, with days of slavery, with the hardships of the black man . . . we want to rise above that." I would argue that one small step towards "rising above that" is Martin's novel, which acknowledges black suffering but which embraces Wilson Harris's concept of the "Unfinished Genesis of the Imagination", by its creative re-visioning of eighteenth-century life to include a black dimension which both surprises and renews our sense of the past; and in the process of renewing and modifying the form and content and imagery of the past, the novel provokes questions about history and writing which are of contemporary relevance to other ethnic communities – in this case the Jews – and, therefore, strives for a "universality" more compassionate and enquiring and uncertain than the "universality" dismissed by Achebe in his book *Morning Yet on Creation Day*. There, "universality" was, of course, synonymous with supremacist Western values. As to Selvon's protest against protest, Martin's achievement is his resistance to a ready sense of victimization and a refusal to moan against minority or marginalized status. As Wilson Harris reminds us, it is only when you are in the margins that you can tilt the plane on the centre. At the centre you grow fat and sluggish and settled in tradition. The weight of being at the margins has the potential of unsettling or revitalizing moribund tradition, moribund not because of innate defects in the texts which lead to inevitable decay, but because of repetitive acts of homage to such texts that make them over-familiar, exhausted by interpretation.

My own concern, in *A Harlot's Progress*, which has a Jew as a leading character, is not with the comic representation of suffering, but with the aestheticizing of it, with Adorno's statement about the impossibility of writing poetry after Auschwitz. Can one give poetic metre to the feet faltering towards the slave ship or gas chamber, or is such a question obscene in itself? But it is a question that engaged Paul Celan, Arnold Schoenberg and others who commemorated the Holocaust in hauntingly beautiful lyric. Paul Celan, later in life, refused to allow reprinting of his Holocaust poem, *Death Fugue*, and "changed his writing style into a . . . less melodious, more disrupted and disruptively elliptical verse" (Shoshana Felman). Celan came to distrust melody and musicality.

And yet the question persists: is what remains of the dreadful history its beautiful expression? Can the Holocaust ever be a resource for art? In a few centuries hence, will we have forgotten the tragedy as just another disaster and marvel instead at the aesthetics of the poem? Or, to put it in a different context, when Ozymandias topples into the oblivion of desert sands, is all that remains the sculptor's gift in shaping the tyrant's cruel face? And, of course, Shelley's sonnet:

> Two vast and trunkless legs of stone
> Stand in the desert. Near them on the sand,
> Half sunk, a shattered visage lies, whose frown
> And wrinkled lip and sneer of cold command
> Tell that its sculptor well those passions read
> Which yet survive, stamped on these lifeless things.
>
> (Shelley, "Ozymandias", lines 2–7)

CHAPTER 9

Introduction to Edward Jenkins's *Lutchmee and Dilloo: A Study of West Indian Life* (2007)

I

ON 4 JANUARY 1836, JOHN GLADSTONE (father of the future British prime minister), owner of two British Guianese sugar plantations, wrote to a firm in Calcutta seeking a supply of labourers under a contract of indenture. Two years later, the first batch of 396 Indians arrived, and between then and 1917, when the system of indentureship ended, more than 238,000 "coolies" were shipped to British Guiana, in excess of 40 per cent of the total number of indentured Indians taken to the region.[1] The only reason for their presence was to maintain the plantation system by their labour. The newly emancipated African slaves abandoned (or were threatening to abandon) the plantations in droves, leaving behind them the great symbols of tyranny, the canefields, canals and sugar factories. They settled in free villages, the names of which expressed their idealism and aspirations: Better Hope, Good Fortune, Friendship, Perseverance. Those who made their labour available to the likes of Gladstone wanted proper wages and employment rights. The plantocracy, accustomed over the centuries to dealing with an enslaved labour force, would not countenance their demands and sought workers who could be coerced into productivity by whip, Law, Bible or whatever means lay at hand. And so began what the British Secretary of State Lord John Russell called, in 1840, "a new system of slavery".[2]

The Indians came from different castes, though the majority were from the lower end of the scale, people specializing in fieldwork and agricultural cultivation. The overwhelming majority came from the United Provinces (Uttar Pradesh and Bihar), with a lesser number from Madras (Madrasis were seen as "inefficient labourers, with reprehensible social customs" and were recruited only when there were insufficient North Indians available).[3] A very high proportion were Hindus, the rest being mostly Muslims. Whatever their linguistic, religious and social differences, they were lumped together as "coolies" and packed off to the Caribbean:

> In the same manner that slavery brought together Africans of different religions and linguistic affiliations, so did indentureship create a mélange out of Bhojpuri speakers and Tamils. Beef-eaters were bundled together on the same ships and on the same estates with those to whom this practice was abhorrent. Low castes now became *jahagis* (shipmates) with twice-born Brahmans, and Aryan-descended North Indians rubbed shoulders with Southern Dravidians with whom they had little intercourse in India. On this later re-visit to the middle-passage, a melting-pot was created which broke down some of the barriers existing in the homelands. In the new environment, Hindus could be found celebrating the Muslim Shia observance of Muharram in which even Afro-West Indians participated vigorously.[4]

Several factors led to the Indians' signing indenture papers, leaving their homeland and crossing the *kala pani*, the dark ocean, which was forbidden territory since the crossing meant a loss of caste affiliation, a loss of the security of community.

Undoubtedly many villagers were fooled by the *arkatis* (recruiters), who spun tales of fortunes to be made in a new, nearby place (for the *arkatis* would certainly have kept quiet about the *kala pani*). Walter Raleigh's ancient description of Guiana as El Dorado would have been evoked, consciously or unconsciously, to excite their imagination, the possibility of glittering wealth in powerful contrast to the drabness of their existence: "It have so much gold there that you don't have enough hand and neck and foot to wear bangle. You wish you have ten hands like Lord Shiva, and even then you run out of skin."[5] The majority, however, emigrated for very practical reasons. They were fleeing from natural calamities which bred famine or epidemics such as cholera, smallpox and the plague. Or else they were fleeing from man-made adversities of economic, caste and gender oppression, from "landlords, moneylenders, husbands, wives, or mother-in-laws, or from some task or family obligation . . . women did have solid reasons for wanting to migrate, and consequently made a conscious decision to leave, to escape painful, empty domestic lives, economic hardships, the social stigma of early widowhood, the odium which descended upon those who had brought inadequate dowry".[6] It would have taken little effort for the *arkatis* to persuade such people to abandon their villages and seek new and better lives elsewhere, lives unencumbered by debt, the burden of caste and other stigmas.

The immediate challenge facing the migrants was how to accommodate themselves to the new landscape while maintaining aspects of social, cultural and family structures which created their sense of Indian identity. The numerical disparity between the sexes led to new stresses on family life. The immigration ordinances stipulated a ratio of two females to five males, but in practice women were extremely scarce. In 1851, for instance, the ratio was a shocking twenty-three females to one hundred males. The sexual imbalance led to crimes of passion, including wife murders in extreme cases. The Agent-General's report of 1875 stated that "the disproportion of the sexes is the greatest cause of the deplorable large number of wife murders which are perpetrated notwithstanding every precaution being taken by removal or otherwise which can be taken to prevent them".[7] The new practice of polyandry (sometimes forced upon women by estate managers in the hope of keeping the peace) invariably led to outbreaks of jealousy accompanied by violence. But women were not unremittingly victimized in the plantation environment. Some used their scarcity value to negotiate better conditions for themselves in the domestic sphere, threatening to leave their husbands for other male partners, should their material ambitions remain unfulfilled.[8] Sometimes, their voluntary association with white overseers sparked off riots by Indian men: "The withdrawal of even a single woman from the Coolie dwellings to the overseer's lodge is regarded with jealous eyes by her fellow countryman, and when it was remembered any female over childhood was already the actual wife of one of them, it is evident that no surer way could be found of sowing the seeds of discontent and riot."[9]

The trauma of accommodating to the new environment was deepened by the hostility of the black population, who attacked the newcomers as scab labour. Afro-Guyanese argued that the Indian presence depressed wages, and the Indian habit of frugality and asceticism gave them an advantage since they were willing to survive on very little. The Afro-Guyanese had absorbed the consumerist ambitions of the British. They had been brought up to live in a "British fashion", which was relatively costly.[10] Moreover, Indians had been given land in lieu of a return passage home upon expiration of their indentureship contract, to encourage the retention of their seasoned labour. The freed Africans, however, had to purchase Crown lands, the cost of which was prohibitively high. Hospital, housing and schooling provisions on the plantations, albeit rudimentary to say the least, also created resentment on the part of the Africans, who had had lesser privileges under slavery and as free men and women were left largely to fend for themselves. In short, the Indians were seen as stealing Africans' rightful inheritance, and the newcomers and interlopers were accorded legal protections and material privileges denied to slave and ex-slave populations. That Indians were mere pawns in an Imperial economic enterprise, wholly powerless to address, much less remedy, black demands and aspirations, did little to stem ethnic hostility. And apart from linguistic and cultural differences which impeded dialogue, the very self-contained structure of the plantation prevented fruitful and satisfying intercourse between Indians and Africans. The plantation, within whose boundaries Indians were effectively imprisoned, and the free African villages were worlds apart. Maintenance of difference was a central strategy of British administration of its subject peoples, since one group could be played against the other in a system of "divide-and-rule".

Many factors sustained Indian communities against despair and disintegration in the hostile new environment, but two were outstanding. Firstly, their psychological sense that the period of indentureship was relatively short, and that in five years' time they could either return home as moneyed people, or acquire land and become property owners. Hence their extraordinary feats of sacrifice in terms of severely curtailed expenditure and patterns of consumption. Every member of the family worked at every opportunity, and the saving of wages for future investment was a supreme Indian discipline. Secondly, their stubborn refusal to surrender the ancestral religions and convert to Christianity. Henry Kirke echoed the opinion of several other missionaries and observers when he wrote that "the attempt to convert the Hindoo and

Mahommedan immigrants to Christianity has been an utter failure".[11] Muslims established mosques and continued the practice of teaching Arabic to their children so that the Koran remained central to their lives. They continued to celebrate their traditional religious festivals. Hindus regularly enacted the stories of the *Ramayana* in popular folk festivals, stories they knew by heart since it was related to them constantly by their pundits in temple settings. If the Koran provided an ethical framework within which Muslims could conduct their lives, irrespective of place of settlement, the *Ramayana*'s power was the power of the mythical. Its story of banishment, exile, displacement and perilous new encounters among strange and hostile tribes, and the eventual, if arduous, triumph of good over evil, and the ushering in of a Golden Age, nurtured the imagination of Hindu Indians, providing them with symbols to sustain their spirits in the midst of plantation miseries.

II

On Christmas Day in 1869, George W. Des Voeux, former stipendiary magistrate in British Guiana, then Administrator of the Government of St Lucia, wrote a lengthy letter to the Earl Granville, Secretary of State for the Colonies, detailing abuses in the indentureship system which needed urgent remedies. The 134 numbered paragraphs of Des Voeux's submission called attention to various malpractices, ranging from inadequate medical facilities for Indians to the authoritarianism and bullying tactics of planters in the legal administration of justice. Without specified reforms, Des Voeux argued that the colony would suffer labour unrest and erupt into violence. A year later, a Royal Commission of Enquiry was set up to investigate the substance of Des Voeux's criticism of the indentureship system. John Edward Jenkins, a radical young barrister, was sent to British Guiana by the Aborigines Protection Society and the Anti-Slavery Society, to observe and report on the proceedings of the Royal Commission.

Jenkins, the son of a Wesleyan Missionary, was born in Bangalore, India, in 1838, the very year that the first batch of labourers left India for British Guiana. His family emigrated to Canada, and Jenkins was educated in school and university there, first at Montreal High School and then McGill University. He moved to Britain in the 1860s, qualifying as a barrister in 1864.[12] He soon became involved with the National Association for the Promotion of Social Science, an organization which was "truly mid-Victorian in spirit: zealous, enquiring and humane . . . an effective pressure group as well as a vigorous forum for social discussion".[13] In 1866 Jenkins presented a paper to the Association, on the legal aspect of sanitary reform. Two of the hallmarks of Jenkins's political and writing career over thirty years were first revealed in his paper. Firstly, his concern for the plight of the common people, exposed to diseases because of the apathy or intransigence of local and national authorities, is linked with a range of other social causes: in the opening page he places the agitation for public health improvements in the context of other reformist movements – "emancipating Negroes, enfranchising householders, and abolishing oppressive taxations".[14] Such connection between national and international issues was to recur in later writings, showing the breadth of his reformist vision. In 1872 in his *Discussions on Colonial Questions* he linked the suffering of the English agricultural class to that of African slaves, Indian indentured labourers, child workers in South Africa and Polynesians exploited by their English masters.[15] Two years later, contemplating the conflict between capital and labour which threatened to engulf Europe and its Empires in social conflagration, he wrote: "This portentous question is beginning to shake the very pillars of society in every part of the civilised world. The Coolie, the Negro, the immigrants in the Western lands, the English artisan and peasant, the French and German workman, all alike are conspiring together to demand for labour a larger reward, a better coparcenary with capital."[16]

Secondly, the tension between the rational and the emotional, between the documentary and the literary. His paper on sanitary reform was closely argued; as befits a newly qualified barrister on his first major public brief, various statistics and tables were marshalled to give objective support to his opinions. Jenkins, however, on occasions could barely contain his feelings for the victims of neglect, and his anger at the inaction of the authorities. In these moments, his mood found literary form and his prose swelled with pity and outrage: "The stench from the watercourse was at times unbearable – there were some houses and stables round which the overflowing feculent matter of dungheaps and *cloacae* lay in stagnant pools, not only sending up a continuing miasma, but being absorbed into the walls of rooms in which human beings were living, eating and sleeping."[17]

Pity and outrage were the features of his first novel, *Ginx's Baby*, published in 1870, the very year he set off for British Guiana to investigate the coolie condition. The novel, "a pathetic satire on the struggle of rival sectarians for the religious education of a derelict child",[18] was a vast success and Jenkins became a controversial figure overnight. It was a Victorian best-seller, running into thirty-six editions by 1876, making it as popular as Edward Bulwer-Lytton's *Pelham* and Thomas Hughes's *Tom Brown's Schooldays*.[19] O.G. Rejlander, the renowned studio photographer, made a photograph of a howling and destitute baby which sold 60,000 prints and 250,000 cartes-de-visites in 1870.[20] The Education Act of that year, arguably the most important piece of social legislation in Victorian Britain, was influenced by Jenkins's novel. Given his fame, his interest in international affairs and his commitment to the destitute, it is no wonder that the Aborigines Protection Society and the Anti-Slavery Society chose Jenkins to report on indentureship. That he accepted the brief was testimony to his idealism and to his moral and physical courage. "I was going alone beyond seas for indefinite months, into strange regions, with black reputations in health matters, and on business of deep importance", he wrote.[21] His statement echoes any number of descriptions in Victorian imperial fiction of the English hero embarking upon an epic adventure on behalf of race and nation, but Jenkins was no clichéd Imperialist. When he composed his statement he was confessing to the anxiety and pain of leaving his family behind, especially his two infants. And his intimacy with health issues meant that his fears of malarial Guiana were dreadfully real rather than a matter of Imperial rhetoric.

III

The Coolie: His Rights and Wrongs, published in 1871, was a work of monumental detail, its 446 pages the most comprehensive account of the indentureship system in the nineteenth century. Specialist readers – members of the Aborigines Protection Society, the Anti-Slavery Society, the Colonial Office and the like – would have found in it very substantial material for consideration, but Jenkins's work was also aimed at the general public. Hence the inclusion of two woodcuts and commentaries in the introductory chapter, summarizing in easily graspable pictorial form the grievances of the labourers.

Jenkins's attempt to make his work accessible to the reading public is also evident in the literary style of his writing. His report is part travelogue, part adventure tale, and he seeks to give character and idiosyncratic qualities to the people he encounters. He casts a novelist's eye over his fellow passengers, seeking out particular details: "The poor French lady who sat moaning in the cuddy, the stout Dutch dame who, for forty-eight hours, rested her double chin on her ample bosom in a state of adipose imbecility, the pretty Hamburg girl, belle of the voyage, whose pink cheek faded for a short time."[22] He records with a novelist's ear particular conversations on board ship, catching the individual idioms of speech: "Last time I came out – eh? there were three Bishops and about twenty ecclesiastics – eh? going to the council. There was great fun – eh? The Archbishop of L—— was one – eh? He was a comfortable little man – eh? He liked well his glass – eh?"[23] As he sails through the Caribbean Sea, his pen grows excited at the exoticism of the islands: "For three days we steamed past the wondrous islands, furrowed, ribbed and riven, lifting up their shaggy heads into the clear sky, whilst below they nourished here and there in pretty laps an exquisitely bright green vegetation."[24] Finally there are the picturesque descriptions of the lush, strange landscape of Guiana and finely drawn portraits of the coolies: "Down the trench comes a coolie wading to his breast, dragging a load of floating brushwood for his home fire. The sun flames upon the water and glints over his slippery limbs. Next an Indian woman, choosing the same damp causeway, who, with pretty modesty, dips up to the neck in the brown water, and watches us soberly with her great black eyes."[25]

Woven into these novelistic passages are details of wages, the diet of workers, acreage under cultivation, hospital conditions, and statistics of how many hogsheads of sugar are produced, how many puncheons of rum, casks of molasses, bales of cotton, cubic feet of timber. The effort to give literary colour to social and economic data ultimately fails; although the prose is at times heightened by exquisite descriptions of plantation life, it finally succumbs to the weight of documentary detail. The shift is sometimes abrupt, with Jenkins reining in the momentum of his literary sensibility, suddenly bringing a fine description of landscape to documentary closure: "Round the corner of the wall and past the lighthouse we glide into a river – the broad, brown river –

and at our left reach away the flats, the stellings, the stores and sheds, the low white jalousied houses over which, everywhere, graceful cabbage-palms spread their green wings. This is Georgetown, Demerara. Thermometer 85 degrees Fahr., time 5.00 P.M."[26]

Such shifting between styles is not evidence of flaws in composition; the whole of Jenkins's writing career was to seek a marriage between the modes of literature and reportage. He was "a writer inhabiting the important no-man's-land between fictional and documentary writing",[27] and as such belongs to an honourable tradition originated by the "father of the English Novel" and professional journalist, Daniel Defoe. At the time of writing *The Coolie: His Rights and Wrongs*, Jenkins belonged to a group of socially committed authors, under the publishing house of Strahan and Company. Alexander Strahan had gathered under his wing novelists and periodical writers like William Gilbert and poets like Alfred Tennyson. As Strahan put it, his aim was "supplying such literature as will not ignobly interest or frivolously amuse, but convey the wisest instructions in the pleasantest manner, and supply it in such form that it will find its way to tens of thousands of British homes to be well thumbed and dog-eared by the children and the grown people, on the journey and at the fireside".[28] The use of illustrations and the insistence upon literary quality to excite the imagination of readers, especially when the subject was potentially as dry and specialist as labour reform and sanitation, were the distinguishing features of Strahan's publishing house. Jenkins's *The Coolie* is an exemplary Strahan publication in its conscious mixing of the genres of travel writing, adventure story, comic caricature, economic tract, legal report and socially concerned journalism.

IV

It was to be expected that Jenkins's *The Coolie* would provoke hostile responses from apologists for the plantocracy. His book was criticized for "containing much grotesque sensationalism and spurious sentiment, many baseless insinuations, and misrepresented facts".[29] The anonymous author ("West Indian") of the pamphlet *The Coolie in Demerara* went to great lengths to counter the charge that indentureship amounted to a new system of slavery. Checks and balances instituted in India, he argued, involving Emigration Agents, the Protector of Emigrants, magistrates, medical doctors and other officials of government, meant that indentured labourers were afforded proper protection against misrepresentation, fraud and forcible removal: "The regulations are so elaborate and stringent that it is a sheer impossibility for a single coolie to find himself on board ship and bound for the British West Indies except by his own free will and consent."[30] As to the highly emotive charge that mortality aboard the coolie ships was excessive, he conceded that a couple of ships did fare badly in 1869, but no more so than ships bound for Australia with white emigrants. In any case, lengthy sea journeys were inevitably perilous, so deaths were inevitable, whatever preventative measures were put in place. Furthermore, it might well be, he proposed, that the emigrants were carriers of all manner of diseases contracted in India from the effects of famine, hurricane and other natural disasters: "The influence of these dreadful visitations might be lurking unseen in a number of emigrants before departure, to be developed during the voyage; thus causing a comparatively large number of deaths, which mortality would, in all human probability, have taken place among the same people had they remained at home."[31] All in all, the deaths are a drop in the ocean, considering that the majority of emigrants arrived safely at their destination.

V

Jenkins, by all accounts a forceful and confident campaigner, would have shrugged off "West Indian's" criticisms for what they were – sophistry born of smugness, with "West Indian" blinded to moral values by the dividends to be reaped from the sugar plantation and the immigration system. The remarks which would have stung Jenkins, given his literary sensitivities, would have been those relating to the aesthetic merit of his writing. "Social characteristics have presented", West Indian wrote, "a ready field for the satirists of every age and time, from Aristophanes to Jenkins, and it was not to be expected that the latter would refrain from using his tremendous power of adjectives in regard to the general condition of the people on the estates of Demerara." Such bracketing of Jenkins with a revered ancient like Aristophanes is obviously sarcastic, and there is the added charge that coolies are not worthy subjects of proper literature (which in any case Jenkins cannot achieve since he is so excessively wordy and hyperbolic). Jenkins, West Indian continues, was deemed "by some of his friends [note the malice of the qualification "some"] with much good nature and unconscious sarcasm, the Swift of the nineteenth century, and he manages to make good his claim to the title by forcibly-feeble writing." The pun on "force-feeding" would have been a potentially withering criticism, especially given the effortlessly biting wit of Jonathan Swift. Compared to Swift, Jenkins is accused of being a bore: "when he is not sensationalist he is dull", and it may very well be said of his work, "one-half will never be believed, the other never read".[32]

Such scathing criticism, however, rather than routing Jenkins, only provoked his resolve to press home his case, in literary form. In the preface to *Lutchmee and Dilloo*, he admits with characteristic modesty and sensitivity that his report on coolies had a certain "natural dryness", and that what is needed is to express the problems of indentured labour in a "concrete and picturesque form", giving flesh and heartbeat and animation to otherwise dry data. To write a novel on coolie life would be an audacious project, since, Jenkins himself observes, "The field is a new one for fiction." The great challenge would be to persuade the Victorian reader that the coolies were a subject worthy of literature.

Such conviction created ground-breaking work, one in which the Guianese coolie in particular and the Indian diaspora in general are for the first time in English fiction portrayed with a degree, however limited, of psychological realism and aesthetic artistry. The Indian enters English literary history in the characters of Lutchmee and Dilloo, a young married Bengali couple, who, through adventure and misadventure, find themselves in British Guiana as indentured labourers. Their relationship in Bihar, India, is an idealistic one. Lutchmee is a picture of physical symmetry, with her "light-brown oval face, with its regular eyes, arched eyebrows, delicately-chiselled nostrils and well-turned mouth and chin". Jenkins's interest in the Victorian pseudo-science of phrenology is evident in the way he links Lutchmee's outer beauty with her inner character. Dilloo is suitably presentable, his handsome and manly features reflecting nobility of spirit. Their physical and spiritual characteristics are Europeanized,[33] in terms of ideal beauty, but their qualities are equally derived from Hindu religious texts. Lutchmee is an image of the *Ramayana*'s Sita, in her loyalty and her devotion to her husband, whose prowess and courage make him a Rama figure. Their spiritually pure love is threatened by the ugly, uncouth and dark-skinned Hunoomaun, a Ravana figure who lusts after and will abduct Lutchmee, given the chance. Jenkins reconstructs Hindu scripture with breathtaking audacity, for in the *Ramayana* it was Hanuman, the monkey-god, who rescued Sita from Ravana and returned her unblemished to Rama. Hindu mythology is also paralleled with Greek mythology: Hunoomaun resembles Ravana but is also described as a satyr intent on chasing and raping a nymph. Jenkins's reference to ancient Hindu religious texts may be fleeting or indirect (he quotes from the *Gita Govinda* and mentions the laws of Manu) but in the context of Victorian celebration of Indian culture they are of considerable significance. Victorian scholars like the Oxford don Max Müller wrote glowingly of India's ancient civilization, drawing parallels between Eastern and Western classical achievements, in art, architecture and literature. Müller wrote of a common origin for all Indo-European languages, relating Sanskrit to Greek and Latin. He summarized his appreciation of the Aryan heritage of India thus: "If I were asked under what sky the human mind has most fully developed some of its choicest gifts, has most deeply pondered on the greatest problems of life, and has found solutions to some of them which well deserve the attention even of those who have studied Plato and Kant – I should say India."[34] Jenkins was, of course, hardly as adulatory of India as Müller, but he was obviously as aware of India's rich literary heritage and artistic equivalences and relationships with Western classical traditions. Lutchmee and Dilloo may be nineteenth-century indentured coolies, but they are descendants of High Civilization.

The British governing class of India and the Guianese plantation owners paid no heed to such heritage. Jenkins details various malpractices in India which converted the indentureship project into a system of financial abuses. In Guiana itself, the plantation environment destroys the idealized love between Lutchmee and Dilloo. Dilloo grows furious at the constant cheating of his fellow labourers: they are given extra work, their wages are unjustly reduced, they are cheated of adequate housing and medical provisions, they are subject to the whims of managers and magistrates. Dilloo degenerates into an angry, murderous character, beating his wife and threatening to chop her to pieces with his cutlass. The plantation treats him like an animal, and he becomes one. Jenkins writes, with scathing passion:

> It is hardly possible to conceive how the scientific or unscientific – it matters little what we term them – arrangements of an artificial system of indenture, with the laws that defined and regulated it, had succeeded in moulding out of a manly, tender, generous and loving character, a hard, unnatural and ferocious savage. We have not been without instances in Christian lands where circumstances and conditions have thus distorted most promising natures.[35]

The achievement of *Lutchmee and Dilloo*, however, is not the detailing of social and economic injustices but the revelation of emotional, psychological and philosophical shifts in the character of the Indians. They are not wooden stereotypes but people who respond vividly to their changing conditions. If Dilloo's nature is constrained by bitterness and hatred, Lutchmee senses the possibility of an existence above and beyond domestic chores, wifely duties and the closed, ghettoized space of the plantation. Her intimacy with the overseer Craig, whom she nurses back to health, provokes a radical awakening of spirit. The passage reveals a nascent feminism, a nascent defiance of patriarchal structures, whether those of the plantation system or inherited from India.

> The life was new. It brought into her life fresh human elements, feelings she had never experienced before: ideas – novel, sweet, piquant . . . Dilloo's sudden hint to her to prepare for her return home struck in harshly upon this contented, delightful peace. It woke her up to the fact that the agreeable season must soon close – it brought her back to common life and to her wifely duties – and, *though she could not analyse the meaning of the feeling*, Dilloo's request disquieted her with a conscious unpleasantness. She would rather not have been reminded by him that he had a claim on her superior to the charming engagements of her recent life.[36]

And yet, Jenkins himself is not radical enough to give Lutchmee her own voice, her own emotional and intellectual control over the narrative of her experiences. Hence "she could not analyse the meaning of the feeling". Earlier in the novel, Jenkins, writing of Lutchmee's nursing of Craig, had also denied her agency: "this strong youth . . . excited in her mind a sort of fascination which it would be hard to define . . . She was too natural to attempt to define these feelings to herself . . . Had Lutchmee been able to analyse her own feelings . . ."[37] In other words, while Indians are subject to sympathy, subject to admiration, subject to psychological growth and moral enquiry, that is what they remain in Jenkins's novel – subjects, albeit rebellious ones.

VI

In his own time, Jenkins was attacked for being a communist and a revolutionary. He was plainly not. He was, instead, a social reformer, a defence barrister for the underdog and prosecutor of the governing class. He is certain, in *Lutchmee and Dilloo*, that it is "European energy"[38] which brings order and civilization to the jungle environment of Guiana. In his *Discussions on Colonial Questions*, he stated unequivocally that the colonies could be productive and Empire could flourish only if "organised and applied under the direction of Europeans".[39] His overriding concern was the elimination of the injustices which corrupted the ideals of Empire. His limitations are obvious in his depiction of Africans. He wrote of Guiana's "large, lazy, prodigiously sensual and fecund black population".[40] In *Lutchmee and Dilloo*, he reduces the African characters to brute stupidity, his descriptions of their behaviour being as objectionable and vile as any found in the racist rantings of his Victorian contemporaries. Sarcophagus, for instance, is a brainless animal, incapable of intelligible speech, much less writing: "If you tossed him a bundle of words, he used them as a gorilla would use a bundle of sticks. He unaccountably mixed and twisted them up together, he tore them to shreds between his teeth."[41] Indians fare better in that they are sometimes given ornate speech indicating lofty feeling. Ultimately, however, they are denied the capacity to fictionalize their own world, with Jenkins remaining steadfastly in charge of the narrative.

Later in the novel, Jenkins dismisses some coolie complaints against the plantation as "obviously ridiculous fictions".[42] In *The Coolie: His Rights and Wrongs*, Jenkins had made a similar charge against the Indian and Chinese labourers giving testimony before the Committee enquiring into their affairs. Their petitions are "written on all sorts of paper – brown, straw, candle-box, cartridge, etc., one on a tiny slip of scarlet torn off a wall or cut from a book . . . Asiatic ingenuity and craft were sometimes plainly written between the lines, and although some of them may have been based on facts, the Commissioners found on testing them that many were built on fiction".[43] Jenkins's accusation is that they "enhance the effects of their narrations"[44] by colouring and dramatizing their grievances, but is this not what Jenkins himself is doing in his own ways in writing his novel? The fact is that the coolies were *writing* for the first time, thus authorizing their lives. If they fictionalized their lives, it was an attempt to give such lives the kind of psychological nuance and depth and drama that Jenkins declared to be his intent in writing the novel. Jenkins, however, will not give credence to their "narrations", much less space in their novel for their expression. *His* is the master script. *He* writes of and for them. They remain indentured to his authorial voice.[45] It is deeply ironical, then, to learn that Jenkins's novel was soon forgotten and Jenkins himself written out of the history of Victorian literature. The only aspect of him which survives in the English language is the word "jinx", from *Ginx's Baby*, but even this fact has been hitherto unrecorded by etymologists.[46] As a descendent of one of Jenkins's indentured coolies it is now my curious privilege to make this fact known, to recover his voice and to bring him once more into print, into the life of English letters.

Part 2

INTERVIEWS WITH
DAVID DABYDEEN

CHAPTER 10

A Talk with David Dabydeen
(1995)

FELICITY HAND, UNIVERSITAT AUTÒNOMA DE BARCELONA

Felicity Hand: Is it possible to discuss black writers or black characters in fiction without considering racism?

David Dabydeen: Unfortunately no, because the sort of social circumstances and contexts in which black writers operate are charged with race. I said "unfortunately" because V.S. Naipaul[1] once wrote that race is not a great enough theme for literature, or words to that effect – I might be misquoting him. I think what he was trying to say is that just to write about race is to be reductionist; it is limiting your art to a singular, monolithic experience, so while the white society in which you live might impress certain racial marks upon you, nevertheless, the burden on the black writer is to transcend those designations or categories. Which means, ultimately, writing *out of* experience rather than *from* experience. This can be extremely difficult, but in some ways it can be deeply liberating because then you are writing purely imaginatively, you have as your subject a purely imaginative one. That could be a real liberation, a real emancipation in a sense, maybe the final emancipation. The first emancipation was in 1833,[2] and that was, if you like, a physical and social emancipation. Now, perhaps, a psychic emancipation has to come about if we are to be really and genuinely post-Columbian. Writers like Wilson Harris[3] have been arguing this for years, that we can't be trapped in hurts and history; even though white society defines us with false historicism we have to somehow transcend, rewrite and revise. Those are the challenges: imaginative liberation, liberation of the imagination. The negatives, of course, are that you can't cease to be what you are because, at the end of the day, you are your despised colour, you are your despised appearance as well. And you don't really want to abandon responsibility to certain ethnic experiences, because if *you* don't write them, who will?

FH: Doesn't all this mean, though, that you're all jumbled up inside, that you're never certain of who you are?

DD: Well, let me just think about this for a minute. You see, C.L.R. James, who was one of our writers and intellectuals, wrote that we West Indians are creatures of our colonial inheritance in that we were made and manufactured in Europe by the Europeans. Other writers like Edward Brathwaite have argued a kind of native position, which is that we retained our Indianness or our Africanness and those qualities went through profound modifications and hybridizations, which resulted in what is called the New World person. What we should be looking at are the processes of transformation and creolization that created this new state, this New World person and *not* keep emphasizing the European ingredient. In fact, what we should start considering are the ways in which contact with Africa and India altered the European psyche profoundly – in other words, the impact we made in creolizing them, exciting them, teaching them, remaking them, liberating them from strictures of form, language, aesthetics and so forth. I hardly need to mention our influence on Stravinsky, Picasso, Modigliani, D.H. Lawrence, and modernism and postmodernism in general.

FH: Your second novel, *Disappearance*,[4] is set in the English countryside and has an English woman who, in her passionate intensity, seems almost a creole character. Why did you write about the countryside?

DD: When ex-colonial writers deal with England, they are terrified of confronting the English landscape, the English rural landscape, and so the bulk of writing is set in cities. No black writer, apart from Naipaul, has ever dealt intimately with the English rural landscape, with village life, and this is because the English landscape is an archetype of the English identity and we are still made to feel that we are immigrants and therefore outsiders. It's interesting to note that in Naipaul's novel *The Enigma of Arrival* (1987) he cannot look at the Wiltshire landscape except through the eyes of Constable and Wordsworth. When he sees a character moving about the landscape, he automatically thinks of Wordsworth's leech gatherer. We still have not got away from being trapped in the allusions that have been inherited, the European allusions especially. Our identities are so fluid that I think you can say we are made of a set of allusions. We echo Europe, we echo India, we echo Africa. We are just like one of T.S. Eliot's allusions in *The Waste Land*. I don't have the sense of being *rooted* in England's rural landscape, but I have a sense of being able to *describe* that landscape, like Naipaul, through Constable and the Romanticists. Although I can't yet *live* the rural experience, I can *describe* it, or imagine it. The real change in England will come about only when we actually begin to live in its cottages and add a dash of "blackness" to the "greenery and pleasantry".

FH: Hostility towards blacks can be traced back to Elizabethan times. Would you agree that fear and distrust of blacks is an innate characteristic of the white British? Would you agree that it is something that lies dormant for, maybe, generations, but will at a particular time burst out?

DD: I think that demonology about blacks in the English imagination has replaced the demonology about wild men. I think the Negro replaced the [medieval] green man; the black man replaced the Green Knight, if you like. It was green and then it was black. A whole empire was centred around this demonology, and the black has remained the symbol of darkness and disorder in the English psyche up to today. There seems to be a need in England for recognition and description of the Other, of that which is not yourself and yet, at the same time, that which is the deepest echo and reflection of yourself. The black man has satisfied that need for the description and recognition of the Other. I think of Conrad's *Heart of Darkness*, when Marlow, describing the blacks in the bush, said that the horrible thing when they danced and yelped was that they were not different, that they were ourselves, they were reflections of us, and that *that* was the horror. Blacks in the bush were our – and by "our" I mean English – capacity for obscenity and for a kind of a revelry and carnival that were not permitted here. So it seems to me that the white encounter with blackness was a way of the whites transgressing all the boundaries – Victorian, Edwardian or whatever – that circumscribe their own existence. These are sexual boundaries, mostly. I think there was a kind of release into the world of lasciviousness that was not permitted. It was Conrad's phrase "going beyond the boundaries of permitted aspiration". I think Africa and blacks, paradoxically, allowed the liberation of the white imagination, whilst the blacks themselves were being incarcerated in baracoons and slave ships and plantations.

FH: If we consider that, in Britain today, roughly 10 per cent of the population belongs to what we might call a "cultured elite" and that, among this 10 per cent, non-whites are underrepresented, how do you feel about belonging to this elite?

DD: I'd say that I quite enjoy the ironies of having been definitely invited to join the white elite, in that through a university like Warwick, which is an English institution, you gain access to other English institutions and you think that this is a beginning of a new movement in England towards a kind of egalitarian society. Or is it that you have just been drafted in to add colour to panels or colour to boards and committees? You are never quite sure at any one moment whether there is a deep liberalism in the society in which you live, whether it is just a masquerade of liberalism. This is exactly why the British Empire lasted for four hundred years and it outlasted other empires, because the British were Janus figures. They were able to show a deep decency in a sense of justice – there were white colonial figures who were radical in the context of their own times, concerned, Christian, compassionate – and yet there were other aspects of the colonial experience that [were] brutal and brutish. Sometimes that brutishness emanated from those very Christian gentlemen and gentlewomen, so I think the poor native was totally confused and didn't know whether to have a reverence and respect [for] the decent foreigner who at other times exhibited a dumb brutality. Why the Empire lasted for so long was because, as colonized people, we could not resolve the contradictions in the British character. Today you are constantly being pulled in two directions in terms of your attitudes towards England. You recognize a genuine liberalism in society and at the same time you come up against all kinds of manic and depressive violence. It may well be that that kind of schizophrenic experience has impeded radical action on the part of the black community. We really ought to have blasted the place apart by now, don't you think, after the centuries of treating us as niggers? Poor Enoch Powell and his unfulfilled prophecy of the Tiber–Thames foaming with racial blood!⁵ To be serious, though, we don't kill white people because we are human and we recognize their own humanity. The greatest gift we can give white people is a sense of their own humanity.

FH: Would you agree that being British today has changed dramatically [from] being British thirty or forty years ago, that now it seems that the periphery is taking over from the centre?

DD: The first thing we ought to do is to get rid of these critical terms like "centre" and "periphery" because, the more we use them, even though we claim to be using them with a degree of subversion, what we are really doing is to concretize them, legitimize them. The centre has always been peripheral in a way, because if you look at the colonial conquest of India, it was deeply superficial, if I can put it like that. Values from the centre – if the centre was England, the colonial power – had minimal impact on Indian culture, on the Indian imagination. Today, the great writers of India are not those who write in English; the great writers of India are those who write in their own languages and remain deeply inaccessible to the English, as the English have to make an effort to understand them. Most people don't speak the English language in India; things go on as they have always gone on, they go on in an Indian way. So the centre was peripheral even though the centre likes to think that it had conquered the globe. It just scratched the surface of, in this case, Indian culture. On the other hand, you could argue that the periphery, which was Indian in this case, had a tremendous impact on the English. The English started building, creating architecture, like the Brighton Pavilion, that was influenced by Indian forms. They started setting up at Oxford and Cambridge schools for Sanskrit studies, Eastern religious studies and so on. You could argue that you could not have got a writer like Laurence Sterne with that sort of saga-like way of writing, digressions all over the place, coming back to the core narrative, and digressions again, unless Sterne had possibly encountered something of Indian stories, and ways of telling Indian stories. Even today India is a hallowed destination for the English traveller. So you could argue that England, the centre, was more affected by the periphery, that the periphery was more centred than England, and that the centre, England, was more peripheral in India. At the end of the day, though, we just have to get rid of these distinctions which merely fuel an immature rivalry and competitiveness. We should avoid simplistic and hateful rivalries. Certainly some of the best writing in England now is being done by people who have a colonial background, but these authors don't write out of vengeance. Of course, there is that nice sense of retaliation in, for example, Ishiguro's *The Remains of the Day*,[6] where he takes a kind of quintessential English symbol, the butler, and slowly reveals all kinds of fascism that lie beneath this surface of servility. But Ishiguro writes with such restraint and grace that after a while you marvel at the style and form of his novel rather than at its retaliatory content. At the end of the day he is a writer and has married art and polemics with supreme ease. The real retaliation, therefore, is in his command of English prose.

FH: It appears that the differences separating the West from the so-called Third World are increasing instead of diminishing. The West has knocked down the Berlin Wall but has built another "European" or "Western" wall in its place. This "wall" represents an insurmountable barrier, getting high[er] and higher all the time. Would you agree that East and West or North and South have never been so far apart as they are now?

DD: You mean the Kipling cliché that "never the twain shall meet"? I think that the main barrier is no longer a cultural barrier, in the sense that texts and people who construct or write those texts are becoming more accessible. Writers travel all over the world and can be made accessible to different language groups. There is no longer a kind of cultural arrogance associated with writing in English, unless, say, people in India want to believe that somehow their writing in native languages is inferior. That's their business; to me that's their failure if they believe that. I think that the wall is no longer a cultural one, since our literature is increasingly being received in Western societies. I am being optimistic, of course, for the sake of my own sales. The barrier is definitely economic and ecological. I mean, the West is slowly destroying not just large parts of the planet, those parts that are specifically in the Third World by a kind of an indiscriminate, almost a brutish use, of resources. America produces nearly a third of the carbon dioxide that threatens the globe. That is shameful. I mean, what is it – they breathe more deeply, they breathe more heavily than the rest of us, or what? I'm sure they consume most of the oxygen as well! So they just consume, they just waste, don't they, and all the stuff that they waste comes from resources in the Third World. So we are slowly poisoning and destroying the Third World, ecologically. There's drought and famine, and all those phenomena – climatic changes that threaten the very existence of certain islands and certain countries. I mean, Guyana, where I come from, is below sea level, and if the ocean [rises] another few inches, that's the end of Guyana, never mind Guyanese literature. We'd have to be writing from boats! And the writing's bound to be up and down – you know, with the waves! The West will find all sorts of stupendous technological ways of survival: they built Thames barriers; they'll build pyramids of technology to save themselves. Economically, of course, the fact is that we still bleed the Third World. There's more money coming in from debt repayments into the West than there's going out in terms of new loans. That's taking from poor people; it's as simple as that. Every year, I've forgotten how many billions come in from debt repayment, and how many billions go out in loans. There's more billions coming in than going out in loans. That's just robbing the poor. It's like mugging a beggar: the next day you give him ten pence or whatever, a couple of dollars, to bandage his wounds, and then you mug him again! They talk about the blacks in Western societies being the muggers – blackness in this country is associated with mugging – but the mugging is much more unsubtle than snatching an old woman's handbag. It's very unsubtle; it's just the banks grabbing chunks of rainforest, and chunks of people's hard-earned foreign exports.

FH: Is it still a sign of success for a "Third World" writer writing in English to become a "name" in Britain?

DD: It's unfortunately true: an Indian writer in India tends to be more known when he or she is legitimized by the West, legitimized in terms of critical receptivity, and I think that this is still one of the shameful legacies of colonialism that we slowly have to purge ourselves of. However, having said that, it's good to be read by anybody. It's a privilege to be read, so that if more people are reading you in England than are reading you, in my case, in Guyana, for whatever reason – the main reason being economic: they can't afford the books in Guyana, and we don't have the publishing systems to produce very cheap books for markets that can only afford books at that price – as an individual. I'm still glad to be read, and to receive royalties that accrue from that. So whilst your question has a wide political dimension, I think the individual writer has to get on with the business of writing and being read by whoever reads you.

FH: In your novel *The Intended*,[7] why is the main character so enamoured of Englishness?

DD: I wanted to show how that character misrepresents what English is by taking on [the same] official English definitions [that the English have for] themselves. The English define themselves in terms of a heritage of language, a very glorious heritage of achievement, of elegance, of order, of civilization. This black character, who wants to be English, gravitates towards the myth of England rather than trying to seek out the reality of England. I wanted to write about a black character trapped in myth, because it seems to me that most of the white characters in fiction written in the colonial period – by Buchan, Henry, Ballantyne[8] and so on – those white characters are trapped in myth, about what Africa is, and what India is, and what they themselves are in terms of being English, so really I just wanted to show how that process of myth-making is still relevant in England today, and to make that myth-making the business of this particular black character. I find him very infuriating myself, because what he does have, being an outsider, is a romantic sense of what England should have been, how it should have lived up to its images. I think he wants to recover nobility in England; he doesn't want to see England in terms of what it is today, the violence and disorder and discrimination and sexual violence. He wants to see England as a place of order and civil values and common decencies.

I thought it was rather poignant that he is trapped in the myth of England that the English never believed in, because if they believed it in previous centuries they wouldn't have gone out and colonized in the ways that they did. They would have gone out and given Shakespeare and Milton and the best of England to other people. The best of England only arrived in the Caribbean in spite of the English. I think you'll find that the best of English literature was actually taken in spite of the colonial powers-that-be. The people from the Foreign Office, the Colonial Office, were not interested in taking the best of England; they were just interested in taking the money. They were interested in the East India Company and the Royal African Company. Shakespeare and the Bible only got to the Caribbean because of individual acts by eccentric Englishmen who actually believed in English values. Or else it was very important to provide a justification for colonial robbery, and justifications lay in the sense of England's glory and in a sense of responsibility towards the "dark races". So Shakespeare and Milton were then taken over as part of the imperial process.

Anyway, coming back to *The Intended*, the protagonist's black friends say to him, "You're only a coon in the end; don't think that Oxford will give you anything." So there's this kind of chorus of satanic voices, a litany of satanic voices off-stage that keep undercutting his desire to be proper, to be a proper Englishman. I was interested in the comedy of the clash between this litany of satanic voices and his own public voice – [his] pronouncements about the beauty of England – and his own private voice, which actually tells him that he is being silly.

FH: Is Patel right when he says that "all they [the British] have over us is money"?[9]

DD: I would say that the saddest thing about England, as opposed to other places in Europe I visit, is you get a sense of an absence of rich culture. There is culture but it can strike you in your more ungenerous mood as being philistine culture. People hardly read, people hardly sing; even in churches people don't sing, they don't celebrate, there's no joy. When I go to Italy, the culture is apparent in the architecture, the culture is apparent in the food. I just think that after twenty years of living in England I'd have to say that it's philistine compared to the rest of Europe, and I also have to say that the English are very proud of this philistinism, the fact they have access to no other language but English and even then only a "half-English", because most people in this country can't speak English. They speak a kind of yob English, you know, it's "Chelsea, Chelsea, Chelsea", it's a kind of primitive chant. So there is a kind of paganism in this society which I find, not disquieting, but terrifying.

Whenever you confront the pagan it is terrifying – these chants at football matches, this yob language on public transport, this sub-cultural violence. The lower orders do as much violence to language as the BBC once did. Even when they curse you racially they do it in a yob language, all grunts and gutturals. I don't mind being cursed but sometimes I wish they would curse me grammatically or in felicitous language. You get a sense of living in an inarticulate community rather than in a community of language. The British Asians speak four or five languages, and inevitably are bringing a richness to the country, and they bring religion and they bring God back into England. Nobody gave a toss about God before. You opened the papers and they would be writing that Jesus was a homosexual or Mary was the mistress of Pontius Pilate, and nobody cared, but the Muslims care about spiritual life. So, apart from bringing ancient languages into the society, they have brought spirituality into the society; they have brought morality into the society. Margaret Thatcher talked about a return to Victorian values. Well, all these things that we talk about in our public political discourse, like family values, language values, spiritual values, are what the Asians are reintroducing in society. So, if England is philistine, the way out is to listen to what the Asians are saying and [to find] out who they are. Asians can be as narrow-minded and cash-oriented as anyone else, but they also come bearing richer gifts.

CHAPTER 11

Interviewing David Dabydeen (1995)

CHELVA KANAGANAYAKAM, UNIVERSITY OF TORONTO

Chelva Kanaganayakam: Let's begin with your long poem "Turner", which is in many ways a remarkable work. A painting provides the immediate context, but how did the poem itself originate? Why did you think of writing a poem that encompasses both Africa and India?

David Dabydeen: Although it is a poem about our history, and about the loss of memory, for me it was also about being an immigrant in Britain, and what migration meant in terms of forgetting where one came from. Migration entailed a dispersal of my family. I have family all over the world now because of the whole process of decolonization. The CIA and the British government "fixed" Guyana's history. They fixed it historically and, when they left, they fixed who would be in positions of power. As a result of that political corruption, we all had to flee. So we migrated to various places, wherever we were given a visa. So, in a sense, you never see your family for years and you only go to their funerals. Although "Turner" was a poem about a dead African, for me it was about today, about how our history is fixed by other people and how it leads to separation and irreparable losses in terms of not being able to go back home; we have lost the language and gestures and habits of what used to be home. That was the immediate impulse.

CK: I can understand your rejecting the world created by "Turner", but you reject the African world as well.

DD: Yes, I reject any notion of home that is idyllic. When I talk about not having a home, I don't mean that if I had that home that would necessarily be comforting or comfortable. I don't believe in any ideologies of return based on a pattern of romance. I don't believe in the fictionalization of the past.

CK: But don't you need a sense of the past to validate the present?

DD: Yes, I do. Except that in the West Indies we have fabricated a sense of the past by replacing what we lost with a kind of romantic fiction. India was a desperate and, in some ways, turmoiled place. We were also enslaved in the caste system and the women were enslaved in the sati system. I have no romance about India or Africa. In other words, I would rather have a home that is real.

CK: In short, you reject anything exotic or essentialist as a substitute for home?

DD: "Exotic" is the word I am looking for. To exoticize is to play into people who fixed our history.

CK: It is interesting that you bring up India because in "Turner" you mention the character Manu in an African context. Did you deliberately make that Indian and Hindu connection in Africa?

DD: The poem is about the African experience, which is the parent experience of the Caribbean, but it is not entirely about the African experience. It is about the Caribbean, particularly the Guyanese West Indian experience. If you read the poem carefully, you will find that the landscape that the African imagines with a cow being central to it is an Indian village landscape.

CK: Yes, I was struck by that unusual juxtaposition.

DD: Even the reference to the *juti* necklace connects with the Indian *choota*, a kind of ritual pollution. I took Indian words from a slightly different context and changed them. "Turner" is, for me, a very Indian and African poem. The reference to Manu was pure intuition. I knew the name "Manu" and I wanted an Indian name, but I never realized that Manu was the Noah of Indian mythology until I read a review of the poem in a newspaper by an Englishwoman who knew Hinduism very well. It was a kind of intuitive process. A happy accident. I didn't have the idea of the Flood when I wrote the poem.

CK: Did you have the hegemonic aspect, the Brahmanization of India, in mind when you included the name?

DD: Not really. At the same time, in a sense, I did, because I grew up in a Hindu environment as a child. So some of the ideas of codification and canonization were in my mind. I grew up in England among immigrants and some of them were Hindus. One picks up memories as one goes along. That is something that a critic would probably read into the poem. I believe that, at the end of the day, as Derek Walcott has said, it is all an accident.

CK: The Walcott comparison is interesting, because he constantly used the sea as an important metaphor. That is quite central to "Turner" as well, and you use the sea image in a very curious kind of way to talk about new beginnings. At the same time, you have a strong sense of the past. Is the sea an important trope because of the geography of Guyana?

DD: The sea is important because Guyana is below sea level. One is constantly aware of the sea as a threat, as a place of great peril – the sea as a place which drowns little boys. A boyhood friend of mine drowned in the sea. I don't swim; I never could. The idea of the sea, for me, was also Adamic; we don't have the Garden of Eden, which was how the Caribbean was described by Jean Rhys. I wanted the Garden of Eden to be the sea, which has no landscape, no land, no nationality or ethnicity. A sea is a place of erasure. I wanted that to be the place where Adam could be born. It didn't work out that way. It was a stillborn child and a dead African in the poem. The sea becomes an empty Eden in the poem.

CK: With the vague possibility of something life-giving emerging from the sea?

DD: There is that possibility, although the poem denies it. I would hope the music of the poem offers some element of hope, even though the theme is bleak.

CK: The sea is used very differently in the novel *Disappearance*.

DD: Do you think so?

CK: In that novel the sea is a threat of a different kind, and human effort is always directed at erecting dams and controlling the destructive potential of the sea.

DD: Yes, but the novel ends with the hope that the sea will wash away the dam, break it into neat pebbles and make humanity realize that it is a dot in the cosmic landscape. In *Disappearance* the idea of the sea as erasure is present, and hence it symbolizes the condition of erasure. The sea has no trail back to Africa or India.

CK: As a metaphor for countering notions of nationalism, that sea becomes useful.

DD: For me, it is very important. It is also a very beautiful metaphor of the possibility of total originality. Not only erasure, but absolute originality.

CK: Is it because it contains life and death?

DD: The sea has no memory in the way land has memory. You can't mark the sea. When the *Titanic* sank in 1917 it was an enormous blow to British prestige and British industrialization. The *Titanic* symbolized the greatness of Britain, and the sea – excuse my language here – just fucked it up. The sea sank the *Titanic* and put Britain at the bottom of the ocean. I like the enormous power that the sea has to deny nationalistic and imperialistic efforts.

CK: Does the poetic become political?

DD: Of course it does. It becomes a weapon against all forms of tyranny because the sea resists all enclosures. Even the land cannot enclose the sea. At the top of the Himalayas the stone is corralled, because the Himalayas used to be below the sea at one stage. I couldn't believe it. That was remarkable. The sea in the Caribbean used to be a land mass running from the Andes to Miami, and then the sea washed in and those islands are the tips of mountains.

CK: The texture of *Disappearance* at certain points reminded me of Naipaul, particularly of *The Enigma of Arrival*. Did you expect the reader to make that connection?

DD: Sure, it was a conscious nod in Naipaul's direction. After writing the first novel, which was consciously untidy and creole, replicated on the structure of creole movements that have no grammar, I wanted to write a very English novel. The model is obviously Naipaul. It has three parts and twelve chapters. It is very engineered and it shows its hand and reveals itself as a piece of engineering. Obviously that is very much like Naipaul, because he is a beautiful engineer of prose.

CK: The politics of Naipaul is probably very different from what you were trying to advance?

DD: I think Naipaul is very narrow in his response to life and living. I think there is a deep honesty in him, but I also think it is miserable. It is a kind of misery about Naipaul that I can't stand. Even with all the bleakness, one needs to believe in some kind of life force. You have to believe in consciousness and beauty, and I don't find that in Naipaul. I wanted to create a character who was Naipaulian. The engineer was a version of Naipaul.

I just finished a third novel in which the main character is called Vidyar. And he is very weak and vulnerable and concerned with money. He can't make love with relish. In my mind I was thinking of a Naipaulian character. I grew up on a diet of Naipaul. The first West Indian novel I read was by him.

CK: I guess he was an important influence or presence?

DD: Absolutely. For an Indian in the Caribbean, Naipaul was a father figure. One tends to hate father figures.

CK: There is an important difference between the narrative modes of the first novel and the second. One is a form of realism and the other is more poetic in its structure. Do you have a preference for one over the other? How do these relate to "Turner"?

DD: I don't know. "Turner" took about four years to write. I started it in '89 and completed it in '93. I wrote it in bits and pieces, a couple of hours at a time. In the meantime I was writing prose and I published a couple of novels. I was much happier with "Turner" than with the two novels. Novelists tend to write travel writing between novels. I think poets write novels between poems. It is a way of killing time.

CK: Was the poem a greater challenge?

DD: Much more, and it was more joyous. It was much more emotional. My instinct is for poetry.

CK: In your introduction to *Slave Song*, you talk a great deal about language and the need to use a certain kind of language. And in "Turner" you don't employ that kind of nation language but rather something more formal.

DD: Yes, I use a language that plays with blank verse with echoes of the iambic pentameter.

CK: Did that constitute a problem?

DD: Not really. I write in creole and English. It is not one against the other. The novel I have finished is partly in creole and the rest in English. Twenty-five pages are in creole. It depends on who is speaking. If it is a Guyanese canecutter speaking, I use creole. "Turner" couldn't be written in creole because it was writing to Turner; the whole idea was to use the language of Turner, which was very English. It didn't start as a creole poem. If it had started that way I could have continued it.

CK: You [have] also mentioned that medieval verse has been an important influence in your writing. How did that come about?

DD: Well, when I was young I was obsessed with medieval alliterative poetry. I remember being overcome by the kind of energy and lyricism of that language. Medieval poetry was very much like the creole. The medieval period, too, was beautiful and innocent. I wish I was a medievalist without all the slavery stuff. It was all pre-colonial, about the green man, not the black man. You almost begin to love England when you read medieval literature.

CK: The poems in *Slave Song* re-create the rhythm of the people. Was this rhythm created by you or were you drawing on an indigenous tradition? Was there an oral culture that you were tapping into?

DD: I think it was both. It was an attempt to put down on paper something of the music of those peasant villagers with whom we grew up. At the same time, there are all kinds of English rhythms that come in as well, like the medieval alliterative tradition. If I were to read the poems again I would probably pick up a lot of that medieval rhythm. I acknowledge it in the notes.

CK: So you blend that with the indigenous?

DD: Yes, but it was not a conscious effort. Those medieval lays, those wicked little songs about getting up in the morning and your mistress is around and realizing that your wife is somewhere else, all those traditions of mischief in the appropriately named "lays" are also part of the influence.

CK: Among the issues you deal with, one is that of ethnicity. For other writers from the region, including Wilson Harris, that issue isn't central.

DD: It is something I am trying to move away from, but you are right: it is central. In a way, if you come from the other end of the earth, which is Guyana, and the centre is England, you know that you are marginalized. Every Guyanese knows that he or she is marginalized. You can't get away from ethnicity. Was it Seamus Heaney who talked about the difference between the expression of grievance and the expression of grief? I am not going to make being in the margins a source of grievance because, like Wilson Harris, I believe that it is not until you are in the margins that you can tilt the plane of the centre. Being in the margins gives you an enormous amount of weight. So I believe in writing out of the freedoms you get by being in the margins.

CK: But specifically the kind of ethnic tensions that are very much a part of the political life of Guyana?

DD: Everything I write implicates that kind of racial violence in Guyana. I grew up with it. I was about ten or eleven when people started killing each other. I was very conscious of that kind of intimidation and terror. The novel I have just finished is very open about that kind of racial feeling. I write openly about Indian people calling black people niggers. At one level it is as simple as that.

CK: But isn't there a need to come to terms with that?

DD: Absolutely. The only way to do that is to write about it. I get attacked from both sides. People say the novel is anti-black or anti-Indian. You write according to the way you remember. I also believe that all this is very temporary. There is a tremendous effort that people make to live together and transcend these differences. You see it in Guyana. We don't have genocidal tendencies. We had that bitter episode in the sixties. But, that apart, I can't think of any instance where we killed each other openly like they do in Sri Lanka or India. We might call each other "coolie" and "nigger" and worry about who is getting the money and who is running the government, but there is a tremendous decency as well. I have a friend who told me that why we live together is because we were all reduced to the lowest common denominator. Then a kind of humility develops.

CK: One final question that has to do with the treatment of women in both your novels. This is particularly true of *The Intended*, although it is true of *Disappearance* as well. You seem to portray women as both emotionally and even physically stronger than men.

DD: I guess it is not that the women are stronger than the men; it is just that the men are weaker than the women. The men fumble; they are always inept. I am being autobiographical as well here.

CK: Is it a result of the colonial past, the kind of pressures that men had to face?

DD: There are all those theories about impotence, and so forth. There is probably a certain element of truth about a certain kind of impotence. I use the term "impotence" quite a lot. There is self-mutilation as well as a feeling of helplessness. The men in Guyana were the ones doing the fighting for political freedom. They were given access to education. They were also being beaten and humiliated. That creates in the eyes of their wives and girlfriends a kind of humiliation. Maybe there is a historical basis. I was more interested in the idea of men being weaker.

CHAPTER 12

"A Certain Obligation": An Interview with David Dabydeen (1999)

CLARISSE ZIMRA, SOUTHERN ILLINOIS UNIVERSITY, CARBONDALE

Clarisse Zimra: You have been a versatile writer. You started very properly as an art historian, the author of scholarly studies. Then you switched pursuits, alternating between fiction and poetry. I know – because you've said so in public readings – that you are reluctant to talk about the work in progress until and unless it is firmly fixed in your mind. What could you tell us about the piece you are working on these days?

David Dabydeen: What I am writing just now? It is a novel set in eighteenth-century London, for which I got the idea from a painting by William Hogarth, *A Harlot's Progress*, which he painted in 1732. So, here is what I do: I take the black character in this painting, I take him off the frame, so to speak, and I give him a biography.

The novel, too, is called *A Harlot's Progress*. It is about the possibility of love between this black man and this prostitute from the painting. But I'm only at the very beginning: I've only done about a quarter of it, and so you never know – *I* never know – how it will turn out.

CZ: How did it come about?

DD: Very simply. It had to do with doing something about the black presence in Britain, a presence that does not just happen post–Second World War but, really, goes back several centuries. It is a literary excavation, as it were, of an aspect of Britain that has remained much neglected – and that is that, at the height of the slave trade, blacks were present in very sizeable numbers in the major cities of Britain.

CZ: We could say that you've been keeping up with your initial interest in the subjects of Empire. It builds, too, on your academic writings as an art historian, does it not?

DD: Indeed! As an academic, too, one keeps in touch; otherwise there is a kind of schizophrenia, isn't there, between the academic world and the creative world? One must use the academic world creatively, or use it as a springboard for ideas. However, I don't honestly believe I am doing much academic work anymore – as a person, that is, not intellectually of course – in that I tend to think imaginatively, which is what one must do when it comes to black history, which is essentially absent data. One has to fill the gaps by acts of the imagination. This is how one manages to flesh out history, since it is data that does not exist, or does not exist anymore, so that it prods one to create a narrative.

CZ: I am sure you know that this is very much Toni Morrison's own position about the willed re-creation of an absent past that, she argues, must be the moral obligation of the writers. I am thinking, in particular, of the strong essays that make up the collection *Playing in the Dark*.

DD: No, I did not know. Intellectually, as well as imaginatively, I agree: this is good, because it means that one can actually write about black history with a kind of freedom to re-imagine the possibilities of history, a marvellous freedom as opposed to the stark actuality of certain events.

CZ: Is this where you are, when you say you might be only a quarter done with this novel because you do not know where or when it is going to end?

DD: Oh yes! I *think* I'm at the first quarter, but I also *know* that it goes as you write; something happens, and one learns to continue along that line, I suppose. But I definitely don't know, at this point, how it will end; nor do I even know how the characters will develop.

CZ: Do you find, then, that characters have a life of their own which might appear later in the writing that you had not anticipated?

DD: Sure, all the time . . . because you work – I mean, *I* work – from day to day and ideas pop up as you go along, and you write them down. For instance, some of my black characters end up having autonomy, and things will happen that I had certainly not anticipated. I find, in my very small experience of having written just a few books, that when the book is finished, and you may come to read it six or seven months later, or whenever you'll come across it, I find that these characters will surprise you.

Really [*he laughs*] . . . You'll put the thing down, and you'll think, "My God! This must have been some serious red wine I was having!" or whatever. You will be surprised by what it is you have written.

CZ: Doesn't it depend on the person? I know writers who claim not to reread themselves, or who swear not to recognize some of their characters or some of their own lines.

DD: Well, it helps if you are asked to do readings, doesn't it? You'll have to select your own passages and think about what you are doing, don't you think? And this might be one of the main reasons, although not the only one, that you find yourself rereading the stuff. I agree that it could be, it *can* be, terribly embarrassing to reread your stuff.

CZ: A related area, which is not quite as wilful, has to do with reintroducing characters of yours from previous works. Do you anticipate this, or does it just happen and take you by surprise, as another instance of character autonomy?

DD: Oh, sure. I did think of a dream sequence for this novel. In this instance, I have an eighteenth-century character who has been endowed by some "magical" process – and I am not yet sure how – with certain prophetic powers. He is a black man who has no sense of the past but a tremendous sense of the future in a "magical", a peculiar, kind of prophetic way, so that, really, this is a novel about the absence of the past, because I set parts of it in Africa. I've not thought about it so far, but it is certainly an imagined Africa: it points to the fact that it is imagined. It's certainly not social realism – it's absurd, an absurd Africa.

CZ: This might also be called "magic realism", couldn't it? Is it the eighteenth-century Africa or the modern Africa? Or neither?

DD: Well, you see, my character has to remember his African background: he's been asked to. He's been asked to remember his past, asked to tell his story, so that he can be made to serve the abolitionist purpose. Now, how can he remember an Africa he does not know, or no longer knows? He has to create a story about himself, and a story that will go down well with the abolitionists who want to use him.

So, how can he do it? So far, what I have imagined is that he creates two possible pasts for himself, neither of which he believes in, you see. And these two pasts he creates do complement each other but they are also very, very different, so that he's more or less saying, "Look, *have* whatever past you want, whatever version you want of me!" [*He laughs.*]

CZ: You *are* churning dangerous waters.

DD: Yes, well . . . I suppose I am. I got interested in this paradox because I believe one has to get away from exotica in order to get away from the idea of victimization. In other words, creating a sense of the past that is exotic for a foreign reader leads to victimization. One is merely inventing a past which pulls the heartstrings and conscience and guilt "facility" of white people.

CZ: So that they can atone? Doesn't this feed some of the criticism that has been levelled at you, that you serve the master's purpose only too well? Or, at the very least, isn't it what your character is going to do if he is trying to concoct a narrative that must serve a preordained purpose, even an abolitionist purpose?

DD: I think we must inhabit our postcolonial situation. So far, I have created a character speaking to the abolitionists while resisting the abolitionists' attempt to write his past for him, to speak his past in a certain way. What's happened in the novel so far – remember, I don't know where it's going – is that the abolitionist, a man called Mr Pringle, also decides to write the African past, you see. Therefore, there are three pasts being presented, here, three fictional ones, two by the African himself, and one by the abolitionist.

CZ: Plus the real one?

DD: Plus the "real" one. God knows what will happen next.

CZ: That's quite a predicament. As an art historian, you were already interested in the disappearing black figures and their iconography. Yet, in your interviews, you seem to slip-and-slide, fairly non-critically if I may say, among several concepts of blackness. You go from the use of "black" as a loose signifier of subjugation, the ontological black, to the "ethnic", geopolitical black-as-non-white, the great unwashed of Empire; finally, you sometimes use it as a racial term, one standing for Africa. Of course, I'm looking at these shifts from the standpoint of an American audience, keenly alert to the use of the term. How would you respond to their criticism that you are essentializing the black-as-Other, or, at least, as that which is not Western?

DD: I'm not quite sure what you are saying. I don't see how essentialism can come into presenting three different images of blackhood. The whole idea of this particular novel is to get away from a sense of essentialism, a set of authentic features; to get away from the idea of an authentic background, an authentic history to anything. Hence the idea of creating three different pasts.

CZ: Well, this novel is not finished, so I can't and should not prejudge. What I had in mind was more along the lines of self-presentation and representation. I have read these interviews in which you call yourself "black". I don't know how Britain responds to this, but I do know that a US audience tends to be very particular about such designations.

DD: Of course, the interviews that I have done . . . I would say, these are always different from my creative work; and yet, both modes are fictional, really, whether one is writing fiction or giving interviews – including this one. [*He laughs.*] You see, if you come from a place like Guyana, you cannot say your identity, your ancestry is determined purely by blood. Ancestry, you know, is also a matter of culture; and, having lived in Guyana for at least a hundred and fifty years, *more* than one hundred and fifty years now, people like me can't say that we are "Indian" based purely on blood, even though we may have originated from India. We arrived in an Africanized, creolized situation; therefore, I have absolutely *no* embarrassment in saying that my ancestors are African as well. In the interviews, I use the word "black", I use the word "Indian", quite interchangeably; and "British" as well, you know.

I remember Salman Rushdie writing in *Imaginary Homelands* that he is not a stranger to Britain because his writings share the same themes and concerns that, let's say, Swift shared. You know, the sense, in Swift's case, of the oppressiveness of England in relation to Ireland, whereas, in Rushdie's case, it's the oppressiveness of England in relation to the Empire. In other words, if you have a set of concerns that are particular to yourself but also to a society in which you live, they're not outside of you – of course, you're part of that society. *That's* your home. *That's* your ancestry. It's not just a matter of literary ancestry, even if I think Rushdie would say, "Yes, of course, literary ancestry!" But it's more than that: a definition of who you are, a sense of home that goes way beyond. It's not merely dependent on your origins or your colour, or whatever . . . It's in the cultural situation in which you find yourself. So, I have absolutely no embarrassment, absolutely none. I mean . . . well, I am embarrassed, sometimes, when I present your British passport in the Caribbean to the Caribbean immigration officer.

CZ: Can't you keep your Guyana passport as well?

DD: Yes, of course, I have. But, in certain Caribbean societies, to be a Guyanese is to be seen as a potential illegal immigrant. So, you see, if I went with my Guyanese passport to Barbados, I would probably get a harder time than if I went with an English passport. Of course it's an embarrassment!

Say, when you are in an airplane, for instance, and the stewardess comes around to ask who would like to fill out an immigration form for arrival in Britain, and all the black people around you have their hands up, and you don't . . . you're not at complete ease, you know, with your set of identities, *any* set of identities, or a particular identity. But, at the end of the day, I've only got another twenty years to live, at the most, and I don't want to spend my time being grounded between self-definitions which can be narcissistic as well.

CZ: But you know – we all know – that America is cursed by the urge to choose.

DD: I was actually appalled during my short time in America, when I had to do a reading. I had created an Indian character, you see, a particular type in the poem I had written. This was an Indian character who was presented as the ancestor to the black Guyanese. And some black American in the audience took objection to this. I was *genuinely* surprised, because in the Caribbean, whatever flaws there are in a society, there's always a genuine attempt to find common ground, you see. It may be because we are small and fragile and vulnerable societies that we have to find common ground because we're all immigrants in the Caribbean. Whether an African from the slave period, or an Indian from the indentured period, you're still an immigrant to the society: the land belongs to the Amerindian. I believe this makes us more open – a lot more open – to the definitions of selves and to trying to find bridges of community between different ethnic groups than I think, perhaps, operates in America.

CZ: It is true that the black citizens of the United States, right now, seem to be climbing back into their shells, claiming the Afrocentric core as they increasingly feel left out of the larger society. It is a tactical move, to want an identity to which the larger group cannot lay claim. By extension, anyone who says identity is behind us, or identity politics should not enter, is siding with the enemy.

DD: Sure! When I said I was appalled, I was not appalled by the man's reaction, or the man himself; rather, I was appalled by the situation that creates these seemingly irreconcilable fractures in the fabric of society. When I went to Stanford, and saw that there was a black [residence] hall in Stanford, I was surprised. In the Caribbean, this would be inconceivable, that there should be a *black* hall and a *white* hall. This tells you something about the malaise, the disease of American society.

CZ: And you need to remember, as I'm sure you know, that these halls are created at the request of the African American students themselves.

DD: I know, as I know that people's definition[s] of themselves are always contingent on a set of social or historical circumstances. And I would hope – although, really, it's none of my business to hope this – but I would hope that the race situation in America will transform itself to such an extent that these ancient divisions become redundant.

CZ: Maybe, maybe not in our lifetime. Still, this being the case, how would you then define the Asian diaspora?

DD: How would I define it? Well, I'd have to think specifically of the Caribbean. Maybe this is because, when I, as a member of this Asian diaspora coming from the Caribbean, encountered members of this Asian diaspora in Britain, I found that there was very little in common. I feel much more comfortable in the presence of West Indians – never mind Indo-West Indians –

incomparably more comfortable in the company of West Indians than I feel in the company of Indians from the Indian diaspora in Britain. And, no doubt, in America as well.

You see, the fantastic thing about the Middle Passage for the Asians who left India from 1838 until 1917 and went into the Caribbean, the fantastic, creative aspect, in a way – this involuntarily creative but nevertheless tremendously creative aspect of the Middle Passage – was that we lost all sense of caste, yes? We lost all sense that widows must be burnt, or that widows should be banished to some piece of wilderness or carry the badge of shame forever. Maybe I am being culturally insensitive to the Indian situation in India, but it seems to me we lost some of the most pernicious aspects of our background. So that, in Guyana, now, the divisions, not just between genders, but, say, between Muslims and Hindus, are much less pronounced and *rarely* lead to violence, if at all – certainly not in *my* memory! Certainly, it is not part of the collective history of the Caribbean that there should be violence between Muslims and Hindus. We lost all the stark divisions that lead to murder and violence. So sometimes I think, obviously in a very ironic way, that "the Brits" did us a favour by removing us to the cane fields of the Caribbean. Involuntarily, they created the conditions of our freedom.

Now, an African from America, an African American, would find someone like myself, somebody saying that the Middle Passage was creative, to be appalling. And, quite frankly, because our circumstances are different – and I don't want here to privilege one set of circumstances over the other; they are simply different – I would argue that there are always different Middle Passages. Indeed, I would argue that, even for the African diaspora, there are different Middle Passages.

Some people came over to Britain in the eighteenth century, you know, as visiting princes, or as potential "missionaries" from Africa. This idea that we were all black and lumped together in the dreadful hold of the ship, in fact, is a way of denying the extraordinary variety of peoples and cultures, languages and habits, and hatreds that actually came over in those boats. Many of those survived.

It does give me great joy, when I think of the Amerindians in *my* country, to think that a Carib and an Arawak, long after Columbus had nearly wiped out everybody, still harbour grievances against each other. I find this remarkable. To me, that's the true post-Columbian nature of our survival, that they should still harbour some of the old suspicions against each other. Obviously, they never break into violence, you know. But, whilst I'm saying we should all come together and so on and so on, I think it's nice also just to kind of luxuriate in some ancient grievances, obviously as long as you make sure they don't get into situations of real violence.

CZ: I was not aware that Caribs and Arawaks could still tell each other apart ethnically.

DD: In Guyana. Only in Guyana. I mean, there are those groups who still have retained the ancient languages, for instance. But, no, as for you and me, we would not recognize the differences. Still, there are at least seven or eight distinctly different Amerindian communities, some of whom don't even know there was a man called Christopher Columbus, some of whom have never, never, *ever* been affected by the Europeans, who retain their own ways of seeing the world, irrespective of the "colonial" or the "postcolonial" moment. These markers are absolutely irrelevant to some of these people – I'm thinking, for instance, of the Wai Wai people that we have in Guyana: they don't observe the protocols of imperialism; they don't observe boundaries and flags and visas and passports – so that, when we talk about colonial or postcolonial literatures, and the postcolonial world, sometimes we're being really ethnocentric. We are being "*centric*" because we are ignoring a whole body of experience that was barely, if at all, touched by the outside.

CZ: I was going to call them "outsiders of the Empire". They have an oral tradition and oral narratives, I'm sure. Do they produce written narratives?

DD: I don't know enough about them to know that. What I know is that most of the culture is orally expressed.

CZ: I know the Centre is sympathetic to the projected translation of indigenous languages. Would you try and retrieve some of their texts?

DD: One of the ideas of this university and this Centre for Caribbean Studies is to actually bring these languages and the thoughts that inhabit these languages to the attention of other people. Because [the] Amerindian view, or views, of the world – no, not even "views"; I don't even know if they have a sense of the world. Let's say, the Amerindian views on life that I'm aware of, and so are you, and so are most of us. Should we not, if they want to make them accessible to us, should we not listen to what they have to say?

CZ: The better, perhaps, to make them accessible to each other?

DD: Yes, to make them accessible to each other. This is the other idea, the thought that you translate, say, from Arawak or Macusi. It may well be that, in Guyana, the Amerindians can speak to each other; they may have languages to share certain features of their common experience.

CZ: Have you put any of these in your work?

DD: You mean those people? Yes, I have created a very negative and stereotypical view of the Amerindian in one of my novels: it was as a Bushman, a degenerate. Because, in the Caribbean, unfortunately, we still think of the Amerindian in relation to the "bush" – forest, jungle, nakedness, you know. And so, I consciously employed that stereotype. What I was not sure about was whether I was able to undermine my stereotype, as I wanted to do, within the body of the fiction. And if I was not, then I am in serious trouble. To be honest, I'm not quite sure I have. Not quite sure.

CZ: If you were not, then Benita Parry will let you know! As you know, she has fairly high expectations for your work. Do you want to address her objections?

DD: Well, her objections are that, in the writing that I have done – not in all of it, but in some of the writing I have done – I have not allowed literature to unpick, or deconstruct and dissolve some of the racial stereotypes I've set up, and some of the sexual stereotypes as well. In other words, my writing consciously deals with what we would call stereotypes, which are bodies of feelings. And she is saying that's fine, obviously; but, within the body of literature, whilst it is important to reveal such stereotypes, literature should also subvert them. And she may be right. She may well be right! I am not being modest, because she's the critic and she may be right. And if she is right, it means that what I have written is bad fiction, not "politically incorrect" fiction, but *bad* fiction, because good fiction should be able to create and dissolve simultaneously.

CZ: Did *you* think you were subverting these stereotypes yourself, as you were writing?

DD: I have to say that there is a streak of malice in me – which means, I think, that there is a streak of malice in most people who write or paint. You write or you paint or you do something sometimes just because you want to be obnoxious, just to see what will happen. I suppose it's like a child, or like a dog. Well, I have a dog, and I have learned from my dog that he *enjoys* being malicious just to see what the response will be. So, he will do certain things, and he will look at me as if to say, "All right! What you goin' to do about it?"

Now, obviously, writing fiction is much more dangerous. You're dealing with human beings whose lives may be affected – the worst example of that being, of course, *Satanic Verses*, people whose lives were literally affected by what they saw as offensive. Whether it was or not is another matter; it's neither here nor there. But, obviously, the writer has responsibilities not to inflame the passions of people to such an extent that it leads to violence.

CZ: But you do allow yourself the writing of it, though. You write disturbingly.

DD: This is where Benita is right, I think. Whilst you enjoy being malicious – "malicious" is the wrong term, obviously, here; this is not "malice with intent to commit harm" . . . One writes "disturbingly", as you say; but such is the pleasure of writing that you *must* disturb . . . and you disturb yourself sometimes. Benita is right, in that you also have to offer some kind of counterbalance to whatever the malice is. But it does not mean, therefore, that the writing is boring. I don't think that's what she says, that what you should be doing is writing a safe novel. I think what she's saying is that I should be writing a fuller novel, yes, a more complex novel?

Now, I take her criticism in good form. I don't spend too much time on it. I don't stay awake over it, because, obviously, when I have finished a piece of writing, it's finished, in the sense that it is no longer my possession. When a critic says it is deplorable, what can I do, other than say, "I'm really sorry, you know"? It's done. Benita's criticisms are countered by other people. So I know that critics have their own positions, and that's their business. They're paid six pounds ninety-nine or whatever for the blasted book, so, really [*he laughs.*]; it's out of my domains, now. It's tabled for public discussion, public reading or whatever.

CZ: But don't you – or do you – depend, in however small a way, on a kind of dialogue with your audience?

DD: No, because I think the dialogue with the audience – well, I don't want to say "no" in a harsh way – but I think the dialogue with the audience, sometimes, becomes an act of performance, of playing a part. And, therefore, you can be profoundly insincere with your audience, especially in a live situation where somebody asks questions you feel you can't really answer because you can't really think of an answer. You become clever, or you become highly articulate, or you become highly erudite. In other words, you are showing off, right?

Sometimes you don't so much depend on the dialogue as you're terrified of it – actually, "terrified" is too strong a word; you're anxious about the potential for self-damage. I have to say, not too frequently, I've attracted criticism of the most violent order. I remember one critic who did not like mixed marriage situations in one of my novels; and he really slammed it, in such a way that even I felt embarrassed to go out in public. I remember reading him one night, and I had to take a train, and I thought, "Oh God! Maybe I should stay home!" [*He laughs.*] Or, there was another critic, not liking what I wrote about Turner, because he thought I was damaging Turner's reputation, for instance. He wrote an absolutely scathing review. But then, that's the game, isn't it? That's the game that people should face. In fact, all you've done is to move them; you've actually disturbed them, you know, and that was part of the game that people should actually take you in, on paper, you know.

To go back to the people who are my audience, though. If I have a sense of audience, it's that I must not let them down, in this case, somebody close to me in my life who edits my work. If she says to me that this is rubbish, she's very violently open. If she says this is good, I tend to accept it. I don't want to let her down by writing badly. And I also have to think of the West Indians. The people I am really afraid of, or rather, not afraid but *keen* to listen to, are people like Derek Walcott or Wilson Harris or Olive Senior, who are fellow West Indian writers of a different generation, who have done fantastically creative work. And, in some ways, I am very conscious of being, of feeling, like a second generation to the first generation of Caribbean writers, of having a certain obligation to people like Wilson Harris and Sam Selvon, who's now dead, and George Lamming, and that is the obligation not to write badly; not the obligation not to write maliciously, but the obligation not to write badly.

CZ: Harris is, shall we say, harsh on his female characters, and so are you on yours. There is in your works what I would call the erotics of violence. Does this come out of any cultural or colonial context at all?

DD: I would first of all attempt to deny it [*he laughs.*] . . . the idea that I am harsh on female characters. It depends on which book it is and what the context of the writing is. I mean, certainly in the first collection of poems, *Slave Song*, I definitely wrote in very naked ways about the pornography of empire. Now, I hope I don't invest in the pornography of empire; you really have to be dreadfully honest about what seems to me to be at the heart of empire, which is callousness to the female. There was callousness to the male, too, which was the beatings and the rest of it, and the humiliations; but there is also, at the heart of it, callousness to the female which expresses itself in a variety of violent ways. And I don't mean only physically violent, but people becoming completely subservient and submissive there. Certainly I think of my experience of living in Guyana, and I think of Naipaul's and [that of] other writers who have written about women and the treatment of women. I've never really wanted to write in the politically correct ways about women; but, maybe, I wanted to write about certain experiences of growing up in a colony that revealed itself to me in terms of cruelty towards women. But then, I don't want to write about cruelty to women in a kind of poignant way either. So, yes, it's difficult territory to discuss.

People from the outside quite rightly will observe and critique from their own perspective, so you might have a black American feminist perspective or a Caribbean feminist perspective or a British one, and people will get from it, or *not* get from it, what they bring to it. I find, for instance, a lot of the criticism of D.H. Lawrence absolutely ludicrous, the one that does not take into account the utter genius of the writer. Yet, at the same time, I can see where some of the critics are coming from. There's always a problem of men writing about women, anyway. You can never do it to everybody's satisfaction.

CZ: When you read women writing about men, do you feel the same sense of disconnection?

DD: Not at all. I don't feel, "Oh God! Who the hell are they to write about men?" I don't. I just look for . . . well, at the end of the day it's not about whether you've written correctly. It's whether you've conveyed the complexity of a situation or a character. And if you have conveyed this complexity, then it's neither politically correct nor incorrect. A work of art is complex.

CZ: Do you have the same sense of travail – that is, linguistic travail – that some Caribbean writers say they have?

DD: Not at all. And I think that's because I come from a different generation. The great battles about using creole or English, the great struggle – if you use that bellicose word – the great tension, were already more or less over by the time we came to writing. And creole has no shame, no claim of low status or anything like that for people of my generation. Walcott and Brathwaite had already broken the ground and would brilliantly use the creole rhythms and creole diction.

And then, writing in England, in the 1980s, say, it was already there, this body of literature in England that was written in dialects, Scots, or Northern England, a body of writing that dates back at least to the Middle Ages; the Northeast dialects, for example. There was no shame or low status doing it, either, in writing creole in England. Myself, I did not feel it. So it's not the same for the lot of us, writing at the turn of the millennium. I'd have to say, if I ever feel that my writing is becoming bad, it's because I've sometimes feared that there's not enough creole in it.

CZ: Would you go back to poetry, then, as a way back to creole?

DD: Probably, although I don't know. There are times . . . even in writing fiction, there are times when, if I can't truly get to a kind of a creole voice, *truly*, then I don't feel happy. [*He laughs.*] And even if I write purely English, I try to get a creole in there, somewhere. It depends on the circumstances how you actually creolize it. But you do feel you are betraying something truthful about yourself, if you don't employ it, in terms of rhythms or in terms of an attitude to life. In other words, at the end of the day, you come to trust your childhood, and all the sounds and images of it, more than anything else.

CZ: Is that going to be in your next novel, then?

DD: I hope so. The thing is, because it is set in the eighteenth century, I've got to come up with a kind of a black language and, at the same time, I'm not sure that I've got the ability to write long, really long, passages using this black language. So one may have to create something else. But the last novel that I did [*The Counting House*], the whole lot of it was one big, heavy piece of work, in terms of *work*, right? And I so resented having to work . . . but where I really began to have fun was in the last twenty pages – you may have read them – which were one long splurge of creole. I enjoyed writing those pages, especially the curses. The great power of creole is its ability to curse, you know, to use language in vulgar ways. And I really enjoyed writing that character Miriam, who ends the novel with one loud creole outburst, a long, twenty-five-page monologue in creole, where she curses the world and then ends up by cursing herself. And these last twenty pages were, for me, really joyous. To me, that was the sheer *joy* of it in the act of writing.

CHAPTER 13

David Dabydeen Talks to Mark Stein (1999)

MARK STEIN, OPEN UNIVERSITY

FIFTY YEARS AGO, IN 1948, the SS *Empire Windrush* docked at Tilbury. With 492 West Indian migrants deboarding, large-scale postwar migration to Britain began. Now, the fiftieth anniversary of the ship's arrival is celebrated in Britain. The following interview with Professor David Dabydeen, University of Warwick, raises questions about the celebrations as well as the literature written in the wake of the *Windrush*.

Mark Stein: All over Britain there are uncounted events to celebrate the *Windrush* jubilee. The BBC certainly are doing a lot, and there are the books by Mike and Trevor Phillips, Tony Sewell and Onyekachi Wambu.[1]

David Dabydeen: Special issue of *Kunapipi*.

MS: Special issue of *Kunapipi*, edited by yourself – that's right![2] And there are the readings, festivals, the processions, exhibitions – you name it. The black weekly *New Nation* expresses fears of "Cash-Ins" on this important date. So that's one position. On the other hand, however, there are complaints that the celebrations are actually inadequate, that, for example, the exhibition *"Windrush": Sea Change* at the Museum of London is lacking in scope. People go there and respond, "It's too small. It's ridiculous. I've come all the way from Birmingham to see it, find out about my parents. And it's so small!" How do you feel about it? What is your position on the celebrations?

DD: Well... West Indians always mutter, moan and complain. So it doesn't matter what you put on, we are going to find some point of criticism. I don't think that it's sad. My own understanding of what's been going on is [that] there's been tremendous coverage of the *Windrush* anniversary. The BBC has really highlighted the *Windrush*. The television and radio programmes, the publications. Now people know about the *Empire Windrush* in general. Who would've even known there was a fiftieth anniversary [before the celebrations started]? Now more or less the whole nation knows. The whole nation knows to such an extent that I get race hate mail. Yesterday I received a "nigger-coon" set of cartoons with a leaflet from the French National Front and the German fascists, and a calling card from the British fascists.

MS: Do you get it locally? You think...

DD: It arrived in the post addressed to "Dr Dabydeen, Warwick University". That indicates that at least the events surrounding the *Windrush*, and the *Windrush* itself, [have] actually become embedded in the consciousness of the people. So, therefore, we can't moan and complain. To say that people are cashing in is absolute nonsense. You know black people don't have much commercial value in the society. What, people are gonna buy our T-shirts? Or, are they gonna make a boat called the *Windrush* and sail to the Caribbean? It's just inevitable carping.

MS: What is the meaning of the *Windrush* today? Decades ago it stood for the beginning of post–World War II migration. What does it mean in 1998? What is the status of the SS *Empire Windrush* in the political unconscious of Britain today?

DD: [*Thinking about it.*] The last thirty years that I have lived in Britain, I can say with some conviction that there is a much greater awareness now of people of West Indian origin as full citizens of the country, deserving of the benefits as well as responsibilities of citizenship. For example, the word "repatriation" is no longer part of the political vocabulary. When I was growing up in the seventies in Britain, repatriation was the buzz term, the Powellite term. Now it's totally dead. It's impossible to talk about repatriation. So the fiftieth anniversary of the *Windrush* has really just acknowledged that we are now third- or fourth-generation people. As John Agard says facetiously, "I like grey, / I'm here to stay".

MS: It's interesting, that point, because, in their book, Mike and Trevor Phillips feel somewhat uneasy about the *Windrush* as a myth. The arrival of the *Windrush* can either mean, like you said, "We're here to stay" – but Mike and Trevor Phillips are saying there is a danger, with the celebration as well, that by remembering the arrival one emphasizes the fact that British Caribbean citizens actually first had to arrive. British Caribbean citizens are thus being relegated to the status of arrivants even when they constitute a second, third or even a fourth generation of black Britons. So, is the celebration of the arrival not a double-edged thing?

DD: Well, it's not double-edged at all. I think these are some nice points. But the fact is, we did arrive. There was an arrival. We may have been in the country since Roman times, dotted here and there, a few thousands, but the fact is, we arrived really in 1948 in large numbers. So why not mark the arrival? And, of course, I am an arrivant. I have no problem in calling myself an immigrant. Even though I'm settled here, I was once an immigrant. The modern condition is one of migrancy. We are here to stay but we are also here to move on if necessary, and emigrate and go back to the Caribbean and go anywhere else, with our British passports. So, I think those kinds of criticisms are a kind of carping. I see nothing wrong in saying we are immigrants: we were immigrants. Many of us are still immigrants. Intellectually or imaginatively, we have not settled in the country. I remember Roy Heath, the Guyanese novelist, saying that, although he has been in Britain for forty-five years, he still dreams about Guyana and writes about Guyana and he can't write about England – not because England is unworthy of description in that sense, but because, imaginatively, he is still a migrant.

MS: Is that the same for you?

DD: Yeah, as a writer, sure.

MS: But also in terms of the memories of Guyana? Is that something that has remained more vivid?

DD: Yes, I think of Guyana constantly. I've just come back from Guyana.

The first ten, twelve years of your life are the formative years. I spent thirteen years there. Those are the experiences that form your character. Some people say writing is just about explorations and re-explorations of childhood experiences. So, in a sense, yes, I feel Guyanese . . . The non-writing part of me, the restrained part of me, is Britain. The imaginative part of me is Guyana. But then, one can't have these easy dichotomies either. But you know what I mean; there are grey areas as well.

MS: But in your fiction and poetry you do write about Britain and you've done that since *Coolie Odyssey* and *The Intended*.

DD: Well, the novel I've just finished is called *A Harlot's Progress*, which is based on the Hogarth painting. It is set in eighteenth-century London but it's also set in an imagined Africa. I could not just write about England. It has to be England in relation to Africa, India or the Caribbean.

MS: You're always transcending Britain?

DD: Well, it's not transcending. It's a kind of double consciousness, isn't it? We're all a double-over. Either in the dockyards, lifting all that heavy stuff or Caliban doubled over by the log. Now we're doubled over in terms of an imaginative life.

MS: You're influenced by V.S. Naipaul; for example, *Disappearance* writes back to *The Enigma of Arrival*. Is there a general point one could make about the influence of the *Windrush* writers on the second and third generation of writers such as Cas Phillips, Fred D'Aguiar or Grace Nichols?

DD: I can say it in one simple word: they achieved. Forget their themes or forget their concerns. The very fact that they achieved meant that it was relatively easier for us to publish because there was already Derek Walcott, there was already George Lamming, there was already Sam Selvon, there was especially V.S. Naipaul. However much we criticize Naipaul, let's not forget that he opened up a lot of doors, indirectly, to people like myself. So, you had a sense that there was a body of writing to which you had a certain responsibility. Which also presented a challenge. I mean, how can you write the sea in the way that Walcott writes it? Or how can you write the Guyana landscape in a better way, or with more excellence, than the way Wilson Harris does it? In a sense, we are a poor generation of writers. When you're following Walcott and when you're following Lamming, certainly when you're following Naipaul, how can you achieve excellence? Our literary ancestors really sit on our shoulders. How do you follow T.S. Eliot, you know? Sometimes I think we're just marking ground for another Renaissance in the next millennium. In other words, the presence of these writers who were excellent must breed a certain modesty in us. I hate blurbs now. When I was younger, I liked to have lovely blurbs that said "what an excellent writer". But now I think some of these blurbs are tremendously embarrassing. When I see things like "a great literary giant" in relation to some of my friends or, in relation to me, "a powerful Caribbean lyrical voice", I think, "No! No! No! Come on!" These things are nonsensical, compared to Walcott. Compared to Naipaul, we are still . . . we've only just written four, five novels, two, three books of poems. These judgements should only come at the end of one's career.

MS: But isn't this kind of promotion and hype, which may in fact only be partly justified, resulting from quite a big interest in black British, and in Caribbean, writing?

DD: We must not overstate the achievement of it; some of it is very bad. I mean, there is stuff that I've written, that I certainly would not have written. And so, therefore, it's literature in the making and should be acknowledged as that, rather than lauded as part of a major contribution to a major tradition of English . . . It has its beauties and it has its tremendous failures. We have to be honest enough to cast a cold eye, a critical eye, on what is being written, rather than adopting a kind of adulatory or valorizing attitude towards it.

MS: From which perspective can we do that? With reference to the first generation, one could say, "That is the standard by which the literature that is following has to be measured." But this is only one of the traditions being pursued. You are writing in Britain, within the context of British writing; you are writing within a context of black British literature, but then you're writing after Caribbean writers too.

DD: Yes, but you can read a Russian novel, you can read *The Brothers Karamazov*, and still read it sensitively and intelligently, although it is set in Russia in a time span that is different from yours. I can't come up with a critical aesthetic on the spot. I'm arguing for a close reading of texts, really. And the same sensitivity and critical faculties that have [been] brought to bear on other literatures should also be applied to ours. There can be an over-sensitivity to what we write, and a critical reticence based on the grievances of history. You know, "This is black stuff, so let's leave it alone in case we offend people." I have to say, for some reason, I've been exempt from this "care". I get some severe lashings by these white people. Sometimes I just wish that they would just shut up and go away.

MS: Are you retreating from a postcolonial framework of reading when you are advocating close readings as opposed to a "special interest"?

DD: Well, is it moving away? It is actually trying to say that one can still read the literature within postcolonial frames – though it's best not to impose any kind of frame onto readings. But a postcolonial frame can give a very rich, politically astute reading of the writing. I'm not arguing against that. What I'm arguing for, really, is the end of kid-gloves. Let's have a bloody fight now. Let us now engage in combat, because before I was winning all the time. Because of history you have made some space for me to win. Let's engage in serious dialogue, critical, intellectual, literary dialogue. And then, you see, we are then properly tested and assessed.

MS: Do you want to say something about new poetry and also about your new novel? You said it's just been accepted by Cape, and could you maybe just say what it's about?

DD: The new novel is set in England in the eighteenth century, and it's a rewriting, if that's the word, of a Hogarth painting – a very famous Hogarth painting, the first English painting to represent the lives of the common people in paint rather than in print. At a time when paint was for the depiction of aristocratic life and religious subjects, Hogarth painted prostitutes and lepers, blacks and Jews. [The painting] has an anti-Semitic slant, so I take this up in the novel and explore the Jewish character. But basically it is a rewriting of the scenes of *A Harlot's Progress*, a reconfiguration of them, rather than rewriting. It has a black character as the narrator, so it's England from eighteenth-century black eyes. But, of course, it has resonances of today; it's eighteenth-century only in form.

MS: What's the text's relationship to Equiano's *Interesting Narrative*?

DD: Well, very important! . . . The writer who has really influenced me emotionally has been Equiano. Equiano is somebody who has definitely entered into my writing, almost like a posthumous spirit or a posthumous presence. So it's a novel by Equiano, of course. A novel about writing, a novel about arriving at the state of writing. In the way that Equiano had to in the eighteenth century.

CHAPTER 14

Getting Back to the Idea of Art as Art: An Interview with David Dabydeen (2001)

LARS ECKSTEIN, UNIVERSITÄT POTSDAM

IN THE SUMMER OF 2001 I spent a couple of weeks at the British Library undertaking research for a project that investigated literary configurations of memory in contemporary black Atlantic writing. Among the texts on my agenda was David Dabydeen's 1999 novel *A Harlot's Progress*, which takes its cue from William Hogarth's 1732 series of engravings by the same title. The second plate of Hogarth's prints features a little slave servant to a rich Jew and his mistress, and it is this character to whom Dabydeen gives a voice to retell and re-imagine his life in a complex and contradictory tale that not only writes back to Hogarth, but also to a number of other eighteenth- and nineteenth-century English painters. Dabydeen, who grew up among the Indo-Caribbean community of Guyana and came to London as a teenager, has engaged in dialogues between writing and the visual arts from the very beginning of his literary career. Already in his first volume of poetry, *Slave Song* (1984), he juxtaposes his poems with images, and it is with his long poem "Turner" (1994) – which evolved from a creative engagement with J.M.W. Turner's painting *Slave Ship* – that he achieved his probably most stunning piece of ecphrastic writing. Being in London, I took the opportunity to send David Dabydeen an e-mail, and he readily agreed to talk to me about his work in his office at Warwick University, where he is currently director of the Centre for Caribbean Studies. The following interview was conducted on 14 August

2001. We were well into chatting about the problematic interconnections of aesthetics and suffering, about the role of the visual arts in his writing and other issues, before it occurred to me to press the record button.

Lars Eckstein: Something that has always intrigued me is that your work reveals an increasing involvement with the visual arts. *The Counting House*, as you once said, is based on picture cards of Indian gods; your poem "Turner" is obviously based on a painting by J.M.W. Turner; and your last novel, *A Harlot's Progress*, on William Hogarth. How did that interest in the visual come about?

David Dabydeen: Well, partly it is because I don't like listening to music; it's too trendy. Listening to music is kind of a signal to social class. And I am not musical anyway. And therefore another sense has been developed, which is the visual. But, in a cultural context, it would be practically the absence of pictures in Guyana. The only pictures there are of Hindu gods and goddesses, and Christian pictures of Jesus, and so on. You don't really get Indian art, or African art, because that memory has been more or less wiped out. So I suppose it's the absence of the visual in terms of the fine arts in Guyana that triggered off this great, widening passion that I have for looking at pictures. I can look at pictures all day. The first thing I do when I go to strange cities is to go to the art gallery. It is a little space of colour and form and ingenuity and genius. I tend to remember countries by their painters. I went to Switzerland – it's a fucking boring place, 'cause nothing goes on in Switzerland, you know, apart from making chocolate and money. But they have got Paul Klee, who must be the greatest painter ever, in terms of an enormous, complex vision of his own life, of the world, but, more than that, this stunning, ingenious painterly technique that he has whereby he can invest a small, flat piece of paper or canvas with a kind of a depth you believe is impossible. What I find absolutely fascinating is the way he layers images upon images upon images. It becomes like a *palimpsest*. And how he could do that with a piece of paper, I just find stunning – I remember leaving the Paul Klee museum and thinking, "If I could write as Paul Klee paints, then I would be a great writer". If you could find a form of writing which is layered, endlessly layered, and yet has a kind of narrative thread, or a set of discernible, readable stories, then that would be a triumph.

LE: When you talk about techniques in painting, how far do your narrative techniques correspond with these? I mean, do you take in the visual aesthetics of a work and put it on the page in a one-to-one relationship?

DD: No, it's not a transfer. In "Turner", in the poem itself, I tried to be as *lavish*, if you like, with words as Turner is with paint. So it's a more general correspondence. It is more an artistic correspondence rather than a technical parallel between the work of art as a poem and the work of art as a painting. In other words, you really have to sense, or intuit, the passion behind the laying down of paint rather than the technique of actually laying down the paint. If you can sense that passion or intuit that passion, then in some ways you have to try to convey that on the page, as a writer.

LE: Is there a similar relationship between Hogarth's *A Harlot's Progress* and your novel in that respect?

DD: Yes, there is, in the sense that Hogarth is endlessly creative. Within one frame of a picture you get stories that multiply and teem, and in other stories every detail triggers off a story that then connects up to another detail, which then connects up to another story. So, really, you can spend quite a lot of time "reading" Hogarth. It seems to be some kind of social realism, but then it can be endlessly complicated in terms of being a narrative that changes upon itself, turns upon itself, sets up other narratives, et cetera, within the one frame. So what I tried to do in *A Harlot's Progress* was also to destroy the surface realism of a story by complicating it, by making it almost unreadable – in a sense replicating what Hogarth was doing in terms of endless, complex narratives.

LE: In an early book you wrote about Hogarth you mentioned that *A Harlot's Progress* is a deeply circular set of paintings, and pointed to the endlessly repetitive sense of doom looming over the set because of the dominance of money business. Is that replicated in the novel as well?

DD: There is, in terms of money, yes. Well, two things really: one, in terms of coming back to the idea of Hogarth's narrative structure being complicated – I find writing about slavery can be seriously tedious in terms of the evocation of guilt and just the conveyance of pathos. That's not for art, really; art's got to do something more fascinating. So, in *A Harlot's Progress*, I kind of tried to get away from the idea that there is a story to slavery that is an easy story to tell and an easy story to consume. That's what I learned from Hogarth, how to complicate a narrative. But also in terms of money – one of the major themes in Hogarth's works is the way that materialism affects ethical, moral, imaginative sensibilities. As I've said somewhere else, the cash nexus replaces human relationships. And that's what happens in *A Harlot's Progress*; although it is set in eighteenth-century Britain, it comes out of a Thatcherite period, because I don't think that anybody who grew up under Thatcher as I did for those fifteen years or so – as a mature person, as it were, not as a child – could not have been affected by this greed that she represented, and the way she placed accountancy and commerce, free market values, and a naked capitalism and privatization at the heart of social and political policy. Everything I've written, really, although it might be set in different parts and carrying different characters, is about money. Of course it is concerned about Thatcherite and post-Thatcherite Britain, even though it is set in the eighteenth century.

LE: So you would see your novel as a political novel in the sense that it refers to contemporary society? Because, generally, you seem very hesitant to admit politics into contemporary aesthetical works.

DD: Yeah. But it's political in the sense that politics emerges without being overt. There is a Thatcherite underlay to *A Harlot's Progress*, in terms of me living in the 1980s in Britain under Thatcher [and] being affected by that Toryism. There is definitely the Holocaust and the politics of representation in terms of me creating a Jewish character in a way that is risky. It is a Jewish character who[m] I am conscious of taking a risk with. In other words, I am talking about the Holocaust, I am intimating the Holocaust in *A Harlot's Progress*, and seeing a kind of correspondence with slavery, which is not a politically correct thing to do today, because black people say, "No, this is our history, which is unique to us", and then the Jews say, "What, we are the only ones who suffered". So I tried to create a Jewish character and put him back, obviously, put him in a slave ship where he is adored as a kind of Christ figure, which again is a bit dodgy. But I don't give a fuck, really. At least I was glad to have got a very positive and delightfully easeful review in the *Jewish Chron-*

icle, but I do have a Jewish friend who thinks it is a scum novel. The thing is, we don't do these things with malice. If you're going to write a novel – any novel – but if you're going to write a novel about slavery, you might as well take chances with your themes. I've said before, you can't write about slavery in a flat, flattened way with a sombre, boring prose, with a kind of a parade of grievances or with a display of "look how hurt I am, look at my scars", because, by and large, we writers who write about slavery live fucking privileged lives in the West. Very privileged lives. I'm a Professor at Cambridge; I'm a fellow of the Royal Society. Cas [Caryl] Phillips is a wealthy man who drives a big limousine up and down in New York. What fucking scars has he got? So we have to be honest with the subject and say, "Really, it happened a long time ago to our ancestors". And, once you do that, once you create space between you and a theme, you surrender it to the imagination.

LE: Despite all that, do you still feel some ethical obligation towards the characters that you evoke, even though they lived two hundred years back? You seem to problematize that in your novel. Ellar, one of the African victims of the slave trade and a fairly dominant character in the book, for example, questions Mungo, "Why do you write that I flit and glitter like if I am some winged frivolity? No one will take me seriously now."

DD: The characters in *A Harlot's Progress*, though they are set in the eighteenth century, are really contemporary people that I know. Ellar and all those people are based on people I know who are now living in the Caribbean. So, therefore, you have a kind of ethical relationship – I don't know if "obligation" is too strong a word – you have an ethical relationship with the characters because they are still living. Although the novel is set in the eighteenth century, its concerns are very contemporary in terms of the relationship between the obscure and the centre; it's a relationship between poverty and wealth, powerlessness and power, in terms of Western definitions of these terms. We have our own power, and we have our own beauty, we have our own wealth; but these are not measurable in Western terms. To be a Guyanese writer, for example, is to be seriously obscure – in a sense, always to be doomed to obscurity. So these are the power relations that the novel deals with, even though set in the eighteenth century, to say, really, in a sense, that there is a continuity between the eighteenth century and today in terms of the dominance of certain values, and the way they replace other values, the way they eclipse other values. Yes, in that sense you have an ethical relationship to the work.

LE: Let me come to the issue of aesthetics and the aestheticizing of suffering. You introduced a reading from *A Harlot's Progress* in Tübingen in 1999 with the following words: "I was exploring the idea whether or how you could aestheticize suffering. It has not really been a question for Caribbean writers so far . . . to explore the possibilities of aestheticizing suffering in relation to the slave baracoons and slave ships. It has more been an issue that Jewish writers are faced with when writing the Holocaust – Paul Celan, or Jewish musicians like Schönberg. And of course there is a whole debate about all that [which] brings Adorno in, as to whether there can be poetry after Auschwitz."

DD: Well, it is definitely in Walcott. Walcott is sensuous and beautiful, a writer who is consciously sensuous and consciously ornate and beautiful. In *Omeros* there is this magnificent poetic passage where he sees the black women carrying coal up to the pleasure steamers. They are walking along carrying coal up the gang plank, and then he looks at their feet – you see, he remembers their obviously struggling feet – and he says, "One day when I'll grow up I'll have to give metre to those feet". He will have to convert these human pieces of degradation, as it were, into subjects of poetry. So he is very conscious of what I would call "aestheticizing of suffering". I suppose, not consciously, partly through Walcott I have come to this concern.

LE: In the introduction to your poem "Turner", you accuse the painter Turner of secretly relishing in the suffering that he describes. Adorno, whom you mentioned before, takes a stand against the "blurry metaphysics" in using, in this case, the Holocaust as a backdrop for a display of true humanity or whatever else. Now, I am not claiming that you relish in the suffering that you describe – but have you inserted any mechanisms that prevent such a reading?

DD: No, I don't want to prevent it. When I accused Turner – I don't think I accused Turner, I stated. I just stated that Turner was getting a great deal of pleasure – pornographic pleasure, almost – from the contemplation of that kind of suffering. This is very erotic, that kind of suffering: it is about sharks and blood and women being thrown overboard. You have seen the film *Jaws* – the opening of the film *Jaws* is very erotic, when the shark attacks her and she is naked, you know. So, obviously, at the core of all art is this eroticism. And, yes, of course, when I write about slavery, it arouses me. It must arouse me; that's the fact why I bother to write. All subjects have a potential to arouse you. I've said before in an interview, it's the same accusation levelled against D.M. Thomas and *The White Hotel*, that the rape of the Jewish woman aroused him. The responsibility of the artist is not to deny this arousal, but to be able to convey on paper something of the tragedy of human lives. That arousal is no more dangerous than me saying to you, "I write for money". 'Cause when I am writing I am aroused by the subject, and I am also aroused by the possibility of making money from my writing. And the two go together. But what matters is the writing itself. When you come to sit down to write, it's not to put in mechanisms, it's not to put in blocks and dams and canals and fences – you know, fences in your imagination. When you come to write, the motivations no longer matter, because you are now writing. You have been motivated sufficiently to come to the page. And the responsibility – if you have responsibility – is to write beautifully. That's the only responsibility a writer has. To use words in a way that startles, and disturbs, and moves people. I was reading Evelyn Waugh the other day, whom I always think of as a writer in shit, which he was. But he does have this passionate concern about writing in a writerly manner, rather than writing in a documentary, sociological manner. In a sense, you can say it's a development of the English philosophy of art for art's sake, which was very aristocratic at one stage – in other words, art for the sake of art, to hell with society and politics. I think it is about time we rediscovered the whole idea of writing as a craft, that you have to be responsible to the craft and the idea of beauty.

LE: So, for you, all these political ideas of subverting canons, et cetera, don't matter any longer, really?

DD: No, that's all rubbish, man, that's finished. We've done it, we've been there, we've subverted the canons, we've blown the fucking canons up, we've turned them against ourselves. We don't subvert the canons anymore. Jesus, imagine the kind of novel you would be writing if you would be writing a subversion-of-the-canon novel. Inevitably you subvert the canon, but you don't write a retaliation of another writer. You are writing partly in homage to another writer – well, let me be detailed here. When I wrote a poem about the Turner painting, it was partly in homage to Turner, a great artist who preceded me, and I was aspiring to that condition of greatness. And secondly, if I quarrel with Turner – well, it is not a quarrel; you don't pick a quarrel with a giant when you are yourself a mouse – it is basically really trying to be what now the critics call intertextual, which is trying to see whether from that art something can emanate that you can take and convert into your own creativity. In doing that, in taking from Turner and rewriting it, if you like, or re-visualizing aspects of it, you may well be subverting the canon. But that is not your motive, is it? You can't sit down and be writing out of hatred.

LE: It just seemed to me that the term "subversion" fitted quite well to what you do with the only very quite recently established canon of slave narratives of the eighteenth century.

DD: Yes, I am sure we subvert; of course we are subversive. But what I mean is that, at the end of the day, it is not about counterattacks, there is nothing militaristic. I hate the whole militaristic language of literary criticism, the way we interrogate the canons, as if there are some fucking suspects and I am shining a light on them, you know.

LE: But what you do with the character of Mr Pringle [secretary of the Anti-Slavery Society and editor of Mungo's story] in *A Harlot's Progress* seems quite militant to me. Let me quote this one passage: "Then he [Thistlewood, Captain of the slave ship] slide down by me [Mungo], and I sleep in the feel of his breath. And in my dream a wild cry burst from my lips, as my legs are spread and spread and eels are born from me like ink that drops from Mr. Pringle's pen and stain a trail through the pages." This is a very close connection you draw there between the rape of an innocent slave and eliciting his story – and doesn't it involve a very strong statement against the linearity and forced pragmatism of that genre of the slave narrative?

DD: I'm not denying that – I am not denying that at all – and that when you come to the page, you come with a whole baggage of ideas that are political, sociological, artistic, financial, sexual, et cetera, the whole lot. What I am trying to assert, really, against political theory, is the idea that when you read literature written by, say, Caribbean people, you've got to read it not for its political or sociological content, but for its artistry. When I read Graham Swift, I am not expected to engage in political or sociological enquiry, even though the novel may be about that – it's a Graham Swift novel; in other words, it is a work of art. So I want critics to also look at our works primarily as works of art, taking into consideration their aesthetic complexity, their aesthetics. Not just their politics and their sociology, but their aesthetics. Because I think that we have been mired, sometimes very deliberately, sometimes because we are poor writers, in politics – the politics of history, the politics of the recuperation of memory, the politics of race, et cetera. It's been an excuse for us writing badly as well.... And therefore that appeals to a certain kind of feminist sensibility. You can write shittily and get away with it. What I want to do in my own writing – other people do what they want – I just want to get back to the idea of art as art.

LE: Let me finish up with one last topic that I wanted to talk about with you.

DD: You shouldn't believe in anything I say, by the way. D.H. Lawrence said, "Never trust the teller; trust the tale." Because what you are doing by interviewing me – which is delightful in your company, et cetera – but what you are doing, well, what any interviewer does – is forcing the writer to rationalize what he has done. And writing is such an arbitrary, accidental, anarchic activity at times, fuelled in the case of people like Anthony Burgess, for example – this guy drank about four bottles of vodka or whiskey and then started writing. The sheer delight and anarchy on the page gets lost in an interview because you have to rationalize what you have done.

LE: Well, you probably shouldn't be a believer in interviews, but I think they set you on tracks, and then it is, of course, nice to get to know the person that sits behind the lines of a novel as well.

Memory was the last issue that I really wanted to talk about with you. Taking up the notion of "anarchy" you just brought up, you advocate, quite contrary to all those Holocaust writers or musicians – we mentioned Celan and Schönberg earlier – that to forget is the more important thing than to remember. Could you elaborate on that?

DD: I don't know if I say it as overtly as that, and I certainly don't know whether I believe it with any great deal of conviction. But I think there is something to be said for – and again, I've learned this from Walcott – *creative amnesia*. Because, if you are to remember the past, and you are only to remember it within the framework of suffering, or the framework of grievances, then you are not really remembering the past. The potential that the past has – even though it might have been an aborted potential – for throwing up a bewildering array of stories which deny and transcend that suffering and those grievances, that's the potential I really want to get to. That is something that I learned from Wilson Harris as well, who talks about the "unfinished genesis of the imagination". In other words, there is no one particular point of departure, but even if there was, if you revisit that point through memory, you can choose through your imaginative penetration of material: you can remember it in a different way, even though it never happened like that. You can remember its potential for happening like something else. What I am saying is, for example, in a practical way, when those people were on board the slave ships that we call our ancestors, I can choose to remember them with pathos, I can talk about the chains rattling, I can rattle their chains, if you like, on their behalf. Or I can give them conversations about food; maybe some bloke tied up suddenly remembered something he ate four years ago that caused him toothache, you know. You can give them a bewildering variety of humane and bewildering possibilities. It may well be that the bloke that was being chained up didn't remember having a toothache, but maybe he did. So it depends how the writer chooses to remember, and what the writer chooses to remember.

LE: Does this, let me call it "transfigurative", sense of memory have a redemptive quality?

DD: Yes. I keep using the word "transfiguration"; I keep using the word "redemption", at the end of the day. Because I think all my work has been a kind of a wrestling with Christian images – Christian images meaning the images that I grew up with as a child, which triggered off my interest in art – and then the Hindu images as well. I would say, at the end of the day, I am much more interested in the idea of "soul", an old-fashioned word like "soul". I am much more interested in a kind of spiritual dimension, in a metaphysical dimension to art, than I am in the sociological, ultimately, even though you have to deal with the sociological. But I only try to deal with it so as to transcend it.

CHAPTER 15

A Forced Indianness: An Interview with David Dabydeen (2009)

LETIZIA GRAMAGLIA, UNIVERSITY OF WARWICK

Letizia Gramaglia: You have recently come back from India, where you are spending more and more time doing research, writing and interacting with local scholars . . . but as a Guyana boy, how did you come to a sense of Indianness?

David Dabydeen: How did I come to a sense of Indianness? I think I came to it through cricket and through politics and through literature, because in the 1960s we had the first international Indian Guyanese or Indo-Caribbean cricket star, Rohan Kanhai, so he immediately became a hero for the whole Indian community because he symbolized the movement from the canefield to the world stage. His family were literally canecutters and he came from a sugar plantation, so his progress was completely inspirational to the Indian community in Guyana, and especially to a young boy. I must have been about nine or ten, and I would listen to the radio – because there was no television at the time – whenever he was playing in, say, Warwickshire or a place called "Australia" – we didn't really know where the hell the places were. You listen to the radio and there was your great star playing in these strange places and making centuries. Consciously and unconsciously he was an inspiration to create and to achieve.

At the same time as I was listening to Kanhai, I read my first West Indian novel. This must have been sometime in 1967, which was when V.S. Naipaul's

Miguel Street arrived in Guyana. It was almost mind-blowing because the characters were people you could actually recognize, you know: if you just looked out of the bedroom window you could see Hat and all the other characters, they were us lot, right? I think it was the first time we had a chance – by "we" I mean me, but also young people – to encounter West Indian literature. It was new. Up to that point, we were immersed in the great classics of English children's literature, wondrous stuff by Enid Blyton and others which told of an unfamiliar, and therefore magical and beguiling, land called "England", where children had bicycles and regular meals, with mouth-watering and magically sounding treats like scones and marmalade. Such writing not only excited our imagination, but no doubt made us want to emigrate, especially now that Kanhai was living in England. Naipaul's novel was something completely refreshing – the familiarity of it, the way you could identify with it. Of course, it is a novel that, on the whole, sympathizes with the underdog even though it is scathing in many ways. For example, something I could recognize immediately was the Indian woman beaten by her husband who oils the cricket bat; I mean, that was appalling. One of the more painful features of being a child in the Caribbean was witnessing incidents of violence towards women, since male violence to women was normal. When you then read it in a novel, in a peculiar way it became even more real than the violence, you know . . . So Naipaul grounded me in the sense of an environment and the humility of ordinary West Indians and the male propensity to violence towards women, undoubtedly.

And then the third moment was awareness of our great political leader, the founder and father of our independence movement, who was Cheddi Jagan, Premier of British Guiana, of Indian origin. And again, because he was powerful, because he would travel to meet Nehru, he would travel to Britain, he would go to see Kennedy, and you would be reading about this as a child, he was somebody who obviously occupied the world stage . . . again, from a cane-cutting family, you know. Therefore these three figures cohered in my imagination as a boy, in terms of being iconic figures and figures you should want to emulate.

I should add, of course, the role of religion in creating a sense of Indianness. My folk were a mixture of Christians and Hindus: there was no contradiction in going to church – and even many denominations: my mother went to

Lutheran and Catholic church on different Sundays – and attending the Hindu Temple. I myself was baptized in the local Scottish Presbyterian Church. We held regular *pujas* in our house, and put out the Hindu prayer flags. As children, we thought the *pandit* a comical figure: he'd ride his bicycle with his *dhoti* on, a tricky thing to do. And after the *puja*, we'd climb up and steal the coins [offerings to the gods] attached to the prayer flags. So Hinduism, for me, as a child, was not a particularly serious matter. The only time I rallied to the cause was when a drunken British soldier, in the early 1960s [the British army had arrived to maintain order during the period of inter-ethnic strife], rattled the gate and demanded to know why we were flying Communist flags. We explained they were red Hindu prayer flags, and I took up position behind the kitchen door to pelt him with a stone – the one my mother used to grind massala for our daily curry – in case he didn't budge. Fortunately, he hiccupped away, Hinduism and the massala stone won the day.

LG: Yet, in your writing you seem to be able to engage and connect not just with a sense of Indianness, but with a sense of West Indianness, of Caribbean-ness, if you like, which also includes aspects of African, Creole and British culture.

DD: Yes, at the same time I was growing up in a black community, because New Amsterdam is largely black. My day-to-day mates – some of them my heroes in the way they were able to ride a bicycle without touching the handlebars, wield a slingshot with precision, run fast, bat and bowl, or excel at school tests – were black. You were automatically part of the community in terms of language, in terms of playing cricket, in terms of just being children together. So, in a sense, the fact that I could be proud of being of Indian origin because of these three figures – Kanhai, Naipaul and Jagan – and at the same time I could be part of the black society, was never a contradiction, but an enrichment. Of course, at the time you just lived, without thinking of ethnicity or the virtues and challenges of a plural society.

Like other children, I marvelled at the genius of Gary Sobers. I fell in love with my primary school teacher at the age of eight, and still remember her name – Miss Lambert – and boyish longing for her: she was African Guyanese. The hurt of her betrayal – I saw her once in the company of a striking young man of her own age – scarred my childhood. It was our headmaster, Mr Spencer, who encouraged me to study, and Mr Griffiths, the tailor next door who showed me how to put on a tie. I spent countless hours "liming" in Mr Griffiths's tiny tailor shop, listening to his stories about being a pan-boiler in Barbados, and, because he had a smattering of French, learning my first foreign words. He was like a grandfather to me, and when he was frail and dying, he and I would go for walks along the streets of New Amsterdam, he talking about his life, me too amazed by the wealth of his travels and experiences to say anything. So, even though you were aware of ethnic conflicts and so on when you were a child, you don't really, apart from certain moments when there was an outbreak of violence, we never witnessed it but we knew about it, and it traumatized us, but it was taking place elsewhere, but certainly our black neighbours and our black friends were not part of it . . . So one could be Indian and black simultaneously, it didn't really matter; when you are a child you don't dwell on these divisions. Your friend's bicycle and your access to it were much more relevant than his colour. Or bowling him out for a duck was a child's, not an ethnic, triumph. And so, as a result of growing up as such, I have always disliked the idea of tribe, tribalism; tribe, to me, translated into literature, equals diatribe . . . I wanted always to move away from tribe and diatribe, or ethnocentricity. I have always thought there is no point to being ethnocentric: to be a writer you must be eccentric not ethnocentric, eccentric, or even concentric – literally, you can chase your "tail/tale", right? I'm sorry to see Kamau Brathwaite stuck in a 1960s position. In a 2001 interview with my former PhD student, Marcia Burrowes, he said that Indians had not contributed to the making of Caribbean culture. He said, "The Asian presence has to make itself felt; they cannot sit and, you know, be invisible and non-contributing. I mean, the same way I'm conceiving of the *harmattan* and the slave trade as part of Hegelian consciousness and the notion of re-integrational elements, I would like to know how an Asian Caribbean person thinks of their origin, but I don't get that and people complain you're leaving them out. It's not for me, it's not for me to try; I cannot be so arrogant as to try to define an Asian sensibility. It has to come from an Asian. And there's no reason why they, by now, are not contributing to that exploration." That's Selvon, the Naipaul brothers, Rajkumari Singh, Mahadai Das, Ladoo and a host of Indo-Caribbean writers and scholars dismissed out of hand. Let's hope he was being provocative, in which case, blessings to him! I admire the grand sweep of his dismissal! I once tried to bite his ankle by saying, in print, he couldn't write in creole richly, whereas I – a coolie – could. Of course, that was being outrageous; I was being *prappa daag*.

The real argument, though, is that there is no reason why a black writer or intellectual cannot grapple, imaginatively or in a scholarly mode, with issues of Asian identity or culture. We are not trapped in the castle of our skins; hence I write on slavery, Olive Senior writes on the Indian Jamaican woman, Wilson Harris, Earl Lovelace too, et cetera, et cetera. What matters is the richness and integrity of the writing, not the ethnicity of the subject, though a Chinese Trinidadian writing about Chinese Trinidadians, say, may well have things to relate that I can't. But it only means that there are different narratives which can be told differently.

LG: Did you ever get to meet any of your Indo-Caribbean heroes whilst living in Guyana?

DD: No. Jagan and Kanhai and Naipaul were like mythical figures; they existed in deep recesses of the mind and soul. To actually see them would have been sacrilege. Like seeing England, with its scones and marmalade . . . you had to be prepared for such a meeting, in terms of being educated, mannered, well-spoken, the creole washed and gargled out of your mouth . . . At the very least you had to be grown up. The Irish have a saying that a cat can look upon a king; well, in Guyana, a boy like me could not cast his gaze upon people like Jagan. Decades after leaving, sometime in the early 1990s, I revisited Guyana and met Kanhai by accident on the Berbice river ferry. I happened to have a book of my poems in my suitcase and managed to rifle around and retrieve it. I went up to Kanhai with faltering heart. "My name is David Dabydeen. I teach at the University of Warwick," I said. He looked incuriously at me, not seeming to recognize the word "Warwick", though he had batted for Warwickshire for countless years. Perhaps I should have pronounced it "War-*wick*" (the Caribbean way) rather than "Warick". I opened the book to a poem called "For Rohan Babulal Kanhai". "I wrote this poem for you", I said. He held the book, looked at the page, then snarled at me in creole: "You spell me name wrang; it get two *l*'s" ("You've spelt my name wrongly; it has two *l*'s."). I was taken aback by his uncouthness, his refusal to accept homage, refusal to be a benevolent divine figure. He didn't take the book – my offering – but told me to leave it at his mother's house. I never did.

Two years later I met Kanhai again, at State House, the official residence of President Cheddi Jagan. I was present to launch a book of essays by Jagan which I edited, by his invitation. Kanhai was subdued and shook my hand politely. There might have been some shyness on his part when we had met on the ferry. Most Caribbean star cricketers never had schooling, and it might be that Kanhai was intimidated by an academic presence – hence his gruff, self-defensive reaction. It might also be true that Kanhai was wearied by carrying the burden of ethnic pride; he wanted to divest himself of the burden of adulation and be an ordinary Guyanese from a Berbice village. At certain moments he didn't want to be recognized, and so therefore I might well have interrupted his privacy, forcing an "Indianness" upon him – for the poem was about ethnicity.

As to Jagan, I was a guest in his home for five years, between 1992 and 1997, and he made me his Ambassador-at-Large in 1993. I found him to be a man of almost impossible virtue. He wasted nothing, he lived frugally. Unlike many third-world leaders who plundered their national treasury, Jagan died intestate; in other words, he had no property, no money, no estate. He once said, memorably, that "you cannot have a Cadillac lifestyle in a donkey-cart economy", and he tried by the example of his leadership to inspire Guyanese to live with principle. He held out the promise of social and economic betterment, and ethnic unity. He aspired to the "rainbow" ideas of Nelson Mandela, but died before he could alter the Constitution to allow for national unity. Another of his memorable statements made to friends and colleagues was, "What's the point of living if you can't do something to help the poor?" When Jagan died it was no surprise to me to find his image pinned up on the walls of Hindu temples, next to statues of Lord Krishna and the goddess Kali.

I met Naipaul soon after he had written a lengthy article on Cheddi Jagan for the *New York Times*, in which he intimated that Jagan had replaced the Hindu scriptures with Karl Marx's *Das Kapital*. I had invited Naipaul to do a reading at Warwick. I sent the university chauffeured car to collect him. All preparations were made to host this god; just as, in Guyana, the home is cleaned before morning prayers are said to the goddess Lakshmi, so my secretary scrubbed and hoovered and wiped the surfaces of my office, and washed and rewashed the cups which would bear tea and milk for this unique visitor. Naipaul was an uncomfortable god; he fidgeted in my office, scanned the bookshelves and struggled to engage in small talk. I was terrified to speak in his presence in case my utterance was deemed to be vulgar, so we spent an hour before the lecture in an uncomfortable silence. I had forbidden anyone to knock on my door, so the two of us were cloistered in my office. I was very much like the Hindu priest at the end of worship, climbing into a private recess in the temple to communicate with the deity, the worshippers left outside the closed door. Naipaul read brilliantly and received a very warm reception, but it was apparent to me that, like Kanhai, he wanted to avoid meeting people, shaking hands, being in the public limelight. There was shyness about him which he sought to disguise by being brazen, in a Trinidadian mode. For example, he declared that he had never read Wilson Harris, thereby insulting not just Harris but the whole of Guyana, and me. When one eminent Oxford professor, an authority on Trinidad, asked him why he had stopped writing about the Caribbean, Naipaul replied, "Because it is of no importance." These words were not uttered in contempt, [notwithstanding] appearances; it was just Naipaul's way of refusing to engage – probably for the thousandth time in his life – in conversation with critics. He is sensitive, raw-nerved, easily irritated, because he is creative.

LG: In 1969 you left the gods behind and moved to England, right after Enoch Powell's 1968 "rivers of blood" speech . . .

DD: Yes, and in growing up, in England, I eventually gravitated into what is now called "black studies". I did a special study of the black presence in English literature as well as black figures in British art. So my intellectual interests had nothing to do with me being an Indian. It was soon apparent to me, within a month of being in England, that I was not a real Indian. My school friends were from India and Pakistan; they had their mother-tongues. Their homes smelt of incense. I felt much closer to a West Indian identity than an Indian one. At university in the 1970s, I was really more interested in the black diasporic experience because it just struck me as something that demanded original scholarship, and you could spend years getting engrossed in these subjects, you know – blacks in literature, blacks in art – partly because they were overlooked, more or less, by mainstream scholarship. It was a challenge of coming from the margin and moving the subject into the centre: all these things we take for granted now in postcolonial studies. You didn't think of it consciously at the time; all you thought was, this is a risk you are going to take with your academic career, and this was an exciting thing to do, to take the risk and not to do a "normal" set of studies. And then I thought that if I wanted to develop my interest in literature there was no point in doing it at a university that didn't have prestige in Britain, so I took a serious risk, which is, I applied to Cambridge. In those days, you could apply to five universities, but I just applied to Cambridge. So, when I was interviewed, they said, "If you don't get in, what will you do?" And I said, "Well, I will reapply." So, obviously, Cambridge must have felt sorry for this skinny West Indian of slender means – I was in the "Care" of the local authorities at the time – and took me in. So it was always about risk-taking, taking on a risky subject, not something that is considered to be central to literary studies or history of art studies.

LG: What did you move onto after your degree? How did you make your way into writing and into the study of the Indian presence in the Caribbean?

DD: Well, that was all exciting and I finished my doctoral thesis in '82, and then I decided to do something practical. So I left university and I went to work as a community education officer, again taking the risk in Wolverhampton, because Wolverhampton is Enoch Powell territory, he was the MP there for many years. Therefore I just found it fascinating to be able to go to Wolverhampton as a Race Relations community education officer, but quickly realized, after a year, that that was not where the power was – local politics and associations; the power was in universities because universities were centres of tremendous influence... You had to get back into university, so I came back into academic life in 1983, a place at Oxford, funded by [my] signing on for the dole, since it was a non-stipendiary Junior Research Fellowship.

And then I was pushed back into Indianness! I did a talk at London University in 1984–85 on the iconography of black people in British art, and during the coffee break a Rastafarian woman literally braced me up against the wall and said, "Why are you doing our thing? Why don't you do your own thing? Why don't you do Indian? You are Indian. Why are you doing black things?" And I remember being shocked by it! Because, at the time, I was working in

Goldsmith College London, in a black area. I was at home there; I was living in a black home. Sybil Phoenix rented me a room, and she is the grandmother of Lewisham; she is a black Guyanese, and I was at home there, completely at home, until this Rastafarian pushed me against the wall and confronted me with my ethnicity. And I remember being so hurt by that: that very evening – and I don't want to be melodramatic about it – but that very evening in Sybil Phoenix's house, I wrote, within one hour, "Coolie Mother", which is my first Indian poem ever. The previous book, *Slave Song*, was a mixture of Indian and black, more about plantation experience, but this was an exclusively and explicitly Indian poem.

My initial ethnic anger at the Rastafarian woman gave way to the sheer pleasure of composing in words, struggling for the image, the alliteration, the cadence. There was no space for spite or ethnic triumphalism. The poem and its seque[l] – "Coolie Son" – are about East Indian poverty, humiliation, ambition. And, later, when I looked into it, it became apparent that the study of Indians in the Caribbean was at an embryonic stage, very much so, and therefore, if you wanted to be a West Indian intellectual you must also try to fill those gaps in scholarship. Hence I organized at Warwick University, in 1988, a Conference on Indo-Caribbean History and Culture – Cheddi Jagan attended – edited a couple of books on Indians in the Caribbean and wrote a novel on the Indian middle passage, as it were.

LG: Yes, you edited a collection of essays with Brinsley Samaroo entitled *India in the Caribbean*, which I believe marked the beginning of Indo-Caribbean studies as we know it today, took it beyond the realm of the early anthropological studies from the 1960s and 1970s . . .

DD: That is a pleasing exaggeration, but the book insisted on creative writing alongside scholarship. I was catapulted into an arena of great privilege, because the BBC asked me to anchor one of their programmes, some ten years later, a programme on the "coolies", and it was shown on BBC 2 and a few million people watched it, and a day or so later I received an e-mail from a woman called Brigid Wells to say, "I saw your programme. My great grandfather's brother wrote a diary on board the *Hesperus*", which was one of the first two ships to arrive in the New World. The first load of coolies actually to be landed in Demerara was from the *Hesperus*. She said, "He was the ship's doctor.

Would you like to see the diary?" Can you imagine, it was almost like finding the beginning of your beginnings! So, eventually, I met her and we published that diary in 2007, a great moment. And then, quite wonderfully, I received a letter from Sir John Gladstone, inviting me to tea in Haworden Castle in Wales. In his letter he more or less apologized for the Indian trade; he thought that his great grandfather – Sir John Gladstone, who started indentureship, the first Guianese Indians being called the "Gladstone coolies" – maybe didn't treat the Indians as well as he should have, and invited me to tea. Beautiful, lovely handwriting, and obviously a very interesting man, and he actually drew me a detailed map in the letter as to how to get to Haworden Castle, which again is marvellous, because it is like the map from India to Guyana: take a left when you get to Cape Coast, take a right past Mauritius, eventually get to Trinidad and keep going straight ahead to Guyana, right? I haven't had a chance to meet Gladstone yet, because I have been busy in India, having spent several months there recently, partly doing research on the departure of Indians in 1838.

LG: What is the future of Indo-Caribbean studies?

DD: Now [that] we have set up a website, we have set up an Indo-Caribbean Studies Association, with Derek Walcott as a patron, we are hoping to set up a journal of Indo-Caribbean studies, so I am hoping that, towards the latter part of my academic career, if I can get embedded in the academy Indo-Caribbean studies, then at least I will have done something worthwhile . . . not quite equal to Naipaul, Kanhai and Jagan, but in scholarship, yes, hopefully something substantial will remain.

But, having said all that, deep down I am not really interested, as a person – intuitively and emotionally and creatively, I am not really interested in: (a) scholarship, (b) Indo-Caribbean scholarship. I would much rather sit and write my novels, which may or may not be about Indians or blacks . . . I do believe that the moment when you really eclipse the predicament of your ethnicity is when you can write beautifully. I think, and I have argued elsewhere, that Equiano finally emancipated himself not when he bought his own freedom – he became then a free social person – but when he wrote his book, his autobiography, with novelistic features, with a prose that was lush and lucid and moving, that had rhythm and thought and humour and pathos; when he wrote with that beauty – in other words, when he became a writer – he was no longer black. In this book of essays I'm presently editing, there is an excellent work by Matt McCann in which he argues that maybe Dr Richmond, although he said he saved the Indians on board the ship, maybe he didn't, maybe he was just, you know, promoting himself. Whereas I would say that, if you attended to the prose of that passage McCann refers to, its cadences of grief, its rhythms, its repetition – repetitions – its pauses – that is, to its writerly aspects – you will know that either Dr Richmond was an ambitious writer or he was completely genuine. For me, the genuineness of his testimony is reflected in the quality of his prose. Writing is always the test of anything to do with my own being.

Having said all of that about writing, I have decided now to spend as long as I can moving from brown and black to green. I want to be a green man now. I want to look at eco-critical aspects of literature, eco-critical responses to writing. I want to look at medieval literature, and I want to look at the green man as a universal symbol.

I want to write the rainforest of Guyana, and I would like to be a green writer, because the future is not black or brown, the future is green. In my last two novels I have been desperately trying to capture something of the nature of the rainforest, echoing Wilson Harris and writers who went before me. Obviously, I take a boat into the interior but I don't spend the night! Because you don't want to spend the night in the rainforest! You want to go with all your intuitive faculties raw, and then you want to encounter the rainforest, and then, after a few hours, you want to return to the nearest bar, get back to Georgetown and urban safety – bandits are more tolerable than jungle snakes – and then you begin to write. Because you can't research your subject too much, you have to imagine it as well, which is my excuse to return to the safety of Georgetown.

So my new novel, at the moment, although it is revisiting slavery – because you have to keep going back to things – although the new novel is revisiting slavery, I am writing it when I am in India, although it is about the black experience of the Caribbean. I am writing it when I am in India because the frisson, I think, is creative. But then I am trying to make it green. I am greening the novel as I go along . . . and who knows what it will turn out to be!

CHAPTER 16

An Interview with David Dabydeen (2010)

KAREN RANEY, UNIVERSITY OF EAST LONDON

Karen Raney: Are you familiar with the phrase "visual literacy", and if so what does it mean to you?

David Dabydeen: As somebody who is worried about the predominance of ideological concerns among students in their reading of literature, the concept of "visual literacy" worries me tremendously. In my experience of teaching, for several years now, literature is no longer seen as literature; it's seen as the equivalent of sociology. So that, when you talk about metaphor or form, students just shove that into a category called "aesthetics". They don't see that that's what defines literature from, say, journalistic prose, from sociological enquiry. The very fact that we use the word "text", for example, instead of "poem" – at my most extreme I'd say it's a new form of philistinism. The danger is that we will then want to transfer this way of looking at literature ideologically to the visual arts.

KR: So your idea of visual literacy is raking through something for its ideological content?

DD: For its context, for its political and social and ideological contents. I'll give a little example, just off the top of my head. If I were to look at, say, Hogarth's *Shrimp Seller* in the National Portrait Gallery, it's just a sketch. Now, a form of visual literacy would talk about the proletariat or the labouring masses, or the price of fish or whatever, and not quite see the flourish of colours, the vividness of paint, the texture of things. In the same way that, in reading novels and poetry, students don't look at the form and the texture of language anymore, they don't look at metaphoric intensities. They want to see whether, at the level of ideas to do with race, class and gender, this work gets a tick or it goes down the chute.

Now, I've had to put up with that, as a black writer. When I say a "black" writer, I mean I'm a writer, but I also happen to come from the Caribbean, where it's expected that our writings will be impregnated with all kinds of ideological positions. And no doubt they are. But I don't want to be judged as a writer of ideas. I want people also to look at the length of a line of a poem, and whether the length of that line corresponds with the next line. In other words, I accept what T.S. Eliot says, which is that poetry is rhythm; poetry's not ideology. Of course, a poem also says something, and no doubt certain kinds of paintings say things. But there's a whole body of paintings that don't say anything. They don't say anything that could be verbalized, except "God, what a tree!" you know, or "Look at that sunset!"

Then there is a whole body of paintings that demand reading. The work I did on Hogarth was about that. A Hogarth print, for example, demands to be read, and is, in fact, structured as a play, with the different acts – act one, act two, act three – where the characters are actually placed on a stage which is lit in a way that one expects an eighteenth-century stage to be lit. And there are characters offstage. So Hogarth is obviously asking for his painting or his engraving to be read as a piece of drama.

KR: It's interesting that you assumed that the term "visual literacy" meant just the ideological reading. Couldn't visual literacy include more sensual responses as well?

DD: Well, why call it literacy, then? As you know, I wrote a long poem on one of Turner's paintings, *The Slave Ship*, but that was in no way an attempt to write the painting. There was no attempt to match the use of words with the use of paint; that's impossible. In the same way that, when Aubrey Williams, the great Caribbean painter, did a series of paintings based on Shostakovich's music, he said he never tried to match paint with musical notation. It can't be done. The most you can do is try to convey something of the rhythm of the sea, in a poem like "Turner" that matches Turner's epic sense of the mammothness, the colossal energy of the sea. You have to try to manoeuvre your words, or to make them swell; you have to make them grand and epic. But that doesn't mean that you're actually writing paint.

KR: Say a bit about why you decided to write that poem from the painting. Would you have written the same poem from reading a historical account of throwing sick slaves off of ships into the sea? Was it necessary that it came from that particular painting? How did that poem come about?

DD: I think, in this case, this was a painting that asked for verbal interpretation. It wasn't like *The Shrimp Girl*, which is a pure aesthetic, if you like; the most dominant aspect is the sheer use of colour and the vividness of expression. The Turner painting was about a story; it was based on a story. It has been read, whether Turner wanted it to be read or not. I'm sure he wanted the absolute moral horror, but also the grand and epic, the sublimity of colour, to be the immediate reaction of the viewer. Nevertheless, it was taken up and read and read and read. Ruskin read it, a whole lot of critics read it, they applied visual literacy to it, and so there was a whole debate as to whether Turner was pro-slavery or anti-slavery, whether the black person in the foreground was sufficiently visible, et cetera, et cetera. All the race, class and gender issues had entered the domain of that painting. So, in a sense, I felt that it was a legitimate thing to also enter that verbal discourse, if you like, but not in terms of scholarship, which would lead to ideological readings, but in terms of trying to re-create, in words, something of the ambiguity in the painting. But it's not a painting about the slave ship. It just uses the slave ship as a trigger for a whole series of other questions which are particular to colonials, to do with memory and the loss of memory and the recovery of memory and idylls of the past, and how one re-creates the past, how one re-creates a sense of family.

KR: You were quite hard on Turner in the preface to the poem. At one point I think you called him a sadist who relished his sadism in private while denouncing it in public. You suspected this from the intensity of the painting?

DD: Yes, but, you know, prefaces are bullshit. In prefaces, you pretend to be a scholar. In other words, you withdraw from the poem and its ambiguities, and its love for Turner. I hope that that poem confesses a love for Turner and the epic dimensions of his paintings. It was a challenge as a poet to try to . . . how do you match that grandeur? You can't. But you try. And in the very act of trying, you're also paying tribute, a very humble tribute, to the greatness of this painting. So I have no doubts in my mind about the greatness of Turner as a painter. Really, if the poem was ideologically grounded at all, it was against Ruskin. In other words, it was against the person who was not a painter but a critic, the one who sought visual literacy.

KR: It interests me that you are working with word and image from the point of view of a poet. I am interested in how words can be triggers for visual artists, but also in someone who uses a painting as a trigger for words.

DD: It's just that Turner's grand imagination acts as a stimulus to another imagination, from a different culture, from a different period. So, that, in itself, is part of the whole miracle of the imagination, isn't it? How a guy in the late twentieth century and from a different culture could look at a painting like that and still be inspired to write something.

KR: You don't have any trouble with saying Turner was a great painter?

DD: Of course not. I mean, who would? I'm a total amateur, but the first thing I see when I look at a painting is the colour. I like paintings where there's some genius in the use of colour. And I wouldn't find any difficulty, therefore, in saying that Turner is probably – and this is just an opinion that echoes fifty million professional art historians – one of the greatest colourists who ever painted. He inspired people like Aubrey Williams, and inspired, in a sense, the colour of Derek Walcott's poetry.

KR: That's interesting. You see that much crossover from the visual to the verbal arts?

DD: Oh, very much. And I think Walcott, who himself is a painter, was very aware of Turner. Because Turner is an icon in English art, so you're aware of him in the same way that you're aware of Shakespeare; as a colonial you're aware of Turner.

KR: Are you happy with the category of "art"? Haven't art and popular culture converged? Isn't the idea of "art" just elitist and out of date?

DD: I'm not happy with the distinction between high art and low art, or popular and elite art, because, from a Caribbean, a Guyanese or Trinidadian perspective, we wear our art on our bodies; it's as simple as that. We don't have art galleries; we never had a tradition of hanging things on the wall. And it's because of that that we have Carnival, for example, the carnivalesque arts; we have people like Peter Minshall, who designs the Olympic banners, the flames going up, and the masks and everything. Well, this is what we do; art is a carnival. It's meant to have an instantaneous, electric impact on the viewer and the participant. And it's meant to disappear afterwards. You don't hang it up in a museum. If you hung up a Carnival calypso costume in a museum, believe me, it's absolutely dead. It just looks like a lot of sequins. When it's worn by, if you like, the black body, and it's dancing and it's shaking its buttocks and it's rippling, then it has a different impact. I come from the West Indies, where nothing really lasted. It all was made of wood and rotted very quickly. Carnival art is described as popular art; it's not quite high art. But it is. I wouldn't make the distinction between high art and low art in that sense. However, to confuse "popular culture" with art can be an act of philistinism: it's saying I can't assess or appreciate the finer quality of things, that a line from Shakespeare is comparable to one from Donald Duck.

KR: Getting back to the painting of *The Slave Ship*, how would you reconcile those two things – Turner as sadist and Turner as great artist?

DD: The idea of Turner as sadist is partly because I'd read that in Lindsay's book, and discovered that Turner's nude sketches, his more erotic sketches, he himself, I believe, destroyed. So we don't really have a sense of the contradictions in the man. You have a kind of moral grandeur about a painting like *Slave Ship*, and, at the same time, one intuits something a bit more perverse. I said that about Turner and, again, this is a fictional Turner. In racial terms, Turner is a dead white man from the nineteenth century. He doesn't care what I think about him.

But I do think that there was something a bit untidy about his – well, untidy is a moral word – there's something a bit tormented about his sexuality. Nothing unusual there. And, in a sense, if I wrote Turner back into his painting, and made him a sadist, I thought at the time, or afterwards, it was a way of rescuing him from the auction houses and the art establishment that seeks to erase this aspect of Turner's personality for commercial reasons. In the same way that commercial reasons drove the slave trade. So, in a sense, one was hoping to rescue Turner from ideology.

KR: At the same time using him as a kind of quintessential Western white man — the Western artist?

DD: Yes, but that was really a point about the relationship between representation and genocide. In other words — in the same way that Jewish critics have attacked Sylvia Plath for using death camp imagery to describe the traumatic relationship between herself and her father, in the same way that people have attacked D.M. Thomas in *White Hotel*, for seeming to relish Nazi brutality, whilst purporting to criticize it — I thought that Turner, in taking on catastrophe, in a sense, opens himself up to certain charges of savouring the sadis[tic]. So, with this business of representation in relation to genocide, there comes a point where art can be an affliction, when one is confronted with massive moments of suffering. I think it was Adorno who said that, after Auschwitz, there is no poetry, there's only a kind of silence. So, if I stand before a Turner painting, really I should just be utterly silent. There should be no visual literacy; I should just be stunned into silence. There's only the rhythm of the colours that ravishes you.

In this particular painting, because it has a narrative design as well as an aesthetic design, I think it's legitimate to read Turner. But if you look at another Turner, you know, the famous steam train, can you read it? Or can you just see how it dissolves reality?

KR: So you distinguish between different kinds of representations and what you need to bring to them, in a sense. You wouldn't say you can read everything in the same way?

DD: How does one read certain kinds of abstract expressionist art? I think this whole business of visual literacy, the ideological implications and the dangers of that, probably stem from the rise of conceptual art.

KR: Which puts the idea above the execution?

DD: Above the artefact, above the texture. It doesn't take into account a particular thing called a painting that is different from a particular thing called a poem, or a particular thing called an idea, or a philosophy or a concept.

KR: It's eroding important distinctions?

DD: Well, it's just privileging ideas over the body of the art itself. I come back to T.S. Eliot, because we grew up in the Caribbean with Eliot. Even though he was a right shit, you know, he did have a tremendous influence on our early poets and therefore on all of us. Eliot describes poetry as the "direct sensuous apprehension of thought". The direct, sensuous – direct, first of all, then sensuous – apprehension of thought. A poem is its texture, its form, its music and its rhythm; in all that is embedded in its thinking. I believe that conceptual art, or indeed, conceptual poetry, just elevates the thinking bit of it, the metaphysical bit of it, above the body of it, the livingness of it.

KR: If you wanted to teach someone to apprehend sensuously, could you teach that kind of thing or is it something that just happens?

DD: Well, at the end of the day, the final appeal is to the imagination of the reader, isn't it? You can have the theories, Romanticist theories, that art should startle, should present what is familiar in wholly unfamiliar ways, the familiar becomes renewed. You can teach the theories, quoting Coleridge and the rest of them, but ultimately the response is inarticulate. It's impossible to persuade anybody of the virtue of a metaphor. It has to do with the individual imagination. So, ultimately, one comes back to Leavis. I know Leavis is deeply unpopular, for good reasons or bad reasons, but Leavis always used to say, "Just read the book." The final appeal is to the work. Just go and read it. I'm not saying that you just read a poem and then shut up; I'm saying that, because a poem is about words, and therefore seeks a level of interpretation, then it's legitimate for the critic to tease out its ideological or political or social contexts. But if that is all that the critic does, then that is not responding to a poem. You have to respond to what *makes* it a poem as opposed to a piece of journalistic prose, or a philosophical pronouncement.

KR: What's the difference between a poem and a painting?

DD: One uses words and one uses colour, basically. One is more intellectual than the other in the sense that – I use the term "intellectual" in a kind of loose way – one is more allied to the world of ideas. The poem or the novel or the play, because it's using words, is more allied to the domain of abstraction, if you like. And then, of course, music is much more direct. It's just degrees of directness. It also has to do with a totally different media. What you can do with a painting you can't necessarily do with a poem, and vice versa.

KR: What can't you do with a poem?

DD: I saw a Paul Klee exhibition in Zurich. And I thought, if I could write with those multi-layered . . . Don't forget, to my mind, as an amateur, as just an ordinary viewer, it's a flat surface, that's the first thing. So it starts off with the great disadvantage of being a flat surface. And then the painter has to re-create fantastic illusions, to endow that flat surface with dimensions. And that, in itself, is a gift, isn't it? It's not just something technical. The painter achieves that not just by a technical sense of form and perspective, but by colour. Now, obviously, poems are layered and multi-layered and echo endlessly, but it's a different way of echoing. These are fatuous comparisons, anyway, but there's something about paintings – I just want to remain naïve to them. I don't want to apply the pursuit that I have, which is writing, to painting, because for me that would spoil it. That would make it familiar . . . when to me it's utterly different. I just want to savour that sense of otherness, of other art forms.

KR: When you say you don't want to apply words to paintings, I might say, well, that's what you did! In that poem, you've taken a painting, and you've made words in response to it. But that's not what you mean. Your way of applying words to a painting like Turner's is building some sort of loose bridge between the two.

DD: I come back to the belief, which is not necessarily a trustworthy belief, that the Turner painting was only a trigger for other ideas that had to do with very personal things, and historical things that probably were totally irrelevant to the painting. Memory, for example. The Turner painting is not about memory, is it? It's not about the re-creation of family, it's not about a lost mother, it's not about a desire for land and there isn't a stillborn child. So the painting is just something that is inspirational.

I'm writing something at the moment called *A Harlot's Progress*, which is a novel. Now, that takes the little black boy from the second frame of Hogarth's series. He's now the oldest black inhabitant in London in the 1780s, and he has to tell his story of his relationship with this English prostitute called Moll.

And his relationship with a painter called William Hogarth, who once came along and painted them. He sees Hogarth, I think, as being as prurient as I saw Turner, in relation to the slave trade. Now, what does that have to do with Hogarth? That's just my own bizarre imagination, isn't it? It's just the freedom to take something, to acknowledge the origin of it and then reshape it.

KR: But it's important to use those particular characters and names because they occupy that celebrated position in Western art, because they're famous, because they're approved of, is that right? It's a way of dethroning them.

DD: I'm not sure it is. No, I wouldn't say one is kicking against the canon, because I have a great love for Hogarth's bitterness and vindictiveness. I think he probably was an evil man at times, and there's a kind of nasty streak to him. And, you know, I quite admire that. He's a grand old sinner as well. But it's not kicking against the canon; it's just taking a black character who's totally marginal and making him a central character in a narrative. So, if you like, it might be a fulfilment of certain interpretations of the Hogarth painting, a fulfilment from my point of view, because obviously I identify with the little black boy. So, in a sense, what I'm doing is writing autobiography; I'm using the Hogarth painting as a key to unlocking all kinds of private interests that I have. Now, that Hogarth painting demands to be read, this is a narrative work, so, in that sense, yes, one can bring a kind of visual literacy to it. And that's legitimate. But I wonder whether I could do that with, say, a Goya painting, or a Munch painting.

KR: It's been done. I think you can bring ideology to any painting. It's one possible layer of meaning. You can look at a Jackson Pollock and ask what it might have meant to dispense with narrative during the Cold War – abstraction standing for American "freedom" against Soviet Socialist Realism, or whatever. What place, then, does ideology have in your scheme of things? Was there a time when you were quite happy for ideology to be made central, and now you're not?

DD: I think, from my perspective, from a colonial perspective, it has to do with coming to terms with the post-imperial. It seems to me that we bend over backwards to come up with a counter-ideology to that of our parents and our grandparents, out of a sense of guilt and shame. And, for that reason, we chuck Shakespeare out of the window because Othello was probably not black enough, and why did Caliban want to rape Miranda, et cetera, et cetera.. And indeed, it goes not just in terms of race but in terms of certain feminist critiques as well, where you chuck D.H. Lawrence out of the window because maybe Ursula is not quite as independent or forceful as – God knows what. So, in other words, you home in on one small aspect of ideology, and you don't see the art or the work.

KR: Do you then rob yourself of the complexity of artworks?

DD: I think so, yes. Because if I wanted to read something about strong women or weak women or the treatment of women or the treatment of black people, I'd go and read a book of history or a book of sociology. I must say, I'm being a bit extreme. I don't really believe in this nonsense that Haydon White – *Tropics of Discourse* – comes up with, which is that history is emplotment. He says that a historian, in writing history, puts at the margin certain facts and highlights other facts, and therefore creates a narrative, creates a plot, and therefore the writing of history and the writing of fiction become conflated. I think this is patently nonsense. Because a poem about the Holocaust uses different tools, different modes of feeling and thinking, than a historical account about the Holocaust, which tries to be factual, and tries to be objective.

Of course, terms like "factual" and "objective" are now out of the window because of postmodernist theories, which say that everything is relative, there is no origin, and there are no essences. I follow Derek Walcott's line, which is "yes, there are origins, and yes, there are essences". The idea that we don't have origins and essences may well be a Western way of avoiding history. When you come from the Caribbean, and in this I'll just quote Walcott, "we know what essences are". We know what it is to have a roof over our head. I was at a conference in Cologne, when Heidegger's theory of language was used as a way of saying that we can triumph over the colonial experience through a mutual understanding and use of language. In other words, Heidegger says, we live in the house of language. I don't want to live in the house of fucking language. I want to live in a house. You go and tell that to people whose houses have been destroyed by hurricanes, or people in the nineteenth century living in mud shit huts, that they live in a house of language. This is what Derek Walcott says in a brilliant essay, that the art critic goes into a St Lucian hut and sees a little nail and a little piece of cloth hanging up there, and stands back and admires it as a mode of postmodern confusion, when all it is, is a little nail and a piece of shirt. So I think different cultures probably have different imperatives when it comes to reading into things.

KR: That's a legacy of semiotics – to find significance in everything.

DD: To find significance in everything, and not to find the sorrow, the grief in things. I come back to Seamus Heaney, who said that poetry should not express grievance, which is ideology; it should express grief. That's a wonderful, wonderful thing. And, to me, the expression of grief means texture, writing a poem that moves because of the music of the poem or the colour of the poem or the rhythm of it, the imagery of it, whereas grievance is just a surface meaning.

At the end of the day, what I believe about the Turner painting is that it does commemorate the meaning of the death of Africans in the grief of the elements. In other words, the violence of the sea and the sorrow of the crimson sunset and the ship twisted is a way of commemorating the death of the Africans, and giving it meaning.

KR: So any cruel or sadistic impulses are mingled in with this kind of redemption in the form it takes, expressing the experience of the slaves as well?

DD: I think what Turner was trying to do was to say that there are certain kinds of grief, certain kinds of human suffering, that can't be commemorated in words or in images, but can only be commemorated in a movement of elements, if you like. I'm not being romantic; it's a painting about the elements in utter conflict. And, to me, that's his way of commemorating the violence and the grief and the inhumanity of all our colonies. So, if someone is taught the literacy of the painting before being engaged in the violence of colour, then they may have just a partial appreciation of the painting.

At the same time, in my "Turner" poem, I make the character male, but don't forget: in the Turner painting it's a female who's drowning; it's a female figure who's being devoured by these sexual, phallic, monstrous male fish. Obviously there's something kind of sexy there, as well, because we know, looking at the iconography of the art of slavery, that there were a whole lot of images that served the abolition movement, but also acted as a peep show, paintings of half-naked black women being branded or being flagellated.

Obviously, that served the abolition movement, but the flip side was that it was also a bit of eighteenth-century pornography.

KR: I want to ask about your relationship to the English language as your medium. You use a kind of creolized form of English. Do you see it as important to use creole in your poems?

DD: Yes, in the sense that, speaking personally, I enjoy myself most when I write in creole. It's a language that hops and limps and has all kinds of fractures and breakages and absurdities and meaninglessness in it. A kind of absence of grammar. When I say "absence of grammar", I mean an absence of recognizable grammar. With creole I find I can be nonsensical. By "nonsensical" I don't mean stupid, I mean I can just . . .

KR: You can play more?

DD: Yes, I can play more, and I can confuse the past and the present and the future. There's an absence of grammar; you can have all kinds of confusion to do with time. It's the best way, when you're trying to avoid being meaningful.

KR: So it's not for ideological reasons that you would use creole?

DD: Partly. I suppose ideological in the sense that it is the language of the common people. Wordsworth said we should use the language of the common people. And certainly creole, historically, has been used as a way of asserting West Indian identity. I and many other writers who use creole are not interested in its ideological import. That is given; we understand that. We just want to see how far we can go with it.

KR: What it can do?

DD: What it could do in terms of dancing and pissing around on the page and jumping here, there and everywhere, confusing people, and coming back and making sense. You can have soliloquies in creole which can jump from past to present without necessarily being as confusing as, say, reading Beckett, where you have similar snatches of meaning. I think a lot of us use creole just to experience something of the joy of the language, and the grief of the language.

KR: I'm trying to think whether there's a counterpart in visual terms, of working with a visual "creole".

DD: If I had to think of the use of creole in relation to the use of English, I'd think of woodcuts compared to engravings. Woodcuts have a kind of – I don't want to use the word "crude", but it appears to be crude, meaning rough hewn and direct, and almost brutal in its effect.

KR: Rather than refined?

DD: Or vulgar, rather than refined, yes. So I think creole has a kind of directness, sensuousness, almost a "primitive" energy that maybe English hasn't, because of its levels of abstraction, because of its hundreds of years of development. You use what will best serve a piece of writing at a particular time.

KR: I know there are women artists who feel they can't use certain kinds of media because these are so steeped in male art history it's as if they're contaminated. I know this is changing, but there has been that feeling. Some women have said they don't feel that painting is theirs; it belongs to men.

DD: I can't figure that out.

KR: I suppose what I'm getting at . . . in the Turner poem, you were talking about the stillborn child, and trying to reinvent an identity that you said was contaminated and drowned in the sea of Turner and other artists. Are you partly saying that you have to separate yourself from the English language because it's contaminated; it's the language of the oppressors?

DD: No, not any more. You see, I think the burden of that separation was in the previous generation. People like Naipaul and Harris and Walcott, Jean Rhys, they had to face these ideological questions about whether you can use the master's language to describe your own experience. And, you know, the same arguments happen in Africa, where people accuse Chinua Achebe of using English, and he argues that English is an African language; we've been speaking it for three hundred years. And, of course, it's the same in the Caribbean. English is our first language as well, and is as native to us as it is to the English, probably even more native to us in the sense that one of the sad things about England is that many of the indigenous English can't speak English any more; the level of illiteracy is daunting. In the Caribbean, we did learn English, we did learn grammatical structures. When you went to school, you were taught what a subordinate clause was. The English we learned was quaint, because in England it had evolved beyond that into something else. But, no, English is as natural as creole; it was the language we always had. I think we've now reached the stage where we've gone beyond these ideological questions. We had about thirty, forty years of this.

KR: So, in your generation, creole and English are resources that are just available to you, at your disposal?

DD: I don't feel embarrassed at all in using English; quite the opposite. I don't feel embarrassed socially, and I don't feel embarrassed politically, and I don't feel embarrassed philosophically. You can relish any language and try to use it vividly, and if you can't, well, then do something else. The whole of "Turner" was written in English, but I don't see it as being written in English. I keep quoting Walcott. He said, "Yeah, of course I write in English, but sometimes the rhythms are not English." The rhythm of a line might be a West Indian rhythm, but the diction might be English, and, to me, that's fantastic, isn't it?

KR: That's how new forms are created.

DD: Sure. And if a woman could take on a male language of art, as it were, and feminize it, or whatever the verb is, to me, that's marvellous. That's triumphant. But I feel very grateful to people like Harris and Walcott and Naipaul, for writing, and initiating a tradition that us lot can then come along and have a responsibility to. We have a sense that everything is there, because they made it for us; they won all the arguments about the use of English versus the use of creole. So now we can really say, "Anything that is available, I'll have. I'll see what I can do with it."

Notes

Introduction

1. The title of this collection is from a two-part series written and presented by David Dabydeen in 1993 for BBC Radio 4; the programmes presented an immigrant's view of Britain.
2. The Barbadian poet Edward Kamau Brathwaite is sometimes referred to as either Edward or Kamau Brathwaite in subsequent articles and interviews in this collection.
3. David Dabydeen, "Eighteenth-Century English Literature on Commerce and Slavery", 4 (this volume).
4. Ibid., 10.
5. Ibid., 18.
6. David Dabydeen, "On Not Being Milton: Nigger Talk in England Today", 23 (this volume).
7. Ibid., 31.
8. Ibid., 32.
9. David Dabydeen, "On Cultural Diversity", 40 (this volume).
10. David Dabydeen, "Teaching West Indian Literature in Britain", 43 (this volume).
11. Ibid., 56. Emphasis added.
12. David Dabydeen, "From Care to Cambridge", 63 (this volume).
13. The interview with Chelva Kanaganayakam provides further insight into this matter; see pp. 133–40 of this volume.
14. David Dabydeen, "On Samaroo's *Tempus Est*", 74 (this volume).
15. Ibid., 75.
16. Ibid., 77.
17. Dabydeen explores his own concerns with becoming a "green" writer in the 2009 interview with Gramaglia, pp. 173–83 of this volume.
18. David Dabydeen, "Hogarth and the Canecutters", 82 (this volume).

19. Ibid., 83.
20. Ibid., 84.
21. Ibid.
22. The interview with Gramaglia considers this matter in further detail.
23. David Dabydeen, "West Indian Writers in Britain", 88 (this volume).
24. Ibid., 100.
25. Ibid., 101.
26. Ibid., 103.
27. David Dabydeen, Introduction to *Lutchmee and Dilloo*, 112 (this volume).
28. John Mair, "Guyana Don", *BWIA Caribbean Beat* 75 (2005): 52.
29. Felicity Hand, "A Talk with David Dabydeen", 123 (this volume).
30. David Dabydeen, *Turner: New and Selected Poems* (Cape Poetry, 1994), inside front cover.
31. Chelva Kanaganayakam, "Interviewing David Dabydeen", 134 (this volume). Emphasis added.
32. Mark Stein, "David Dabydeen Talks to Mark Stein", 159 (this volume).
33. Ibid.
34. Lars Eckstein, "Getting Back to the Idea of Art as Art", 165 (this volume).
35. Ibid., 167.
36. Ibid., 169.
37. Ibid.
38. Letizia Gramaglia, "A Forced Indianness", 171 (this volume).
39. Ibid., 176.
40. Ibid., 183.
41. *Guardian*, 1 April 2008.

Chapter 1

1. Samuel Johnson, cited in L. Whitney, *Primitivism and the Idea of Progress* (Baltimore: Johns Hopkins University Press, 1934), xviii; *Craftsman* of 1735 reproduced in *The Gentleman's Magazine* 5 (1735): 717–18; John Brown, *An Estimate of the Manners and Principles of the Times*, 2nd ed. (London, 1757), 22; A.S. Catcott, *The Antiquity and Honourableness of the Practice of Merchandize. A Sermon* (Bristol, 1744), 13, 14, 15.
2. *Spectator*, no. 69, 19 May 1711.
3. J.A. Doyle, cited in A.A. Ettinger, *James Edward Oglethorpe: Imperial Idealist* (Oxford: Clarendon Press, 1936), 110; T. Seymour, "Literature and the South Sea Bubble" (PhD diss., University of North Carolina, 1955), 12.

4. See, respectively, *Maxims of Wisdom for Gaining Wealth* (London, 1788), 20; *Put Money in your Purse* (London, 1754), 321; *The Universal Merchant: Containing the Rationale of Commerce, in Theory and Practice* (London, 1753), 6; *A Trip to Leverpoole by Two of Fate's Children in Search of Fortunatus's Purse: A Satyr* (London, 1706), title page, quoting from Butler's *Hudibras*; J. Vanderlint, *Money Answers All Things* (London, 1734).
5. Eric Williams, *Capitalism and Slavery* (Chapel Hill: University of North Carolina Press, 1944), 52, has written that "the profits obtained provided one of the main streams of that accumulation of capital in England which financed the Industrial Revolution". James Walvin, *The Black Presence: A Documentary History of the Negro in England, 1555–1860* (London: Orbach and Chambers, 1971), 8, states that such commerce "underpinned Britain's transition towards an industrial society".
6. See, respectively, Williams, *Capitalism and Slavery*, 30, 51; J. Houstoun, *Some New and Accurate Observations . . . of the Coast of Guinea* (London, 1725), 43; Peter Hogg: *Slavery: The Afro-American Experience* (London: British Library, 1979), 3.
7. *The Case of the Royal African Company of England* (London, 1730), 31; *The Dispute between the Northern Colonies and the Sugar Islands, Set in a Clear View*, 1731 broadside, in *The Goldsmiths Library's Collection of Broadsides* IV, no. 343.3, Senate House Library, London University; *A Letter to the Right Reverend the Lord Bishop of London from an Inhabitant of His Majesty's Leeward-Caribbee-Islands* (London, 1730), 14; *Some Matters of Fact Relating to the Present State of the African Trade* (n.p., 1720), 1.
8. By 1768 the estimated number of blacks in Britain was 20,000 (F. Shyllon, *Black People in Britain, 1555–1833* [London: Oxford University Press, 1977], 102). The figure may have been higher – the *London Chronicle* of 1756 gave a number of 30,000 (D.A. Lorimer, *Colour, Class and the Victorians* [Leicester, UK: Leicester University Press, 1978], 25). The *Daily Journal* of 5 April 1723 reported that " 'tis said there is a great Number of Blacks come daily into this City, so that 'tis thought in a short Time, if they be not suppress'd, the City will swarm with them".
9. Daniel Defoe, *A Brief Account of the Present State of the African Trade* (London, 1713), 55; see also Defoe's *Review*, ed. A.W. Secord (New York: Facsimile Text Society, 1938), IX, 82. Defoe also declares that the British plantations "can no more subsist without Negroes than *England* could without Horses" – see R.P. Kaplan, "Daniel Defoe's Views on Slavery and Racial Prejudice" (PhD diss., New York University, 1970), 120. For the Grosvenor statement, see *Report of the Debate on a Motion for the Abolition of the Slave Trade in the House of Commons on Monday and Tuesday, April 18th and 19th, 1791* (London, 1791), 47.
10. *A New and Accurate Description of Guinea* (London, 1705), cited in M. Craton, J. Walvin and D. Wright, *Slavery, Abolition and Emancipation* (London: Longman,

1976), 222; William Snelgrave, *A New Account of Some Parts of Guinea, and the Slave-Trade* (London, 1734), 160.

11. *Athenian Mercury* 8, no. 30 (1691). See C.A. Moore's *Background of English Literature* (Minneapolis: University of Minnesota, 1953), 153. Edward Long's views are cited by O. Wali, "The Negro in English Literature" (PhD diss., Northwestern University, 1967), 391–92. For Grainger's and Boswell's views, see Wylie Sypher, *Guinea's Captive Kings* (Chapel Hill: University of North Carolina Press, 1944), 59, 169–70.

12. "The African Slave Trade Defended", *The London Magazine* 9 (1740): 493–94, cited by E. Donnan, *Documents Illustrative of the History of the Slave Trade to America*, 4 vols. (Washington DC: Carnegie Institution of Washington, 1930–35), 2:470.

13. *The Letters of the Earl of Chesterfield to his Son*, ed. C. Strachey, with notes by A. Calthrop, 3rd ed. (London: Methuen, 1932), 116.

14. For a sample of such opinions, see *A Brief Discovery . . . of . . . The Island of Madagascar*, in *A Collection of Voyages and Travels* (London, 1745), 2:633; *A True Relation of the Inhuman and Unparalleled Actions and Barbarous Murders, of Negroes or Moors*, in *Collection of Voyages and Travels*, 2:515. The first writes that there are "no ingenious manufactures . . . no arts, no sciences" among the Negroes, that they show no "symptoms of ingenuity"; the second and third writers describe blacks as "idle, sluggish . . . free from having any tillage whatsoever; they make little use of labour or manufactures".

15. Tom K. Meier, "Defoe and the Defense of Commerce" (PhD diss., Columbia University, 1971), 1, 18.

16. Bonamy Dobrée, "The Theme of Patriotism in the Poetry of the Early Eighteenth Century", *Proceedings of the British Academy* 35 (1949): 60.

17. *The Four Kings of Canada* (London, 1710), 46.

18. Moore, *Backgrounds*, 133.

19. Cornelius Arnold, *Commerce* [1751], in *Poems on Several Occasions* (London, 1757), 129. The truth was that the Europeans actively encouraged Africans to fight against and enslave each other by the bribery of tribal leaders – see W. Rodney, *A History of the Upper Guinea Coast, 1545–1800* (Oxford: Oxford University Press, 1970), 102–6, 113.

20. I borrow James Sutherland's words from a different context; see *A Preface to Eighteenth Century Poetry* (Oxford: Oxford University Press, 1948), 89.

21. Poem in *The Gentleman's Magazine* 8 (1738): 158. Joseph La Valée, *The Negro Equalled by Few Europeans* (Dublin, 1791), I, 81–82.

22. *Spectator*, no. 106, 2 July 1711; emphasis added.

23. Details from the *Dictionary of National Biography*.

24. Max Byrd, *London Transformed: Images of the City in the Eighteenth Century* (New Haven, CT: Yale University Press, 1978).

25. T. Marcy, *Eighteenth Century Views of Bristol and Bristolians* (Bristol: Bristol Branch of the Historical Association, 1966), 13; S. Johnson, *Lives of the Poets*, 2 vols. (Oxford: Oxford University Press, 1975), II, 168.
26. Brown, *Estimate of the Manners and Principles*, 192.
27. Thomas Bedford, *The Origin of our Grievances: A Sermon* (London, 1770), 14.
28. M. Postlethwayt, *The National and Private Advantages of the African Trade Considered* (London, 1746), 4. The Quakers declared against slavery in 1727; see T. Clarkson, *An Essay on the Slavery and Commerce of the Human Species, Particularly the African* (London, 1786), viii. For Dunton's change of heart about slavery, see Moore, *Backgrounds*, 135; R. Sandiford, *The Mystery of Iniquity*, 2nd ed. (London, 1730); J. Swift, *Gulliver's Travels* (Oxford: Oxford University Press, 1956), 293, 352; *Boswell's Life of Johnson*, ed. G.B. Hill, 6 vols. (Oxford: Oxford University Press, 1934), 2:476–77; Charles Gildon, *The Life and Strange Surprizing Adventures of Mr. D—— DeF*, 2nd ed. (London, 1719), 14; J. Warton, "Ode to Liberty", in *The Works of the British Poets*, ed. Thomas Park (London, 1808), xxxvii, 15; R. Savage, *Of Public Spirit in Regard to Public Works*, I.301f., in *Poetical Works*, ed. C. Tracy (Cambridge: Cambridge University Press, 1962), 233; D. Defoe, *Reformation of Manners, A Satire* (n.p., 1702), 17.
29. See Sypher, *Guinea's Captive Kings*, 186–89, 215–17.
30. See Peter Fraser's introduction to the catalogue *Africa beyond Africa* (London: Commonwealth Institute, 1984).
31. E.B. Dykes, *The Negro in English Romantic Thought* (Washington DC: Associated Publishers, 1942), 75.
32. The names of Pope and Swift are to be found in the company's subscriptions books, which are now kept in the House of Lords Records Office.
33. Moore, *Backgrounds*, 133.
34. Hans H. Anderson, "Daniel Defoe: A Study of the Conflict Between Commercialism and Morality in the Early Eighteenth Century" (PhD diss., University of Chicago, 1930), 107; Charles Davenant, *An Essay upon the Probable Methods of Making a People Gainers in the Ballance of Trade* (London, 1699), 154–55; Brown, *Estimate of the Manners and Principles*, 217.
35. *Letter to the Right Reverend the Lord Bishop of London*, 15.
36. Dykes, *The Negro*, 75.
37. *Team Work* (Journal of the West Indian Standing Conference) 1 (October 1984).

Chapter 2

1. Thomas Thistlewood was a small landowner in Western Jamaica during the eighteenth century. He chronicled daily life around him until his death in 1786. A selection of his writings can be found in *In Miserable Slavery: Thomas Thistlewood in Jamaica, 1750–1786*, ed. Douglas Hall (London: Macmillan, 1988).
2. Alan Coren, *The Further Bulletins of Idi Amin* (London: Salamander Books, 1975).
3. Joseph Conrad, *Heart of Darkness* (Harmondsworth, Penguin, 1983), 70.
4. Thomas Herbert, *Some years travels into divers part of Africa, and Asia the Great, fourth impression* (London, 1677), 18.
5. John Ogilby, *Africa, being an accurate description of the regions of Ægypt, etc.* (London: the author, 1670), 451; Richard Jobson, *The Golden Trade* (London, 1623), 52; William Strachey, *The Historie of Travell into Virginia Britania*, ed. Louis B. Wright and Virginia Freund, Hakluyt Society, 2nd ser. 103 (London: Hakluyt Society, 1953), 71.
6. Mrs Aphra Behn, *Oroonoko: or, the Royal Slave: A True History* (London, 1688), 20–21.
7. Bernth Lindfors, "The Hottentot Venus" (paper given at London University's International Conference on the History of Blacks in Britain, 1981).
8. L.K. Johnson, *Dread Beat and Blood* (London: Bogle-L'Ouverture, 1975), 56.
9. Mikey Smith, *News for Babylon*, ed. James Berry (London: Chatto and Windus, 1984), 108.
10. Ibid., 113.
11. John Agard, *Mangoes and Bullets* (London: Pluto Press, 1983), 44.
12. Andrew Motion, *Dangerous Play* (Harmondsworth, UK: Penguin, 1985), 41.
13. Edward Kamau Brathwaite, *The History of the Voice* (London: New Beacon, 1984), 10.
14. Walter Mac M. Lawrence, cited in M. Gilkes, *Creative Schizophrenia: The Caribbean Cultural Challenge*, Third Walter Rodney Memorial Lecture, University of Warwick (Warwick, UK: Centre for Caribbean Studies, University of Warwick, 1987), 3.
15. Alison Daiches, in *Third World Impact*, ed. A. Ali (London: Hansib, 1988), 74.
16. C. Achebe, *Hopes and Impediments* (London: Heinemann, 1988), 52.

Chapter 3

1. Philip Thicknesse, *A Year's Journey through France and Port of Spain*, 2nd ed. (London, 1788), 102.

Chapter 4

1. Derek Walcott, address to Association of Commonwealth Language and Literature Studies, University of Kent, 1989.
2. George Lamming, "The Indian Presence as a Caribbean Reality", in *Indenture and Exile: The Indo-Caribbean Experience*, ed. F. Birbalsingh (Toronto: Tsar, 1989), 45–54.
3. Alistair Hennessy and George Lambie, eds., *The Fractured Blockade: West European–Cuban Relations during the Revolution*, Warwick University Caribbean Studies Series (London and Basingstoke: Macmillan, 1993).
4. Meenakshi Mukherjee, "The Centre Cannot Hold: Two Views of the Periphery", in *After Europe*, ed. S. Slemon and H. Tiffin (Sydney: Dangaroo, 1989), 41–48.
5. Derek Walcott, "Caligula's Horse", in *After Europe*, 138–42.
6. See Diana Brydon, "Commonwealth of Common Poverty?", in *After Europe*, ix–xiii.
7. Private communication with author, August 1995.
8. Paul Edwards, ed., *The Life of Olaudah Equiano* (London: Longman, 1983), 80–81.
9. See D. Dabydeen, "Eighteenth-Century English Literature on Commerce and Slavery", in *The Black Presence in English Literature*, ed. D. Dabydeen (Manchester: Manchester University Press, 1985), 26–49 (pages 1–20 in this volume).
10. Aubrey Williams, in conversation with Rasheed Araeen, in *Guyana Dreaming: The Art of Aubrey Williams*, ed. Anne Walmsley (Sydney: Dangaroo, 1990), 43–61.
11. I am grateful to George Simon and Pauline Melville for insights into Amerindian perspectives, and to various essays by George Mentor, Jannette Forte, Anne Benjamin and Desrey Fox, published by the Amerindian Research Unit, University of Guyana. See, too, Andrew Sanders, *The Powerless People*, Warwick University Caribbean Studies Series (London: Macmillan, 1987).
12. I am grateful to Clement Seecharan's excellent study of Indo-Guyanese history, "Effort and Achievement" (PhD dissertation, Centre for Caribbean Studies, University of Warwick, 1989), for information on this and other subjects.
13. Sasenarine Persaud, "Extending the Indian Tradition", *Indo-Caribbean Review* 1, no. 1 (1994): 15–28.
14. Ibid.
15. Seecharan, "Effort and Achievement", 39–49.

Chapter 5

1. "Coolie Mother", "Coolie Son" and "Catching Crabs" all from David Dabydeen, *Coolie Odyssey* (London and Coventry: Hansib Publishing and Dangeroo Press, 1988).

Chapter 6

1. Daniel Defoe, *Robinson Crusoe* (Harmondsworth: Penguin, 1985), 237.
2. Joseph Conrad, *Heart of Darkness* (Harmondsworth: Penguin, 1983), 68–69.

Chapter 7

1. Dated ca. 1735, oil on canvas; Nostell Priory, Wakefield.
2. Mary Webster, *Hogarth* (London: Studio Vista, 1979), 12.
3. Lawrence Gowing, *Hogarth* (London: Tate Gallery, 1971), 40.
4. Ronald Paulson, *The Art of Hogarth* (New Haven and London: Yale University Press, 1995), 120.
5. Ibid.
6. Benita Parry, "Between Creole and Cambridge English: The Poetry of David Dabydeen", in *The Art of David Dabydeen*, ed. Kevin Grant (Leeds: Peepal Tree, 1997), 47–66.
7. David Dabydeen, "The Canecutters' Song", in *Slave Song* (Mundelstrup and Sydney: Dangaroo, 1984), 25.
8. David Dabydeen, "Miranda", in *Turner: New and Selected Poems* (London: Cape Poetry, 1994), 51.

Chapter 9

1. D. Dabydeen and B. Samaroo, eds., *Across the Dark Waters: Ethnicity and Indian Identity in the Caribbean* (London: Macmillan, 1996), 1.
2. D. Dabydeen and B. Samaroo, eds., *India in the Caribbean* (London: Hansib, 1987), 25.
3. C. Seecharan, *"Tiger in the Stars": The Anatomy of Indian Achievement in British Guiana, 1919–1929* (London: Macmillan, 1997), 6.
4. Dabydeen and Samaroo, *Across the Dark Waters*, 3–4.
5. D. Dabydeen, *The Counting House* (London: Jonathan Cape, 1996), 4.
6. Seecharan, *"Tiger in the Stars"*, 31.
7. Dabydeen and Samaroo, *India in the Caribbean*, 30.
8. F. Birbalsingh, ed., *Indo-Caribbean Resistance* (Toronto: Tsar, 1993), 46.
9. Dabydeen and Samaroo, *India in the Caribbean*, 124.

10. Dabydeen and Samaroo, *Across the Dark Waters*, 32.
11. Henry Kirke, *Twenty-Five Years in British Guiana* (London: Sampson Low, Marstn & Co., 1898), 212.
12. J. Poynting, "John Edward Jenkins and the Imperial Conscience", *Journal of Commonwealth Literature* 21, no. 1 (1986): 211.
13. A.P. Stewart and Edward Jenkins, *The Medical and Legal Aspect of Sanitary Reform* (Leicester: Leicester University Press, 1969), 21.
14. Ibid., 80.
15. Edward Jenkins, ed., *Discussions on Colonial Questions* (London, 1872), 8.
16. Edwards Jenkins, *Glances at Inner England* (London, 1874), 75ff.
17. Stewart and Jenkins, *Sanitary Reform*, 82–83.
18. *Dictionary of National Biography*, 1910.
19. G.C. Kinnane, "A Popular Victorian Satire: *Ginx's Baby* and Its Reception", *Notes and Queries* 222 (1975): 116–17.
20. Brian Maidment, "What Shall We Do with the Starving Baby? Edward Jenkins and *Ginx's Baby*", *Literature and History* 6, no. 2 (1980): 163.
21. Edward Jenkins, *The Coolie: His Rights and Wrongs* (London: Strahan, 1871), 15.
22. Ibid., 21.
23. Ibid., 23.
24. Ibid., 26.
25. Ibid., 51.
26. Ibid., 27.
27. Brian Maidment, "Victorian Publishing and Social Criticism: The Case of Edward Jenkins", *Publishing History* 11 (1982): 42.
28. Ibid., 46.
29. West Indian, *The Coolie in Demerara* (London, 1871), 5.
30. Ibid., 15.
31. Ibid., 16.
32. Ibid., 21–22. For Jenkins's sensitivity to literary criticism, see Brian Maidment, "What Shall We Do with the Starving Baby?", 161.
33. See Poynting, "Imperial Conscience", 214.
34. C. Seecharan, *India and the Shaping of the Indo-Guyanese Imagination* (Leeds: Peepal Tree, 1993), 14.
35. *Lutchmee and Dilloo*, 3:275–76.
36. *Lutchmee and Dilloo*, 2:70–71. Emphasis added.
37. *Lutchmee and Dilloo*, 1:265–66.
38. *Lutchmee and Dilloo*, 1:101.
39. Jenkins, *Discussions on Colonial Questions*, 8.
40. Jenkins, *Coolie*, 243.

41. *Lutchmee and Dilloo*, 2:10.
42. *Lutchmee and Dilloo*, 1:138.
43. Jenkins, *Coolie*, 149.
44. Ibid., 153.
45. The two drawings reproduced in *The Coolie* are woodcuts made by a Chinese artist. Jenkins will allow the coolie to sketch out but not *write* or articulate in words his/her story, the pictures being immediate, simple, lacking intellectual depth and subtlety, overstated.
46. *The Oxford English Dictionary* gives an early-twentieth-century American usage for "jinx", but is unaware of the fact that there were at least five pirated American editions of *Ginx's Baby* by 1876. See Kinnane, "Popular Victorian Satire", 116–117. Although vastly popular for many years, *Ginx's Baby* eventually went out of print and was forgotten. Jenkins himself suffered a waning of popularity and his subsequent novels never achieved the same success. He turned to politics and journalism, becoming MP for Dundee between 1874 and 1880, and editor of the *Overland Mail* and *Homeward Mail* from 1886 onwards. He died, a relatively neglected figure, in 1910.

Chapter 10

1. V.S. Naipaul, who was born in Trinidad in 1932, has published over twenty books of fiction and non-fiction. In 1993 he was awarded the first David Cohen British Literature Prize, the most valuable literary award in the UK, which is given in recognition of lifetime achievement.
2. Slavery was abolished in the British Empire in 1834, but it was not until 1 August 1838 that the last imperial serfs, nearly all black Africans, were officially emancipated.
3. Wilson Harris is a Guyanese writer and critic. C.L.R. James, who died in 1989, was a leading Trinidadian novelist and Marxist intellectual. Edward Kamau Brathwaite is a Barbadian poet.
4. David Dabydeen, *Disappearance* (London: Secker and Warburg, 1993).
5. Dabydeen is referring to former Conservative MP Enoch Powell's highly inflammatory speech made in April 1968, in which he foresaw great evil befalling Britain unless black people from the former colonies were barred entry into the country.
6. Kazuo Ishiguro, *The Remains of the Day* (London: Faber and Faber, 1989).
7. David Dabydeen, *The Intended* (London: Secker and Warburg, 1991).
8. G.A. Henry, John Buchan and R.M. Ballantyne are examples of what might be called "writers of the Empire", as their novels, written during the second half of the

nineteenth century or in the early part of the twentieth, tend to portray black characters rather unfavourably and at the same time insist on the racial superiority of the whites.
9. Patel is one of the Asian friends of the nameless narrator of *The Intended*. He continually reminds the narrator of his debt to the black, rather than the white, community.

Chapter 13

1. Mike Phillips and Trevor Phillips, *Windrush: The Irresistible Rise of Multi-Racial Britain* (London: HarperCollins, 1998); Onyekachi Wambu, ed., *Empire Windrush: Fifty Years of Writing about Black Britain* (London: Gollancz, 1998); Tony Sewell, *Keep on Moving* (London: Voice, 1998).
2. David Dabydeen, ed., "The *Windrush* Commemorative Issue: West Indians in Britain, 1948–1998", special issue, *Kunapipi* 20, no. 1 (1998).

www.ingramcontent.com/pod-product-compliance
Lightning Source LLC
Chambersburg PA
CBHW021808220426
43662CB00006B/234